# Religious Schools in Europe

The European Convention on Human Rights guarantees freedom of education, including the opportunities to create and operate faith-based schools. However, as European societies become more religiously diverse and 'less religious' at the same time, the role of faith-based schools is increasingly being contested. Serious tensions have emerged between those who ardently support religious schools in their various forms and those who oppose them. Given that faith-based schools enjoy basic constitutional guarantees in Europe, the controversy around them often surrounds issues of public financing, degrees of organisational and pedagogical autonomy, and educational practices and management.

This volume is about the controversies surrounding religious schools in a number of Western European countries. The introductory chapter briefly analyses the structural pressures that affect the position of religious schools, outlining the relevant institutional arrangements in countries such as Denmark, Germany, France, Ireland, the Netherlands, and Scotland. The following chapters provide a detailed analysis of the discussions and controversies surrounding faith-based schools in each country. Finally, the two concluding chapters aim to provide a bigger, comparative picture with regard to these debates about religious education in liberal democratic states and culturally pluralist societies. This book was originally published as a special issue of *Comparative Education*.

**Marcel Maussen** is Assistant Professor at the Department of Political Science at the University of Amsterdam, The Netherlands. His research focuses on governance of religious and cultural pluralism, transitions of democracy, and fundamental rights and freedoms.

**Floris Vermeulen** is Associate Professor at the Department of Political Science at the University of Amsterdam, The Netherlands. His research focuses on the political and civic participation of immigrants, religious diversity, and policies against extremism.

**Michael S. Merry** is Professor of Philosophy of Education in the Faculty of Social and Behavioural Sciences at the University of Amsterdam, The Netherlands. His primary areas of scholarship are ethics, political philosophy, and educational theory.

**Veit Bader** is Emeritus Professor in Social and Political Philosophy and Sociology at the University of Amsterdam, The Netherlands. He has published widely on citizenship, democratic theory, associative democracy, social inequality, governance of religious pluralism, and various other topics.

# Religious Schools in Europe

Institutional opportunities and contemporary challenges

**Edited by
Marcel Maussen, Floris Vermeulen,
Michael S. Merry and Veit Bader**

LONDON AND NEW YORK

First published 2016
by Routledge
2 Park Square, Milton Park, Abingdon, Oxon, OX14 4RN, UK

and by Routledge
711 Third Avenue, New York, NY 10017, USA

*Routledge is an imprint of the Taylor & Francis Group, an informa business*

Chapters 1–5, 7–9 © Taylor and Francis
Chapter 6 © Marcel Maussen and Floris Vermeulen

All rights reserved. No part of this book may be reprinted or reproduced or utilised in any form or by any electronic, mechanical, or other means, now known or hereafter invented, including photocopying and recording, or in any information storage or retrieval system, without permission in writing from the publishers.

*Trademark notice*: Product or corporate names may be trademarks or registered trademarks, and are used only for identification and explanation without intent to infringe.

*British Library Cataloguing in Publication Data*
A catalogue record for this book is available from the British Library

ISBN 13: 978-1-138-88848-7

Typeset in Times New Roman
by diacriTech, Chennai

**Publisher's Note**
The publisher accepts responsibility for any inconsistencies that may have arisen during the conversion of this book from journal articles to book chapters, namely the possible inclusion of journal terminology.

**Disclaimer**
Every effort has been made to contact copyright holders for their permission to reprint material in this book. The publishers would be grateful to hear from any copyright holder who is not here acknowledged and will undertake to rectify any errors or omissions in future editions of this book.

# Contents

*Citation Information*     vii
*Notes on Contributors*     ix

1. Non-governmental religious schools in Europe: institutional opportunities, associational freedoms, and contemporary challenges     1
   *Marcel Maussen and Veit Bader*

2. The Danish free school tradition under pressure     22
   *Tore Vincents Olsen*

3. Non-governmental religious schools in Germany – increasing demand by decreasing religiosity?     38
   *Annette Scheunpflug*

4. The national management of public and Catholic schools in France: moving from a loosely coupled towards an integrated system?     57
   *Xavier Pons, Agnès van Zanten and Sylvie Da Costa*

5. Religion and education in Ireland: growing diversity – or losing faith in the system?     71
   *Nathalie Rougier and Iseult Honohan*

6. Liberal equality and toleration for conservative religious minorities. Decreasing opportunities for religious schools in the Netherlands?     87
   *Marcel Maussen and Floris Vermeulen*

7. The continued existence of state-funded Catholic schools in Scotland     105
   *Stephen J. McKinney and James C. Conroy*

## CONTENTS

8. What can international comparisons teach us about school choice and non-governmental schools in Europe? 118
   *Jaap Dronkers and Silvia Avram*

9. The conundrum of religious schools in twenty-first-century Europe 133
   *Michael S. Merry*

   *Index* 157

# Citation Information

The chapters in this book were originally published in *Comparative Education*, volume 51, issue 1 (February 2015). When citing this material, please use the original page numbering for each article, as follows:

**Chapter 1**
*Non-governmental religious schools in Europe: institutional opportunities, associational freedoms, and contemporary challenges*
Marcel Maussen and Veit Bader
*Comparative Education*, volume 51, issue 1 (February 2015) pp. 1–21

**Chapter 2**
*The Danish free school tradition under pressure*
Tore Vincents Olsen
*Comparative Education*, volume 51, issue 1 (February 2015) pp. 22–37

**Chapter 3**
*Non-governmental religious schools in Germany – increasing demand by decreasing religiosity?*
Annette Scheunpflug
*Comparative Education*, volume 51, issue 1 (February 2015) pp. 38–56

**Chapter 4**
*The national management of public and Catholic schools in France: moving from a loosely coupled towards an integrated system?*
Xavier Pons, Agnès van Zanten and Sylvie Da Costa
*Comparative Education*, volume 51, issue 1 (February 2015) pp. 57–70

**Chapter 5**
*Religion and education in Ireland: growing diversity – or losing faith in the system?*
Nathalie Rougier and Iseult Honohan
*Comparative Education*, volume 51, issue 1 (February 2015) pp. 71–86

# CITATION INFORMATION

**Chapter 6**
*Liberal equality and toleration for conservative religious minorities. Decreasing opportunities for religious schools in the Netherlands?*
Marcel Maussen and Floris Vermeulen
*Comparative Education*, volume 51, issue 1 (February 2015) pp. 87–104

**Chapter 7**
*The continued existence of state-funded Catholics schools in Scotland*
Stephen J. McKinney and James C. Conroy
*Comparative Education*, volume 51, issue 1 (February 2015) pp. 105–117

**Chapter 8**
*What can international comparisons teach us about school choice and non-governmental schools in Europe?*
Jaap Dronkers and Silvia Avram
*Comparative Education*, volume 51, issue 1 (February 2015) pp. 118–132

**Chapter 9**
*The conundrum of religious schools in twenty-first-century Europe*
Michael S. Merry
*Comparative Education*, volume 51, issue 1 (February 2015) pp. 133–156

For any permission-related enquiries please visit:
http://www.tandfonline.com/page/help/permissions

# Notes on Contributors

**Silvia Avram** is a Senior Research Officer at the University of Essex, Colchester, UK. She obtained her Ph.D. in 2011 at the European University Institute, Florence, Italy, where her thesis was entitled 'Antipoverty Policies in Central and Eastern Europe'.

**Veit Bader** is Emeritus Professor in Social and Political Philosophy and Sociology at the University of Amsterdam, The Netherlands. He has published widely on citizenship, democratic theory, associative democracy, social inequality, governance of religious pluralism, and various other topics.

**James C. Conroy** is the Vice Principal of Internationalisation at the University of Glasgow, UK, where he was previously Dean of the Faculty of Education. He has published widely on a range of research interests that includes religious education, the role of religion and education in state education, models of teacher education, and moral education. His recent publications include *Does Religious Education Work?* (2013).

**Sylvie Da Costa** is a Research Assistant at the Observatoire Sociologique du Changement at Sciences Po, Paris, France. Since 2002, she has regularly participated in various qualitative research studies done by the members of the Observatoire.

**Jaap Dronkers** is Chair in International Comparative Research on Educational Performance and Social Inequality at Maastricht University, The Netherlands. He has previously held positions at the European University Institute, Florence, Italy, and the University of Amsterdam, The Netherlands.

**Iseult Honohan** is Senior Lecturer in the School of Politics and International Relations at University College Dublin, Ireland. Her research interests include political theory, civic republican political theory, citizenship, and migration and diversity.

**Marcel Maussen** is Assistant Professor at the Department of Political Science at the University of Amsterdam, The Netherlands. His research focuses on governance of religious and cultural pluralism, transitions of democracy, and fundamental rights and freedoms.

**Stephen J. McKinney** is a Professor in the School of Education, University of Glasgow, UK. His research interests include faith schooling, Catholic schooling, and the impact of poverty of school education. His most recent publication is *Education in a Catholic Perspective* (with J. Sullivan, 2013).

# NOTES ON CONTRIBUTORS

**Michael S. Merry** is Professor of Philosophy of Education in the Faculty of Social and Behavioural Sciences at the University of Amsterdam, The Netherlands. His primary areas of scholarship are ethics, political philosophy, and educational theory.

**Tore Vincents Olsen** is Associate Professor in Political Theory in the Department of Political Science at Aarhus University, Denmark. He writes on immigration and integration issues, Danish political culture, education, democracy, and the European Union.

**Xavier Pons** is Associate Professor at the University of East-Paris Créteil, France, member of the Laboratory of research on governance (Largotec), and Associate Researcher at the Observatoire Sociologique du Changement at Sciences Po, Paris, France. He works mainly on the transformations of the governance of education systems in France and in Europe, especially through evaluation, with a special focus on the role of policy tools, professional groups, knowledge, and discourses in the policy process.

**Nathalie Rougier** is a Research Assistant in the Robert Schuman Centre for Advanced Studies at the European University Institute, Florence, Italy. Her research interests include inter-group and inter-cultural relations, integration and acculturation processes, and stereotypes, prejudice, and discrimination.

**Annette Scheunpflug** holds a chair on Foundations of Education at the Institute of Education, University of Bamberg, Germany. She works on the anthropology of education, globalisation, and educational quality.

**Agnès van Zanten** is Senior Research Professor at the Observatoire Sociologique du Changement at Sciences Po, Paris, France. Her main research areas are class, elites and education, school segregation and school choice, transition to higher education, widening participation, and educational policies.

**Floris Vermeulen** is Associate Professor at the Department of Political Science at the University of Amsterdam, The Netherlands. His research focuses on the political and civic participation of immigrants, religious diversity, and policies against extremism.

# Non-governmental religious schools in Europe: institutional opportunities, associational freedoms, and contemporary challenges

Marcel Maussen[a] and Veit Bader[b]

[a]Department of Political Science, University of Amsterdam, Amsterdam, The Netherlands; [b]Department of Philosophy, University of Amsterdam, Amsterdam, The Netherlands

> The European Convention on Human Rights guarantees freedom of education, including opportunities to create and operate faith-based schools. But as European societies become religiously more diverse and 'less religious' at the same time, the role of religious schools increasingly is being contested. Serious tensions have emerged between those who ardently support religious schools in various forms and those who oppose them. Given that faith-based schools enjoy basic constitutional guarantees in Europe, the controversy surrounding them often boils down to issues of public financing, degrees of organisational and pedagogical autonomy, and educational practices and management. This introduction to a special issue on controversies surrounding religious schools in a number of Western European countries briefly introduces structural pressures that affect the position of religious schools and sketches the relevant institutional arrangements in the respective countries. We then go on to introduce some of the main concerns that frame the relevant debates. The paper concludes by introducing the various contributions in the special issue.

## Introduction

In the context of increasing religious and cultural diversity of European societies the role and functioning of religious schools is often brought up in discussions about the structure of education systems, and in connection with concerns about social cohesion, immigrant integration, democratic citizenship, non-discrimination, and equal educational opportunities for all. International human rights law, the European Convention on Human Rights (ECHR) and the European Court of Human Rights (ECtHR), as well as most liberal-democratic constitutions and courts, oblige states to permit freedom of education in all their consequences for religious schools (de Groof 2012).[1] But educational systems vary widely with regard to the ways they recognise and finance religious schools, and the types and degrees of public scrutiny and control that are exercised over these schools. Across Europe religious schools have varying competences to decide on the curriculum, teaching materials, internal school regulations (e.g. with regard to dress or gender segregation), the recruitment of teachers, the selection of pupils, and so on.

This diversity of institutional opportunities for faith-based education is in itself the outcome of political struggles and different trajectories of formation of mass education systems, which developed from the late decades of the eighteenth century onwards. Until then, education had mostly been a matter of the church. Sometimes the provision of general education was mostly government led, for example in Prussia and France, whereas in other countries schools were set up with modest involvement of the central government, for example in Scandinavia and New England. In the context of state building, governments increasingly sought to employ a system of mandatory popular schooling to create a more homogeneous nation and raise virtuous and loyal citizens. Many rulers, such as the Dutch King William I (r. 1813–1840), believed that in order to play a role as a nation-forming institution, the school should teach a 'liberal', non-sectarian, Christianity. In a country such as France, on the other hand, a more rigorously secular system of public schools was pursued, for example by the Minister of Education Jules Ferry in the 1880s. State-led education could in principle develop independently or in opposition to church-led education. Religious communities protested against efforts to marginalise religious schools, and both in Protestant and Catholic countries church-sponsored schools were successful in their resistance and continued to reach the majority of the population (Glenn 2012a, 9). In the second half of the nineteenth-century, controversies with regard to the status and funding of religious education culminated in series of 'school struggles', for example in Belgium, France, and the Netherlands. Periods of intense confrontation ended with some form of accommodation (see Glenn 2012a). In some Western countries, including the USA, the period between 1900 and 1945 was marked by the dominance of the state-led 'common school', whereas in others (such as the Netherlands) the 'statutory equality' of religious and state schools was secured in constitutions and laws (in the Constitution of 1917 and the Primary School Act of 1920). In other countries, however, contestation around religious schools would continue throughout the twentieth century. In France, for example the Debré laws of the 1950s created opportunities for recognition and funding of religious schools (mostly Catholic). In 1983 plans to revise the model led to widespread protests in favour of freedom of education, also for religious schools. Ten years later (in 1994) fierce protests broke out yet again when advocates of strictly secular education and *l'école Républicaine* demanded that state schools were given far more financial opportunities than private, religious ones.

Also in the more contemporary period the position of religious schools continues to be subject to debate. European school systems have been affected by a variety of profound social transformations, including secularisation, individualisation, growing mobility, and immigration. Pedagogical philosophies and practices of education have changed, and parents, teachers, school managers, politicians, and society at large now have new ideas and concerns when it comes to providing primary and secondary education to children. Some say that religious schools are once again under pressure and questions are being raised as to their legitimacy in modern school systems. In the Netherlands, for example a series of recent legal amendments were aimed at enforcing more strict application of non-discrimination legislation upon conservative religious schools (with respect to the hiring of teachers and the selection of pupils) and obliging them to teach a more 'liberal' message with regard to sexual diversity (Maussen and Vermeulen 2015). The former leader of one of the Christian parties (the Christian Union), André Rouvoet, wrote in October 2011 that attempts to restrict 'fundamental freedoms of religious schools' were illustrative of a climate in which there was less 'principled room for minorities, and for their opinions and practices' (Rouvoet 2011, 3). Another example is the way immigrant religious schools, above all Islamic schools, continue to encounter social and political resistance (Merry 2013, Chap. 5). Concerns about the spreading of religious hatred and 'radicalisation' of Islamic youth have resulted in increasingly strict supervision of Islamic schools in several countries.[2] However, the situation of religious schools looks rather different when we focus on other trends. For one, the market share of religious schools is stable or growing in countries such as the Netherlands, Germany (Scheunpflug 2015), and England (Hatcher 2011). And also countries that have a reputation as being reluctant to accommodate and finance religious schools, such as France and the USA, have seen an increase in the number of religious schools and have taken steps to make funding more 'fair', i.e. more equal compared to the funds that are being spent on other schools.

In our view the fact that the overall picture remains so fuzzy implies that we need to zoom in more and differentiate between developments in different countries, take into account important differences between school types and between the religions in question (majority or minority, Christian or other, established or newcomer), and specify the aspects of the 'position of religious schools' that we are discussing. This special issue aims to shed light on the developments in a number of West European countries by linking institutional differences, political contestations and broader societal trends and policies.

We begin with a note on terminology. First, we use the term religious or faith school to refer to all schools that have a distinctive religious character, playing a role in the way the school operates, for example, with respect to curriculum, admission policies, selection of teaching staff, pedagogy and teaching aids, internal regulations, and so on. The exact role of the religious ethos can vary in terms of intensity (some schools are more 'nominally' religious others more 'pervasively') and in terms of direction (some schools are more conservative, others more liberal or ecumenical). The schools we are speaking of are primary and secondary schools, teaching all kinds of subjects, mostly preparing their pupils for exams and diplomas that are certified by the state, and attending these schools is at least considered as a way for children to comply with demands of compulsory education. A second important terminological issue concerns whether religious schools should be called 'private' or 'public' schools. Actually, the legal status of religious schools varies. In England Voluntary Aided and Voluntary Controlled schools (most of them Anglican, some Roman Catholic, only very few others) are treated as 'public' or 'state schools'. In many countries they are classified as 'private schools', for example, in the USA but also in Denmark ('free primary schools') and Sweden ('independent schools'). In the majority of countries their legal status is neither fully public nor private but somewhere in-between; such as 'special' or 'bijzonder' (in the Netherlands), 'with contract' in France ('sous contrat') and Spain ('concertadas') (different from 'private schools' that do not receive public money), or 'national schools' (also called 'denominational' or 'faith schools') in Ireland. For us, this is the reason to choose as neutral and precise a term as possible and distinguish between governmental and non-governmental schools. Governmental schools are understood to be owned, run, and financed by (a flexible combination of) governmental (federal, state, municipal) authorities. Non-governmental schools are owned and run by (central or local) organisations or associations whether (partly or fully) publicly financed or not. A broad variety of non-governmental schools exists, not all of them faith-based, for example, schools based on distinctive educational practices or pedagogy. Third, we will use the terms 'associational autonomy' and 'associational freedoms' to speak of freedoms of religious schools, enabling 'those who are engaged with individual schools – their boards and their teachers and administrators – to shape and implement a distinctive educational mission' (Glenn and de Groof 2012,

1). The significance of these freedoms depends on institutional opportunities (including but not limited to constitutional and legal regulations) and the balance of power between relevant actors, *within* school organisations (e.g. between school board, teachers and daily management), *around* schools (e.g. in relations between the school and national and local authorities, teachers' unions, and parents) and *within the wider society* (it matters, e.g. whether the school belongs to the majority religion or to an immigrant minority religious group). The significance of school autonomy will also depend on other factors, such as prevailing education policies or ideas about the ways schools should be administrated and how states should monitor quality and performance.

We begin this introductory article by discussing the major societal trends that, over the past 30 years or so, have come to affect the position of religious schools. We then go on to discuss the broader features of the situation and institutional opportunities for religious schools in Western Europe, especially concerning the countries included in the special issue. Against this background we discuss some of the issues that have come up in contemporary debates about religious schools. We conclude by introducing the contributions included in the special issue.

## Structural pressures on religious schools

What we will tentatively describe as the 'position' of religious schools in European educational systems is related to various factors, including their relative 'market share', their perceived legitimacy in the wider society, levels of financial support and school autonomy. This position has been changing since the 1960s as a result of structural changes and societal transformations. Even though the exact nature of these social trends varies between countries, four broader clusters of factors should be highlighted.

First, European societies have been undergoing important transformations in terms of their composition. Their populations now look different in terms of age, religion, class, ethnicity, and so on, but also in terms of prevailing socio-cultural values, lifestyles and worldviews. These changes include, for example, 'secularisation' (decline of church attendance, decline of church membership, decline of people positioning themselves as religious) and the emergence of all kinds of new ways of 'believing and belonging', individualisation and rising levels of education, growing social and physical mobility (including migration), growing importance of sub-cultural identities (including sexual identities and life-styles), further diversification of cultural pluralism (including ethnic diversity), growing importance of post-materialist values and related political and social identifications, diversification and greater dynamic of forms of family life and personal relationships, and so on.[3] In addition, new patterns of social inequality have emerged, some of which are tightly connected to differences in cultural, religious and ethnic background. These changes have profound consequences for the institutional arrangements via which liberal-democratic states aim to accommodate societal pluralism, also in education.

These structural transformations in European societies are intimately connected to a second cluster of structural factors that is also generating institutional reorientation. These are transformations related to the sphere of politics, such as mediatisation and personalisation of politics, changes in party systems and party-political configurations, including: the declining role of confessional parties, growing volatility of the electorate, emergence of new political and value conflicts, the emergence of populist parties, and so on (Kriesi 2010; Mair 2013). These transformations are connected to changes in public opinion, both at the level of elites and of citizens. For our purposes, especially the renewed politicisation of religion and cultural pluralism is of importance. There is a seemingly growing influence of 'secular progressive' voices in public and political debate (Schuh, Burchardt, and Wohlrab-Sahr 2012), and, on the other hand, anti-Islam rhetoric articulated by right wing populist leaders has become a constant in public debate, finding resonance among a substantial part of the electorate. Even though there is significant variance between European societies in this respect, the growing prominence of 'secular voices' sets off Europe as a whole against the USA. However, we should note that we cannot simply conclude that greater visibility of secular ideas in public debate is illustrative of a further trend of 'decline of religion' (for the Netherlands, de Hart 2014). Notice should be taken of the opinions and values of increasingly substantial immigrant communities, that are, however, up till now, far less vocal in most European public spheres. Moreover, some recent mobilisations by religious groups, such as the massive demonstrations against same-sex marriages and teaching on gender and sexual diversity in France (Battaglia 2014) or the protests against speech that is considered offensive to religious people (Maussen and Grillo 2014), stand to show that religion is still an important social and political rallying force in Europe.

Third, there have been profound transformations in the relations between state and society, altering the configuration of governance in domains that are traditionally also of relevance to religion, such as health and mental care, education, social support and relief, leisure, and so on. A major factor has been the expansion of modern welfare states after the Second World War, followed by a period of contraction and neo-liberal reforms since the late 1970s, and more recently giving way to a new phase of 'welfare state recalibration' (Hemerijck 2013). In this context, institutional arrangements that structured the roles and interactions between the state, civil society and the market, based on specific views about the role of religion and religious organisations therein, have come under pressure. The so-called shift from 'government to governance', and new ideas about the most effective and efficient ways of producing of all kinds of public goods and services have also affected the possible role of faith-based institutions (see Van Bijsterveld 2011). With regard to management philosophies and styles, many European countries have been implementing new public management (NPM) inspired models of marketisation and privatisation to their bureaucracies and public service organisations. Reforms were intended to introduce economies of scale, rational 'company like' management based on clear targets, objectively measured output, systematic use of assessments and accountability systems, further professionalisation, the introduction of quasi-markets, and so on (see Whitty and Power 2000; Whitty 2009; Dronkers and Avram 2015; Pons, Van Zanten, and Da Costa 2015). These changes have affected education systems in many ways, and have altered the configuration and understandings of basic freedoms. For example, nowadays parents often act as consumers scanning the educational market for the optimal offer for their children. Schools have obtained more (or perhaps better: a different kind of) 'autonomy', for example, over their budget, in view of enabling them to develop a distinctive profile, optimise their achievements and market their product, whilst being subject to steering-at-a-distance on the basis of performance indicators and budget controls (for the UK, see Hand 2012). In the Netherlands, for one, this has led to a renewed understanding of the freedom of education, shifting away from its nineteenth- and twentieth-century image of non-governmental school as 'owned' by the parents, towards individual parents exercising freedom of choice on a market (National Education Council 2012). However, we hasten to add that this is but a broader trend, which has had different policy consequences and met different responses (see the contributions on Denmark (Olsen 2015) and France Pons, Van Zanten, and Da Costa 2015).

A fourth major cluster of factors triggering changes in the field of governance of cultural and religious diversity and education is 'Europeanisation', and especially the ways issues of cultural and religious diversity are embedded in supranational human rights regimes, involving notably the ECHR and the ECtHR and, increasingly also the European Court of Justice and the EU Charter of Fundamental Rights. In the context of religious education, it has been observed that a human rights perspective on religious governance may contribute to an individualised understanding of religious freedom rights, in tension with collective understandings of those rights (Hunter-Henin 2011, 4). Particularly important for the debates on school autonomy are EU directives and initiatives to combat discrimination, but also the signals by the European Commission to member states asked to guarantee religious freedom and educational opportunities for 'vulnerable groups', including children from a migrant background (Foblets and Alidadi 2013).

In order to situate the impact and significance of these structural tends as well as of public debates and contestation around religious schools we begin by setting the stage and highlight some of the commonalities and differences, the structural problems, and the ways they are framed and dealt with in the countries that are included in this special issue.

## Religious schools in Europe: institutional opportunities and patterns

As we mentioned, supranational and constitutional obligations demand that liberal-democratic states guarantee freedom of education for religious schools. Even states that have been characterised by a near monopoly for governmental schools, such as Sweden, Norway, Bulgaria, Italy, and most Swiss cantons, have increasingly acknowledged the right to freedom of education, which is mostly interpreted as the right of parents to choose a particular type of school for their children and the right to create and operate faith-based schools. We do not intend to give a full-scale historical or synchronic map of all educational systems but only sketch the most important existing options in order to locate the countries and case studies in a comparative perspective. In order to do this systematically we focus on (1) legal status and 'market share', (2) opportunities for public financing, and (3) the types and degrees of public scrutiny, control and associational freedoms of religious schools.

### *Legal status and 'market share'*

The legal status of non-governmental religious schools differs. Historically and constitutionally this status has often been shaped via the incorporation of church-sponsored schools in modern, mass education systems, and has been strongly stamped by country-specific church-state ideologies and institutions.[4] In Denmark religious schools are institutionally recognised as 'private' schools or 'free primary schools', a category of schools that is controlled and funded by the government and which includes, besides religious schools, also academic-oriented grammar schools, progressive 'Free Schools' and boarding schools (Wiborg 2012; Olsen 2015). In the context of a church-state regime shaped by the Reformation and the creation of an established Lutheran Protestant church (in 1536), the Danish education system was initially heavily biased in favour of a public school dominated by the established church (called the Danish People's Church since 1849). The so-called 'free school tradition', led by reformers such as Grundtvig and Kold, emerged in the nineteenth century as a protest against this state dominance and criticised the role religion played in the curriculum. With the legal recognition in 1855 of the right of parents to assume responsibility for the education of their own children and create 'free schools', the institutional opportunities to create non-governmental schools became extremely good, which benefitted both those wanting to found non-religious schools and those intending to found minority *religious* schools (e.g. Catholic schools) (Rangvid 2008). In Germany a variety of statuses exists for Christian religious schools, which can be 'governmental schools' (interdenominational Christian (called *christliche Gemeinschaftsschulen* in some Länder) or confessional (*Bekenntnisschulen*) (usually Catholic, sometimes Evangelical)), or non-governmental schools accepted in the public system, meaning their confessional identity is limited to their periods of religious instruction and clerical influence is limited. Besides there are non-governmental religious schools, which are independent but sponsored by the state (Glenn 2012b). In light of German state-church traditions, which are based on the recognition of the autonomy of churches combined with openness for state-church partnerships that tend to be formalised and corporatist, it is not a surprise that on the whole these institutional opportunities are most favourable for *Christian* religious non-governmental schools (Monsma and Soper 2009, 169ff.). In strictly secular France religious schools are 'private' schools, but they can enter into a 'contract with the state', which creates substantial opportunities for public funding, and obliges schools to comply with the national curriculum. In Ireland *all* primary and the vast majority of secondary schools are non-governmental, and the vast majority of primary schools, that are called 'national schools', is religious (mostly Catholic) (O'Mahony 2012). The fact that primary schools have a 'patron' (often a local Bishop) and the fact that there is great institutional bias in favour of Catholicism fits in the wider pattern of the Irish state-church regime, illustrated by the fact that Catholicism was until 1972 officially recognised as 'the religion of the majority'. In the Netherlands religious schools have the legal status of 'special' (*bijzondere*) schools, which is guaranteed by article 23 of the Dutch Constitution. In line with the prevailing church-state regime, in which a neutral state seeks to accommodate religious and secular worldviews on an even-handed basis, religious school have statutory equality with governmental schools (Maussen 2014). In Scotland the Presbyterian Church of Scotland functions as the national church without being an established church. Initially schooling was primarily a matter for parishes. When an important wave of Irish immigrants settled in Scotland in the nineteenth century, there was a relative openness to dissenting Protestants and Catholic schools, but state grants only accounted for 10% of the required sources. The 1918 School Act incorporated Catholic schools into the state system, while providing safeguards for the associational autonomy of these schools. A dual system emerged because Church of Scotland schools were incorporated into the 'secular' or 'non-denominational' state sector, whereas Roman Catholic schools remained recognisably confessional. Nowadays, non-governmental, independent or 'voluntary' schools, most of which are Catholic, are almost everywhere recognised by local educational authorities into the public system of 'state schools' (Flint 2007, 257–258; Glenn 2012c; McKinney and Conroy 2015).

With regard to the 'market share'[5] of religious schools, the countries that are included in this special issue are spread along the continuum from very high to very low percentages. In Ireland, the market share of religious schools is extremely high, and in the Netherlands the proportion is very high. Denmark and Scotland rank in between, and at the lowest end we find France and Germany. The relative market share of religious schools, as well as the diversity in types and denominations, depends both on social and historical factors (including the religious composition of the population and the demand for this type of schools) and on institutional opportunities. It is to these institutional opportunities that we now turn.

## *Public financing*

Empirically, the overwhelming majority of states with liberal-democratic constitutions publicly finance non-governmental religious schools.[6] But the modalities of financings are perplexingly complex and diverse, depending on *who* is financing *how, when,* and *what.*[7] As with governmental schools, in most states the public funding of non-governmental religious schools is divided in various degrees between federal, state, local, or municipal authorities, which may or may not have an independent tax-base. Governmental authorities are financing religious schools either directly (by fixed or flexible subsidies for facilities, number of enrolled students, and so on) and/or indirectly by granting schools certain tax-exemptions or by paying vouchers and/or grants for students or tax-credits to parents. Financing can be constitutionally and legally obligatory and enforceable by court action or at the discretion of administrations. It can be lump sum or expense related, it can be contractual (like in France, Portugal, Spain, and Iceland), it can be withheld under specified conditions, or it can be directly to schools or to networks or associations of providers, as for the 'systemic schools' in Australia. It is usually restricted to 'non-profit' schools. It can be ex ante and/or ex post, it can be conditional on property and capital of school owners or not, and it commonly is conditional on school type. Finally, many different costs can be financed (by different authorities, to different degrees, under divergent conditions): capital costs for construction of school building (premises), costs for maintenance, operational costs and costs for administrative/supportive staff, for teaching staff (and additional training courses etc.), for inspection, for schoolbooks, school meals, uniforms, transportation, and for many extra-curricular activities.[8] Most systems combine direct subsidies for schools, teachers and staff, and for the number of enrolled students with indirect subsidies for students and parents (like vouchers or tax-credits). This mixed approach allows more stability and predictability to run schools without making them insensitive to considerable changes in student enrolment, and it allows better public control of what schools actually do, for instance with supplementary funding for 'poor, minority, and immigrant' students.

The upshot of the complexity and lack of transparency of public financing of religious schools within states and among states is that it is difficult to exactly calculate the comparative overall amount of public money for non-governmental religious schools in relation to governmental schools. Roughly the following picture of groups of countries emerges (cf. also Rogers Berner 2012): Some states (Austria, Belgium, England/Wales, Ireland, and the Netherlands) cover virtually all costs (full funding), the Scandinavian model (Denmark, Finland, and Sweden) is characterised by large subsidisation. Partial funding is known in many other countries as well (e.g. Australia, Germany, Hungary and countries where public funding depends on contracts, as in France or Spain). Finally, a few countries still do not allow non-governmental schools to receive public money (no funding: Greece, Bulgaria, most Swiss cantons).

The fact that nearly all European states are willing to finance non-governmental schools seems to be in stark contrast to what happens in the USA, but also on the other side of the Atlantic things are changing. In the USA, pupils of religious schools have rights to publicly funded services, such as special education assistance, transportation or textbooks, depending on location and need. The Zelman ruling of the Constitutional Court in 2002 allowed indirect public funding via vouchers. Furthermore, since 1992, 42 states have enacted legislation for charter schools. They are, like traditional public schools, directly subsidised by a combination of primarily state and local taxes based on their student enrolments but receive, like private schools, autonomy from a variety of rules and regulations while being accountable to the requirements that are established in the charter (Green, Baker, and Oluwole 2013, 303). By 2012, there were roughly 6000 charter schools educating some two million students. The 'hybrid' character of these non-governmental, non-profit schools has created lots of troubles for American Courts and lawyers. 'Charter school supporters, private charter school boards, and Educational Management Organizations' emphasize their public nature to be eligible for funding under state constitutional law, while emphasizing their private characteristics to evade federal and state statutory requirements that apply to public entities' (Green, Baker, and Oluwole 2013, 336) with regard to protections of employees and students. Their opponents argue that they are really private schools that are therefore ineligible for state public funding.[9] In addition, there are ongoing discussions about the ways in which religion may play a role in school and after-school programmes, and also about whether these schools can have strong partnerships with faith-based organisations (Schlikerman 2014).[10]

One may conclude that public financing of religious schools is an 'emerging international legal norm' (Glenn and de Groof 2002a, 578). This is expressed in most detail in the *Lüster Resolution* of March 1984 of the European Parliament representing 'the high-water mark, to date, in the international recognition of an *effective* right to education freedom, supported by its appropriate share of public resources' (Glenn and de Groof 2002a, 578). The variety in degrees and types of public funding of religious schools is also represented in the countries that are discussed in this special issue.

In Denmark, rough estimates indicate that between 75% and 85% of the costs of non-governmental schools are funded, depending, among other things, on the fee payments by parents and whether schools are entitled to special subsidies for some pupils (Rogers Berner 2012, 119).[11] In Germany, the procedures under which and the amounts of public funding for non-governmental schools vary greatly between the *Länder*, going from about 55–85%. However, in some *Länder* religious schools are part of the 'public system' (meaning equal funding), and mostly non-governmental *religious* schools receive more public resources than non-governmental pedagogically distinctive schools, allowing the former to keep their tuition fees lower (Glenn 2012b, 218). In France, both national and local governments subsidise non-governmental religious schools, although what is being subsidised (salaries, operational costs, cost of building, or renovating facilities) varies according to the type of contract a school has with the state (see Pons, Van Zanten, and Da Costa 2015) and also depending on the local political climate. Yet, parity in funding of public and non-governmental schools is the norm, as was illustrated by the so-called *loi Carle* of 2009 that 'imposed on communes of residence the requirement to share in the operating costs of private elementary schools on the same terms as apply to public schools' (Legrand and Glenn 2012, 186). In the Netherlands, non-governmental religious schools are funded according to identical and equivalent criteria as governmental schools.[12] Ireland has a complex system of state funding. In primary education, for example, the Department of Education pays salaries directly to teachers (but schools are their legal employers) and gives grants directly to schools to meet their day-to-day running costs. In the past, costs of buildings were provided by churches who remain owners of the schools, but the state has paid for building of schools since 1999. State payment normally does not cover all running costs; most parents make what is called a 'voluntary contribution' to running costs. The state does not pay for uniforms, books, materials, school meals, and so on, except in the case of some grants, based on need. School transport costs for those living outside a radius of a school are also paid by the state. In Scotland, the 1918 Education Act created the opportunity for non-governmental Catholic schools to be incorporated into the system of state schools, which effectively happened from 1928 onwards. This means that these religious schools are state funded.

## School autonomy, public scrutiny, and freedoms: types and degrees

The extent to which non-governmental religious schools have effective opportunities to 'do as they please', or in other words, the scope and limits of their associational freedoms, should be understood against the background of the way countries seek to strike a balance among freedoms of parents 'to make fundamental decisions about the education of their children', the autonomy of people running individual schools (boards, teachers, daily management), and responsibilities of governments to oversee education in the light of the interests of society and children (Glenn and de Groof 2012, 1). The ways these balances are struck and the ways inevitable trade-offs are being made vary between educational systems. In the case of religious schools, educational systems have to deal with the following main tensions:

(1) The right to freedom of education interpreted as parental choice can conflict with the (proto-) freedoms of pupils, increasingly gaining in 'autonomy'.
(2) Organisational, educational, and pedagogical freedoms of religious schools may conflict with principles and rights of non-discrimination.
(3) Associational freedoms of religious schools to select students can be in tension with rights of equal educational opportunities for all.
(4) Educational/pedagogical freedoms of religious schools may conflict with demanding requirements of teaching and learning democratic citizenship and democratic virtues.
(5) Far-going decentralisation or autonomy of schools and teachers (in general, for religious schools in particular) combined with the monitoring and guaranteeing of educational performance, is a challenge for educational systems in general.[13]

Religious schools that are publicly financed are legitimately subjected to more extensive forms of control and accountability.[14] The main impact of the 'public trust theory', in our view, lies in rules requiring schools to be non-profit organisations (actually imposed in all countries) and in legitimate control of financial affairs: private schools may waste their own money if they so wish, but publicly financed school are accountable and should respect standards of efficiency and effectiveness. However, the differences between private and publicly financed schools are less evident with regard to the selection of teachers and students. Private religious schools, which are not publicly funded, still are subjected to basic non-discrimination legislation in employment and student selection, for example, they cannot discriminate on the basis of race and ethnicity. All religious schools, publicly financed or not, may argue for mission-based and circumscribed exemptions. The differences between public and private schools are even weaker regarding matters of content and pedagogy:

if schools want their exams to be recognised, they have to teach the minimal cognitive content of the curriculum. In the end, the moral intuition that public funding of schools also makes a huge difference in terms of content-control seems correct only *prima facie*.

To grasp the ways educational systems at certain moments in time find institutional ways of balancing these various concerns and tensions in exercising public scrutiny and to remain sensitive to the ways things work out in reality (not only formally or legally), one should in a stepwise approach disaggregate the shaping of associational freedoms of religious schools.

At the first level, the associational freedoms of non-governmental religious schools are shaped by the (earlier mentioned) legal status and the ways international and national constitutional arrangements protect educational and associational freedoms. At this level, one should be sensitive to distinctive traditions of governance of pluralism in the respective country, and specifically to the ways these have developed in the field of church–state interactions and in the educational field. Different religious groups struggled with the state about the provision of mass education, and the predominant outcomes vary between countries. For example, in the Netherlands Calvinist groups demanded quite successfully the right to be 'sovereign in their own set' (the phrase used by the nineteenth-century neo-Calvinists Groen van Prinsterer and Abraham Kuyper). The Catholic ideology of 'subsidiarity' was played out in the educational domain in the Netherlands, Belgium, Scotland, and Germany, but with different results. Interactions between dominant churches and the state developed differently in countries such as France, Germany and Britain, which has affected the opportunities for religious education. Besides, many of the Scandinavian countries, Germany (and the Netherlands to a lesser extent), have known important and influential movements of educational reform, ranging from the Free School movement in Denmark, to Rudolf Steiner-inspired Waldorf schools, to distinctive pedagogical programmes (including Montessori). These have given wider legitimacy to the idea that schools essentially belong to parents, not to the state, and strengthened the idea that a plurality of forms of education is essential to a free society.

At the second level, one needs to look at the broader (contemporary) system of governance employed in the educational domain. Systems of educational governance range from specified and strongly centralised, nearly full regulation and control with little or no autonomy in nearly all regards (in France, in Italy before 2000), to minimal regulation and control.[15] Fairly high degrees of associational autonomy in specific regards, for example, the freedom to recruit teachers or to select and admit pupils, can go hand in hand with nearly no autonomy in other regards, for example the freedom to shape the curriculum and select teaching material. The latter is the case, for example, in the Netherlands. In view of protecting educational freedom, the challenge is finding the least invasive or obtrusive but still effective ways and means of public regulation and control. Regulation and control of accreditation ranges from the pole of detailed specification in advance to more lenient rules and practices, and shorter periods between recognition and public financing. In some countries, accredited schools are controlled regularly (e.g. in England/Wales once in six years) in others only after a 'notice of complaint' or when withdrawal of financing or accreditation is more or less imminent. In addition to general curriculum guides or frameworks, accepted in most countries, some require curriculum plans specifying in detail not only subjects but also courses, or prescribe a minimum number of lessons, or even prescribe textbooks and teacher guides.[16] The more detailed these regulations and controls are, the less autonomy for teachers and schools generally, for religious schools in particular. In addition, the requirement to document all kinds of aspects of educational activities and to give account for a great number of internal decisions results in extra man-hours and costs, which is especially problematic for smaller schools. Opposition against this tendency is mounting even inside governmental schools. Alternatives are 'outcome driven approaches' or output regulation and control favoured by 'pro-choice' authors as 'smart regulation'. They require final attainment targets following from general curriculum guides or frameworks but leave schools and teachers – also in governmental but particularly in non-governmental schools – 'free to express its distinctive character and its method of teaching and to a considerable extent in the content of teaching, as well as in other aspects of school life' (de Groof 2004, 172). In order to make outcomes comparable and to test whether cognitive and non-cognitive achievements live up to minimum standards, they also require common, state or nationwide examinations[17] at least at the end of primary, secondary, and high-school education. The kinds of exams differ widely (oral, written, from multiple choice to open essays, course-work) regarding different subjects.[18] The 'pedagogical climate', 'atmosphere', 'ethos', or 'culture' of schools, related to the character of interactions in classes and in schools, as well as the actual learning of civic and democratic virtues, could be controlled, if at all, by external inspections in classes or schools (Eisengruber 2002, 70, 82). Some countries, for example France, go very far in this regard (at least in theory), others are much more reluctant.[19] Inspection, particularly unannounced state-inspection, is clearly the most effective method if one really wants to know what is actually going on in classrooms and schools, but it is also the most invasive one.[20]

At the third level, one should look at specific societal and political trends and incidents that may matter a great deal for the significance and scope of associational freedoms of religious schools in a given society. The founding of schools by religious newcomers (Muslim, Hindu, Sikh schools) has triggered discussions on religious schools. 'Radicalisation' among Islamic youth has become a key concern leading to increased scrutiny of Islamic schools. Fluctuations in public opinion and perceptions may thus have an effect on opportunities for all religious schools, or for a specific sub-category (such as orthodox schools or Islamic schools).

At the fourth level, one should take notice of the ways balances are struck at the level of individual schools (and specific sectors or types of schools). As we have mentioned, 'the school' is in itself a complex actor, making decisions and policies in a field with other actors (such as parents and inspectors) and with many incentives to be sensitive to the ways the school is being perceived by the wider society. For example, increasing societal concerns about anti-gay intolerance in the circles of conservative Christian and Muslim communities have resulted in several initiatives of religious schools to find ways of speaking about these topics. Given that schools are dealing with children and young adults on a daily basis, there are sometimes remarkable difference between the ideological and 'scandalised' tone of public-political debates, and the ways schools pragmatically search for ways of handling sensitive topics and issues.

In the contributions to this special issue several of these levels will be discussed, but here we limit ourselves to giving a rough impression of the ways a balance is struck between associational freedoms and other principles and concerns in the respective countries.

Denmark has a system with the highest overall amount of associational freedoms for religious schools. The constitutional right to freedom of education (Art. 76) implies ideological and pedagogical freedom, economic independence, freedom in staff recruitment, and freedom of selection of pupils in relation to religious and philosophical beliefs (Olsen 2015). In addition, the Danish educational system is fairly radically decentralised and puts a strong emphasis on 'the rights of parents (not the state) to have their children educated according to their preferred ideological outlook'. However, the emphasis on the rights of parents in education and the tradition of 'Free Schools' have over the past 15 years been challenged by policies imposing more conditions for the reception of state funds on non-governmental primary schools and closer monitoring of these schools by the state. Besides concerns about academic standards and mandatory civic education, in the case of Islamic schools state monitoring is also connected with government anti-radicalisation programmes. For Germany, the effective associational freedoms of governmental and non-governmental religious schools vary greatly between the *Länder*, because the latter have full responsibility for education and can therefore opt for diverging arrangements. Non-governmental religious schools have in most states substantial freedoms when deciding on the use of resources, but limited opportunities to choose teaching methods and decide on curriculum. They may also select teachers, but those whom they employ should be certified, and in selecting pupils they should not privilege children from wealthier families (Glenn 2012b). The French school system is predominantly government led and centralised, and, in comparative terms, parents, local authorities, and teachers have little opportunities to decide on nearly anything with respect to the ways schools operate (Legrand and Glenn 2012). For non-governmental schools that have a contract with the state, the degree of autonomy depends on the type of contract. Schools with a 'simple' contract can employ teachers on the basis of a private contract, they should comply with 80% of the national curriculum, and there is no obligation on behalf of municipalities to provide financial support. Schools with an 'association contract' have less autonomy; they should follow all rules and teach the entire curriculum, their teachers are either civil servants or under contract with the state, and they receive identical funds as governmental schools (Pons, Van Zanten, and Da Costa 2015). In Ireland, the Department of Education sets a broad regulatory framework within which schools in receipt of State funding are required to operate. The regulatory framework includes the curriculum, the governance structures for individual schools and the timeframe within which they are required to operate. While the country has a centrally devised curriculum, schools have considerable autonomy in deciding on the teaching methods and assessment methods to be used. However, national externally set and marked examinations, run by the State Examinations Commission, apply to all students at the end of lower second level education and on completion of upper second level education. The particular character of the school makes a vital contribution to shaping the curriculum in classrooms. Adaptation of the curriculum to suit the individual school is achieved through the preparation and continuous updating of a school plan. The selection of text books and classroom resources to support the implementation of the curriculum is made by schools, rather than by the Department of Education and Science or the National Council for Curriculum and Assessment.[21] Schools in general appoint their own teachers, and have a somewhat controversial exemption from the conditions of equality legislation and discrimination on grounds of religion. They can also select among pupils on grounds of religion, but not on other grounds.[22] The Netherlands also has a strong constitutional guarantee of educational freedom. Non-governmental, denominational schools (*bijzondere scholen*) are subject to the same general education regulations and quality standards as governmental schools, and they should employ certified teachers, but they have some opportunities to select teachers and pupils on the basis of their religious and philosophical views, to have some say on curriculum in relation to the religious identity of the school, and to impose rules with regard to dress and behaviour in the school context. However, the Dutch educational system is also fairly centralised and all schools have to respect qualitative standards set by the Ministry of Education, including, for example, the subjects to be studied, the attainment targets of examination syllabuses, the content of national examinations, the number of teaching periods per year, etc. (Versteegt and Maussen 2011, 13). In the Netherlands, the issue of autonomy of religious schools is now widely debated, especially with regard to conservative Christian schools and Islamic schools. In Scotland, non-governmental, Catholic schools negotiated a firm position for their associational autonomy around the 1918 Education Act. They retain influence over staffing, curriculum, ethos, and inspection (Flint 2007, 258).

## Religious schools: key issues, basic tensions, and public debates – outline of the special issue

In the above we have discussed the ways in which educational systems provide opportunities and obstacles for the creation and operation of religious schools. The empirical contributions in this special issue explore different tensions that have arisen in various countries, and which have given rise to public debates, policy changes, and sometimes legal and constitutional amendments.

Obviously, the way these tensions are framed and the way in which problems are perceived, not only depend on such structural tensions but also on developments of the country-specific institutional arrangements, political opportunity structures, and the ways in which political contestation and public debates around minority and majority rights develop. Although the articles have different focuses, depending on the salience of particular issues in specific countries, it is possible to detect common themes in them. When questions are being raised about (some specific) religious schools, we mostly encounter three main issues. First, debates about the performance of this type of education compared to other (governmental or non-governmental) forms of non-religious education. These debates on performance may touch on all kinds of aspects: cognitive achievements (including mastery of the language of the 'host society' in the case of children with an immigrant background), 'teaching of citizenship and tolerance' and 'preparing pupils for life in liberal democratic and pluralistic societies'. Second, in what ways does the existence of religious schools relate to patterns of ethnic, religious and socio-economic segregation? What are the consequences of having separate religious schools and what are normative arguments for and against 'voluntary separation'? Often religious schools are said to be illustrative of minorities' strategies of 'isolation' or 'self-segregation', if not as institutions that are illustrative of 'backwardness', 'gender discriminatory ideologies and practices', and 'religious fundamentalism'. In nearly all countries the contrast space to this danger of segregation is constructed around concepts such as 'common citizenship' and 'integration', which are seen as a crucial goal of education and often connected to the need for common, state schools (see Merry 2013, 2015). Third, often questions are being raised with regard to the outer limits of religious and educational freedoms for religious schools. One of the broader underlying questions, then, is to see whether indeed this type of school and it organisational practices should continue to be 'tolerated' or whether there are grounds for more forthcoming forms of recognition.

# RELIGIOUS SCHOOLS IN EUROPE

In 'The Danish Free School Tradition under Pressure', Tore Vincents Olsen explores how the right to fund non-governmental 'free schools', including religious ones, and to have them funded by the state, functioned as one of the strongest expressions of Danish 'free-mindedness' or tolerance. It allowed parents to choose a school for their children according to their own ideological, religious, cultural, and pedagogical convictions. However, the existence and associational freedoms of these schools are now under debate. New clauses in the law on free primary schools demand that they 'shall prepare the students to live in a society like Denmark, with freedom and democracy'. Monitoring mechanisms have been reinforced to ensure that private schools live up to academic standards and teach 'freedom and democracy' to a sufficient degree. The article analyses the debate about Danish free schools and about Muslim schools in particular and discusses the extent to which the legislative changes have reduced the autonomy of non-governmental schools.

Annette Scheunpflug addresses the increasing demand for religious schools in Germany in an article entitled 'Non-Governmental Religious Schools in Germany'. Against the broader background of institutional opportunities for religious schools in the governmental and non-governmental sector, the issue is raised why in the context of increasing 'secularisation' and 'decline of belief' the demand for faith-based schooling is on the rise. As the article demonstrates, the demand of parents for non-governmental religious schools is not primarily driven by religious considerations, but is motivated by concerns about educational profiles of these schools, the wish for social distinction, and better performance.

In 'The National Management of Public and Catholic Schools in France: Moving from a Loosely Coupled Towards an Integrated System?', Xavier Pons, Agnès van Zanten, and Sylvie Da Costa analyse changes in the management of private Catholic schools under State contract since the 1980s. Building on ongoing research about comparing policies of accountability in France and in Quebec, the authors show that the introduction of NPM approaches and instruments in the field of education did not have a significant influence either on the public management of State-controlled non-governmental schools or on the coupling between the public and the private sector. The management of Catholic schools is still mainly based on a consensual regulation through inputs, which leads to a loosely coupled system of management of private and public schools.

Nathalie Rougier and Iseult Honohan examine the evolution of the state-supported denominational education system in Ireland in the context of increasing social diversity in an article called 'Religion and Education in Ireland: Growing Diversity – or Losing Faith in the System?' The article explores the capacity for incremental change in a system of institutional pluralism hitherto dominated by a single religion. In particular, challenges to the historical arrangements that emerged in two recent contentious issues are analysed: cuts in special funding for Protestant secondary schools, and proposed diversification of the patronage of primary schools, revealing pressures on the dominant role of the Catholic Church and on the privileged place of religion in education. They find a shift towards a more varied pluralism, or greater 'diversity of schools', in which multi- or non-denominational schools now feature more prominently, rather than towards either a secular system or privileged recognition of religious schools. These developments entail a change in the historical balance of religious equality and freedoms; from leaning more towards collective religious freedom and equality among religions, to tilting more towards individual religious freedom and non-discrimination.

# RELIGIOUS SCHOOLS IN EUROPE

In 'Liberal Equality and Toleration for Conservative Religious Minorities. Decreasing Opportunities for Religious Schools in the Netherlands?', Marcel Maussen and Floris Vermeulen begin by observing that liberal, democratic states face new challenges in, on the one hand, balancing between principles of religious freedoms and non-discrimination and, on the other hand, in balancing these constitutional principles with other concerns, including social cohesion, good education, and immigrant integration. In the context of increased dominance of a 'secular' native Dutch population, there are demands to reduce 'exceptions' for (orthodox) religious groups. The article focuses in particular on public debate and jurisprudence with regard to conservative religious schools, including their right to select and refuse pupils (the debate on the so-called 'duty to enrol' (*acceptatieplicht*)), teaching on sexuality and sexual diversity, and the possibilities for schools to refuse hiring staff who do not support the school's philosophy (e.g. in relation to sexual orientation). The article concludes by arguing that the Netherlands is undergoing a shift in the conceptualisation of religious freedom in relation to liberal equality, which in the longer run may destabilise a tradition of toleration and substantial collective freedoms for conservative religious groups.

In their contribution entitled 'The Continued Existence of State-Funded Catholics Schools in Scotland', Stephen J. McKinney and James C. Conroy begin by locating the Scottish debate in the history and development of the faith schools debate in the UK, particularly England and Wales. The debate in Scotland has distinctive features that need to be understood. The article then focuses on a critical examination and analysis of two key contemporary themes concerning state-funded Catholic schools in the Scottish context. The first theme is the continuation of government funding of Catholic schooling. The second theme, which is more distinctive to Scotland and has some links to the debate on faith schools in Northern Ireland, concerns the allegations that Catholic schools are associated with sectarianism.

The remaining two articles in the special issue are not case studies of specific countries but aim to provide a bigger, comparative picture. In 'What Can International Comparisons Teach Us about School Choice and Non-Governmental Schools in Europe?', Jaap Dronkers and Silvia Avram begin by observing that states have right to supervise non-governmental schools that they finance and to seek to guarantee that the quality of organisation and teachers are not lower than those in governmental schools. Four basic arrangements exist of non-governmental and governmental schools in Europe: integrated educational systems of public and non-state schools, denomination supportive educational systems, limited support non-governmental schools, and educational systems with segregated public and non-state schools. The article then draws on an analysis of empirical data to explore three main topics: parental background and the choice for non-governmental schools, non-governmental schools and their cognitive outcomes, and non-governmental schools and their non-cognitive outcomes. It concludes that there are important differences between non-governmental-*in*dependent (without state grants) and non-governmental-*de*pendent schools (with state grants); that school choice for non-governmental-*de*pendent schools is more related to socially mobile parents, whereas schools choice for non-governmental-*in*dependent schools is more related the reproduction of social classes; that in a majority of European countries non-governmental-*de*pendent schools are more effective cognitively than governmental schools, but that non-governmental-*in*dependent schools are more effective cognitively only in a few countries and more ineffective in a larger number of countries. Also non-governmental-*de*pendent schools are not more effective non-cognitively than governmental schools.

In the final contribution entitled 'The Conundrum of Religious Schools in Europe', Michael S. Merry examines in detail the continued – and curious – popularity of religious schools in an otherwise 'secular' Europe. Various motivations underwrite the decision to place one's child in a religious school and the article then delineates what are likely the best empirically supported explanations for the continued dominant position of Protestant and Catholic schools in twenty-first century Europe. Merry argues that institutional racism may well inform both parental assessments of school quality as well as selective mechanisms many mainstream religious schools use to function as domains of exclusion. He then distinguishes between religious schools in a dominant position from those serving disadvantaged minorities and argues that the latter are able to play a crucially important function other schools only rarely provide, and hence that vulnerable minorities may have a reason to value.

## Acknowledgements

This introductory article builds on our comparative report 'Religious Schools and Tolerance' in Bader and Maussen (2012). The articles on Denmark, Ireland, and the Netherlands build on studies that were conducted as part of a European Commission, DG Research, 7th Framework Programme, Socio-Economic Sciences and Humanities, Research Project 'Tolerance, Pluralism and Social Cohesion: Responding to the Challenges of the 21st Century in Europe' (ACCEPT PLURALISM) (2010–2013) (call FP7-SSH-2009-A, grant agreement no. 243837), Coordinator: Prof. Anna Triandafyllidou, Robert Schuman Centre for Advanced Studies, European University Institute. Most articles were presented during the workshop 'Tolerance and Faith-Based Education in Europe: Liberalism, Freedom of Education and Equality' held at the University of Amsterdam on 23–24 May 2013.

We thank the authors of the various contributions in this volume for comments and suggestions for their respective countries in this introduction.

## Notes

1. See OSCE (2004), especially the section on Religion and Education.
2. See Olsen (2015) on Denmark and see also the recent debate on the growing influence of radical Muslims in state schools in Birmingham. See Gilligan (2014).
3. For a broader overview of some of these structural social changes, see Norris and Inglehart (2011).
4. We introduce the countries included in the special issue in alphabetic order throughout this article (Denmark, Germany, Ireland, France, the Netherlands, and Scotland).
5. We draw here on the estimates of 'market shares' provided in the various contributions in this volume and on Bader and Maussen 2012. This is, depending on existing information and evidence, a very rough estimate indeed because, obviously, it makes a difference whether one takes percentages of students or of the number of schools. In the Netherlands, for example, many non-governmental schools (particularly Montessori, Islamic and Reformed schools) have much less than average number of students so that the percentage of non-governmental schools is higher than the percentage of students. Still, the overall estimates give an indication of the relative importance of the non-governmental religious sector.
6. Normatively speaking, two sets of reasons are commonly taken to be the most convincing ones: First, in all cases in which majority religious schools are recognised and publicly financed *equality before the law* requires a fair and even-handed treatment of all religious schools (Bader 2007, 160). Second, if states depend considerably on religious schools to live up to their obligations to provide education for all (for whatever historical or recent reasons), i.e. if religious schools meaningfully *help to realise mandatory public services*, fairness requires that they should be equally publicly funded.
7. See the country studies in Wolf and Macedo (2004) and the comparative analysis and its results by Glenn and de Groof (2002a, 578ff., 584ff., Chart 2, 2002b, Chap. 9).

8. Depending on the legislation in different countries, public subsidies may cover the full cost or more selective personnel wages and pensions, the functioning costs, equipment, building, loans or grants for capital expenditure, fees, fiscal advantages, and supplemental services for pupils (Glenn and de Groof 2002b, 253).
9. See Green, Baker, and Oluwole (2013) for an excellent overview of the most relevant Court rulings in different states.
10. See also http://www.edreform.com/2012/03/just-the-faqs-charter-schools/.
11. The Danish *taximeter system* comprises four grants: a basic grant (lump sum), a teaching, an administration/operations, and a building grant to cover rent, interest, debt servicing, and maintenance based on the actual levels of verified number of enrolled pupils (Glenn and de Groof 2002a, 190).
12. As a matter of fact, sometimes non-governmental schools receive even more funding than public schools. This is due to inflexibility of the system of financing, in itself a legacy of pillarisation, meaning that sometimes resources should be distributed proportionally between governmental and non-governmental schools. For example, if local authorities in a municipality decide to spent *additional* amounts (almost all funding actually comes from the central government) for staff or material upkeep for the governmental schools (that they administrate!), they must spent the same amount for non-governmental schools (Zoontjens and Glenn 2012, 343–344).
13. Clearly it is not 'autonomy of schools or teachers' in itself that is responsible for low performance, as is clear from Finland (see Sahlberg 2011), where very high degrees of autonomy go hand in hand with comparatively high standards of performance (and, in addition, comparatively low costs). The 'public secret' of the 'Finnish success' is: highly qualified teachers (and the 'trust' they gain combined with 'respect'). This can be compared with the situation in Denmark, where there is high school autonomy but comparatively poor performance while being among the most costly models (Olsen and Ahlgren 2011).
14. In England/Wales, for example, all schools except independent schools are included in inspection regimes (Leenknegt 1997, 107ff; Harris 2004, 102–107), in Belgium only if a school asks for community support and for 'recognition of certificates' (Groof 2004, 166).
15. See Glenn and de Groof (2002a, 596 ff.): Charts for Rating the National Systems with regard to Freedom, Equal Treatment, and Autonomy. See Bader (2007, 279–283). See Dronkers and Avram (2015).
16. Hotly contested cases in this respect are music and drama in conservative religious schools (Jewish, Christian, Islamic), sex education either explicitly or in 'personal, social and health teaching', and, obviously, evolution theory versus creationism or intelligent design. See Maussen and Vermeulen (2015).
17. Hotly contested in federal education regimes, like Germany or the USA. The Dutch regime is fully centralised in this, as in all other regards. Also in Finland, where schools and teachers have an extremely high degree of autonomy, they are 'disciplined' by national exams (see Sahlberg 2011).
18. Yet, one should be aware of two combined dangers. First, one can use common exams as a backdoor strategy to impose statism and professionalist secularism on all schools. This danger can be prevented effectively only by integration of the different educational providers in standard-setting and preparing common exams. Second, one should also be aware of the combined pressure from the side of 'free-choice-parents' and governmental authorities to introduce testing in all schools and classes all the time starting from pre-schooling. This should not be misunderstood as an argument against obligations for schools to provide information on (1) admission of students, (2) curriculum and pedagogy, (3) student achievements, and (4) expenditure and financial information (Witte 2004, 363ff.). Both in Denmark and in Sweden, public ranking of schools is proscribed.
19. For the excessively comprehensive and centralised rules in France, see Meuret (2004, 247ff). Norway seems still to be free of any inspection (Glenn and Groof 2002a, 593) and also of standard testing until the end of compulsory education (Glenn and Groof 2002a, 401ff.) and Finland is free of any inspection (and, by the way, all other types of regulations: it completely trusts highly educated and qualified (and highly paid) teachers). In Sweden and Denmark, there is also no national inspectorate, quality control is left up to parents 'who can select the person who will supervise their compliance' and either may

20. In the case of Islamic schools in Denmark and the Netherlands, there is now more political support for government inspection of civic education and the teaching of democratic values.
21. From NCCA website – http://www.ncca.ie/en/Curriculum_and_Assessment/.
22. Under section 7(3) of the Equal Status Act 2000 schools can discriminate by giving preference in admissions to children of a particular denomination, or by refusing to admit a child where such refusal is essential to maintain the ethos of the school. Under the Employment Equality Act 1998, certain religious, educational, and medical institutions may give 'more favourable treatment on the ground of religion to an employee or prospective employee where it is reasonable to do so in order to maintain the religious ethos of the institution' or take 'action which is necessary to prevent an employee or a prospective employee from undermining the religious ethos of the institution'. See http://www.irishstatutebook.ie/2000/en/act/pub/0008/print.html#sec7.

(Note: item 20 continues from previous page; items above preceded by item about appointing an external evaluator or asking the municipal council to assume this role, based on self-assessments (Glenn and Groof 2002a, 197, 200, 579).)

## References

Bader, V. 2007. *Secularism or Democracy? Associational Governance of Religious Diversity*. Amsterdam: Amsterdam University Press.

Bader, V., and M. Maussen. 2012. "Religious Schools and Tolerance." In *Tolerance and Cultural Diversity in Schools. Comparative Report*, edited by M. Maussen and V. Bader, 87–107. Accept-Pluralism, Working Paper, 2012/01. http://cadmus.eui.eu/handle/1814/20955

Battaglia, M. 2014. "La polémique sur le genre pèse sur les écoles." *Le Monde*, February 14.

van Bijsterveld, S. 2011. *Burger tussen religie, staat en markt* [Citizen Between Religion, State and Market]. Inaugural Lecture. University of Tilburg.

Dronkers, J., and S. Avram. 2015. "What Can International Comparisons Teach Us About School Choice and Non-governmental Schools in Europe?" *Comparative Education* 51 (1): 118–132.

Eisengruber, C. 2002. "How Do Liberal Democracies Teach Values?" In *Educating Citizens: International Perspectives on Civic Values and School Choice*, edited by P. Wolf and S. Macedo, 58–86. Washington, DC: Brookings Institution Press.

Flint, J. 2007. "Faith Schools, Multiculturalism and Community Cohesion: Muslim and Roman Catholic State Schools in England and Scotland." *Policy & Politics* 35 (2): 251–268.

Foblets, M. C., and K. Alidadi. 2013. *Religion in the Context of the European Union: Engaging the Interplay Between Religious Diversity and Secular Models*. Religious Diversity and Secular Models in Europe (RELIGARE). Final Report.

Gilligan, A. 2014. "State Schools Isolate Non-Muslims." *The Telegraph*, April 18.

Glenn, C. L. 2012a. "State and Schools: An Historical Overview." In *Balancing Freedom, Autonomy and Accountability in Education*, edited by C. L. Glenn and J. de Groof, Vol. 1, 3–24. Nijmegen: Wolf Legal.

Glenn, C. L. 2012b. "Germany." In *Balancing Freedom, Autonomy and Accountability in Education*, edited by C. L. Glenn and J. de Groof, Vol. 2, 209–228. Nijmegen: Wolf Legal.

Glenn, C. L. 2012c. "Scotland." In *Balancing Freedom, Autonomy and Accountability in Education*, edited by C. L. Glenn and J. de Groof, Vol. 2, 451–463. Nijmegen: Wolf Legal.

Glenn, C. L., and G. de Groof, eds. 2002a. *Finding the Right Balance. Freedom, Autonomy and Accountability in Education*, Vol. 1. Utrecht: Lemma.

Glenn, C. L., and G. de Groof, eds. 2002b. *Finding the Right Balance. Freedom, Autonomy and Accountability in Education*, Vol. 2. Utrecht: Lemma.

Glenn, C. L., and G. de Groof. 2012. "Introduction to Volume One." In *Balancing Freedom, Autonomy and Accountability in Education*, edited by C. L. Glenn and J. de Groof, Vol. 1, 1–2. Nijmegen: Wolf Legal.

Green, P.III, B. Baker, and J. Oluwole. 2013. "Having It Both Ways: How Charter Schools Try to Obtain Funding of Public Schools and the Autonomy of Private Schools." *Emory Law Journal* 63 (2): 303–337.

de Groof, J. 2004. "Regulating School Choice in Belgium's Flemish Community." In *Educating Citizens: International Perspectives on Civic Values and School Choice*, edited by P. Wolf and S. Macedo, 157–186. Washington, DC: Brookings Institution Press.

de Groof, J. 2012. "Legal Framework for Freedom of Education." In *Balancing Freedom, Autonomy and Accountability in Education*, edited by C. L. Glenn and J. de Groof, Vol. 1, 25–62. Nijmegen: Wolf Legal.

Hand, M. 2012. "A New Dawn for Faith-Based Education? Opportunities for Religious Organisations in the UK's New School System." *Journal of Philosophy of Education* 46 (4): 546–559.

Harris, N. 2004. "Regulation, Choice, and Basic Values in Education in England and Wales." In *Educating Citizens: International Perspectives on Civic Values and School Choice*, edited by P. Wolf and S. Macedo, 91–130. Washington, DC: Brookings Institution Press.

de Hart, J. 2014. *Geloven binnen en buiten verband. Godsdienstige ontwikkelingen in Nederland* [Keeping the Faith? Trends in Religion in the Netherlands]. Den Haag: The Netherlands Institute for Social Research Publications.

Hatcher, R. 2011. "The Conservative-Liberal Democrat Coalition Government's 'Free Schools' in England." *Educational Review* 63 (4): 485–503.

Hemerijck, A. 2013. *Changing Welfare States*. Oxford: Oxford University Press.

Hunter-Henin, M. 2011. "Introduction." In *Law, Religious Freedoms and Education in Europe*, edited by M. Hunter-Henin, 1–33. Farnham: Ashgate.

Kriesi, H. 2010. "Restructuration of Partisan Politics and the Emergence of a New Cleavage Based on Values." *West European Politics* 33 (3): 673–685.

Leenknegt, G. 1997. *Vrijheid van Onderwijs in 5 Europese Landen* [Freedom of Education in 5 European Countries]. Deventer: Tjeenk Willink.

Legrand, A., and C. L. Glenn. 2012. "France." In *Balancing Freedom, Autonomy and Accountability in Education*, edited by C. L. Glenn and J. de Groof, Vol. 2, 175–208. Nijmegen: Wolf Legal.

Mair, P. 2013. *Ruling the Void: The Hollowing of Western Democracy*. New York: Verso.

Maussen, M. 2014. "Religious Governance in the Netherlands: Associative Freedoms and Non-Discrimination after 'Pillarization'. The Example of Faith-Based Schools." *Geopolitics, History, and International Relations* 6 (2): (ahead of print)

Maussen, M., and R. Grillo. 2014. "Regulation of Speech in Multicultural Societies: Introduction." *Journal of Ethnic and Migration Studies* 40 (2): 174–193.

Maussen, M., and F. Vermeulen. 2015. "Liberal Equality and Toleration for Conservative Religious Minorities. Decreasing Opportunities for Religious Schools in the Netherlands?" *Comparative Education* 51 (1): 87–104.

McKinney, S. J., and Conroy, J. C. 2015. "The Continued Existence of State-funded Catholics Schools in Scotland." *Comparative Education* 51 (1): 105–117.

Merry, M. S. 2013. *Equality, Citizenship, and Segregation. A Defense of Separation*. Houndmills: Palgrave/MacMillan.

Merry, M. S. 2015. "The Conundrum of Religious Schools in Twenty-First Century Europe." *Comparative Education* 51 (1): 133–156.

Meuret, D. 2004. "School Choice and its Regulation in France." In *Educating Citizens: International Perspectives on Civic Values and School Choice*, edited by P. Wolf and S. Macedo, 238–267. Washington, DC: Brookings Institution Press.

Monsma, S. V., and J. C. Soper. 2009. *The Challenge of Pluralism: Church and State in Five Democracies*. 2nd ed. Lanham: Rowman & Littlefield.

National Education Council. 2012. *Artikel 23 Grondwet in maatschappelijk perspectief. Nieuwe richtingen aan de vrijheid van onderwijs* [Article 23 Constitution in Societal Perspective. New Directions for the Freedom of Education]. Den Haag: Onderwijsraad.

Norris, P., and R. Inglehart. 2011. *Sacred and Secular: Religion and Politics Worldwide*. Cambridge: Cambridge University Press.

Olsen, T. V. 2015. "The Danish Free School Tradition Under Pressure." *Comparative Education* 51 (1): 22–37.

Olsen, T. V., and S. M. Ahlgren. 2011. "(In)tolerance and Accommodation of Difference in Danish Public and Private Schools." Accept-Pluralism, Working Paper No. 2011/09. http://cadmus.eui.eu/handle/1814/19796

O'Mahony, C. 2012. "Ireland." In *Balancing Freedom, Autonomy and Accountability in Education*, edited by C. L. Glenn and J. de Groof, Vol. 2, 245–259. Nijmegen: Wolf Legal.

OSCE (Organisation for Security and Co-operation in Europe). 2004. *Guidelines for Review of Legislation Pertaining to Religion and Belief*. Accessed May 28. http://www.osce.org/odihr/13993

Pons, X., A. van Zanten, and S. Da Costa. 2015. "The National Management of Public and Catholic Schools in France: Moving from a Loosely Coupled Towards an Integrated System?" *Comparative Education* 51 (1): 57–70.

Rangvid, B. S. 2008. "Private School Diversity in Denmark's National Voucher System." *Scandinavian Journal of Educational Research* 52 (4): 331–354.

Rogers Berner, A. 2012. "Funding Schools." In *Balancing Freedom, Autonomy and Accountability in Education*, edited by C. L. Glenn and J. de Groof, Vol. 1, 115–129. Nijmegen: Wolf Legal.

Rouvoet, A. 2011. "Formele en materiële democratie en de vitaliteit van grondrechten [Formal and Material Democracy and the Vitality of Constitutional Rights]." Paper ter gelegenheid van het afscheidssymposium Groen van Prinsterer Stichting – Tweede Kamerfractie ChristenUnie.

Sahlberg, P. 2011. *Finnish Lessons: What Can the World Learn from Educational Change in Finland?* New York: Teachers College Press, Columbia University.

Scheunpflug, A. 2015. "Non-governmental Religious Schools in Germany – Increasing Demand by Decreasing Religiosity?" *Comparative Education* 51 (1): 38–56.

Schlikerman, B. 2014. "Charter School's Religious Affiliation Raises Questions." *Chicago Sun Times*, February 22.

Schuh, C., M. Burchardt, and M. Wohlrab-Sahr. 2012. "Contested Secularities: Religious Minorities and Secular Progressivism in the Netherlands." *Journal of Religion in Europe* 5 (3): 349–383.

Versteegt, I., and M. Maussen. 2011. "The Netherlands: Challenging Diversity in Education and School Life." Accept-Pluralism, Working Paper, 2011/11. http://hdl.handle.net/1814/19798

Whitty, G. 2009. "Marketization and Post-Marketization in Education." In *Second International Handbook of Educational Change*, edited by A. Hargreaves, A. Lieberman, M. Fullan and D. Hopkins, 405–413. Dordrecht: Springer.

Whitty, G., and S. Power. 2000. "Marketization and Privatization in Mass Education Systems." *International Journal of Educational Development* 20 (2): 93–107.

Wiborg, S. 2012. "Denmark." In *Balancing Freedom, Autonomy and Accountability in Education*, edited by C. L. Glenn and J. de Groof, Vol. 2, 99–109. Nijmegen: Wolf Legal.

Witte, J. 2004. "Regulation in Public and Private Schools in the United States." In *Educating Citizens: International Perspectives on Civic Values and School Choice*, edited by P. Wolf and S. Macedo, 355–367. Washington, DC: Brookings Institution Press.

Wolf, P. J., and S. Macedo, eds. 2004. *Educating Citizens: International Perspectives on Civic Values and School Choice*. Washington, DC: Brookings Institution Press.

Zoontjens, P. J. J., and C. L. Glenn. 2012. "Netherlands." In *Balancing Freedom, Autonomy and Accountability in Education*, edited by C. L. Glenn and J. de Groof, Vol. 2, 333–362. Nijmegen: Wolf Legal.

# The Danish free school tradition under pressure

Tore Vincents Olsen

*Department of Political Science and Government, Aarhus University, Aarhus, Denmark*

> The Danish free school tradition has entailed a large degree of associational freedom for non-governmental schools, religious as well as non-religious. Until the late 1990s, the non-governmental schools were under no strict ideological or pedagogical limitations; they could recruit teachers and students according to their own value base, and were given a large state subsidy. From the late 1990s, a number of legislative changes were introduced demanding that non-governmental schools provide civic education and document the academic value of their teaching programmes. The rules concerning the monitoring of schools were also changed. This article analyses the political justification for these changes and asks to what extent the changes have altered the Danish free school tradition.

## Introduction

In Denmark, non-governmental schools (religious as well as non-religious) have traditionally enjoyed a high degree of associational freedom in terms of ideology, pedagogy, recruitment of staff and students, generous state subsidies and a loose and decentralised control. The freedom of Danish non-governmental schools, officially known as 'free primary schools', is the result of a social and political struggle against church and state domination in the educational sphere that began in the early nineteenth century. The struggle was headed by the 'free school movement', which established and represented a number of free schools from the 1850s onwards. The free school movement achieved its first legislative victory in 1855, when the 'free school law' established the right for parents to choose the school for their children (or teach them at home) based on a general duty to *educate* their children rather than a 'school duty' in the strict sense, *as long as* the education provided was 'equivalent' to public school education.[1] In 1915, this resulted in an amendment to the constitution, which was written into the current 1953 Danish constitution, guaranteeing free public schooling for every child and giving parents the right to provide their children with 'instruction equivalent to the general primary school standard' by sending them to a non-governmental school of their choosing or, alternatively, to home-school them.

The freedom of parents and schools was not established all at once, since the clause demanding education 'equivalent' to the public school could be and initially *was* specified rather closely. From the 1930s and until the 1990s, however, the freedom of the schools increased significantly, providing the schools with considerable ideological and pedagogical freedoms and allowing them to recruit students and staff according to their own value base. At the same time, there was no detailed specification of the subjects to be taught or the educational targets to be reached, and the main responsibility for monitoring the schools was entrusted to the parents, while the state provided the schools with high subsidies (as high as 85% in 1979). Significantly and in continuation of the free school movement's notion of free-mindedness, schools could espouse views that were in 'strong opposition' to those of the majority, ranging from Nazi sympathies in the 1930s to revolutionary views in the 1970s, as long as the schools did not 'act' (with violence) on their views; and this despite the fact that they received state subsidies (Korsgaard and Wiborg 2006, 378–379).

However, in the last 15 years, the state has issued a number of new regulations regarding the free schools and hence on the conditions for running religious school in Denmark. This can be seen as the prerogative of the state to specify once again more in detail what it means for non-governmental schools to provide a 'public school equivalent' education. This article tracks the motivation for this state regulation and the consequences of it, *asking to what extent the associational freedoms of these schools have been reduced or redefined in such a manner that there is a fundamental break with the Danish 'free school tradition'* that evolved since the 1930s and entailed a high degree of freedom of conscience and belief in education. The description of the historical background and the Danish free school tradition is based on secondary sources while the article's main contribution in the analysis of policy changes since the late 1990s is primarily based on legislative documents and interviews with the representative organisations of the free primary school sector.

The present article explores the thesis that the freedom of Danish non-governmental schools has been redefined due to concerns with the competitiveness of the Danish education system in light of (economic) globalisation and due to (partly related) concerns regarding the integration of immigration-based minorities and fears of political extremism; and that the regulative changes for the non-governmental schools thereby partly follow the changes in the regulation of the public school.

## Education on the agenda

In Denmark, education is high on the political agenda for three reasons. First, there is an ambition to maintain and improve the global economic competitiveness of the Danish nation, a political priority since the economic crises of the 1970s (Pedersen 2011a). Furthermore, disappointing results from the Programme for International Student Assessment (PISA) of the The Organisation for Economic Co-operation and Development (OECD) in 2000 – which hit a policy community already concerned with the academic quality of Danish schools – thrust education high on the political agenda. Second, the 'integration' of marginalised groups, especially non-Western immigrants and their descendants, has been a high priority since the 1990s. Non-integrated groups were commonly viewed as a burden on the welfare services. Along with the gradual shift from the welfare state to the workfare state (Torfing 2004), new emphasis was placed on duties rather than rights. Everybody had to contribute to society actively and be able to participate and work smoothly with the institutions of a modern society. It has increasingly been stressed that all citizens be at least familiar with and preferably acquire (liberal) national values (Mouritsen and Olsen 2013). Schools were seen as a place where the socialisation of marginalised groups could take place and where immigrants and descendants could learn the values and practices of Danish liberal democracy (Jensen 2010). This includes the conviction that religion and politics are to be considered separate matters, a belief that some leading politicians somewhat paradoxically base on the national Christian Evangelical-Lutheran culture, thereby indirectly protecting the privileged position in the constitutional order of the Danish People's Church from demands for disestablishment (Berg-Sørensen 2006; Christoffersen 2010; Olsen 2011; Mouritsen and Olsen 2013). Third, particularly since 9/11 there also is a fear of extremism that might lead to terrorism. Particular concern here pertains to Muslims and non-governmental Muslim schools, the fear being that they might function as breeding grounds for extremism (Lindekilde and Sedgwick 2012).

The main focus for the government continues to be the public school, which still takes care of the majority of schoolchildren in Denmark (in 2012, 79% of children in Grades 0–10). Accelerated by a shift to a centre–right government in 2001, the public school system witnessed a relative shift towards increased focus on measurable skills and competences and away from a conception of schools as a place for the general education or *Bildung* of the individual and future citizen (Korsgaard 2010; Pedersen 2011b). In light of the PISA results, the national politicians have wanted to reinforce this focus and have left part of the more decentralised aspects of the public school behind. In 2003, educational goals and guidelines set by the Ministry of Education (ME) were changed from recommendations to teachers to obligatory goals that had to be reached within each subject (Holm-Larsen 2006). The range of subjects included in the final exams of the public school was expanded so it covered not only core topics such as Danish, math and English, but also the natural sciences as well as history, social studies and Christianity studies (Holm-Larsen 2006). Furthermore, the exams were made obligatory rather than optional, and they were made the basis of access to upper secondary education (Holm-Larsen 2006). The logic behind the new 'Common Goals' (*Fælles Mål*) for the public school was that they should facilitate new national tests in the public school at different age grades, rendering it possible to see the extent to which the school population had reached required levels. This was also supposed to contribute to an overall 'culture of evaluation' in the public school system (Holm-Larsen 2006). The latter was reinforced by the publication of grade point averages (GPAs) from each school's final exams so that the public, parents and students would be able to compare schools. Combined with the free choice of public schools (introduced in 2005), the publication of GPAs would create a market-like incentive structure for schools to improve their results. The publication of GPAs for each school has been suspended by the centre–left government that came to power in 2011, however, due to fears of unfair comparisons between schools with very different student populations and the likely negative effects of privileged families de-selecting certain schools with low GPAs. But the Common Goals, national tests and obligatory final exams stay in place since they originally were backed by the Social Democrats (SD), the leading party in the current centre–left government coalition.

The question then becomes whether the developments in public schools are followed or accompanied by similar developments in the regulation of non-governmental schools and the extent to which this leaves the Danish free school tradition, with its large associational freedom for schools, intact. The next section briefly describes the historical background of the free school tradition and lays out its defining features before turning to the analysis of the last 15 years of change in the regulation of the sector. The last section analyses how the changes are perceived to affect the associational freedom of non-governmental schools, including religious ones, by the central representatives of the non-governmental school sector.

# RELIGIOUS SCHOOLS IN EUROPE

**The Danish free school tradition**

The Danish free school tradition gave Danish free primary schools a large degree of associational freedom. The associational freedom of schools depends on the extent to which they are regulated, subsidised and controlled (Bader 2007, 279–283). An important dimension in the regulation concerns what schools are required to teach in terms of knowledge, technical skills, values and virtues and how it is controlled that schools live up to the regulation through input control (control through specification of school teaching programmes), throughput control (control of teaching practices) and output control (control of results). Important is also who is controlling, for example, the state (e.g. ME, central inspectorates), the local administrations (which might be running 'competing' public schools as in the Danish case), the parents or other types of actors (e.g. certified inspectors) or even the schools themselves through self-control. School freedom also depends on the extent to which schools can be selective in their staff and student recruitment. Finally, the level of public subsidy shapes the schools' freedom to pursue their own policies independently of other actors. There is no simple formula for the calculation of associational freedom, but all things considered the less regulation and (centralised) control and the more public subsidy, the larger the freedom is. Based on secondary sources, this section provides a brief sketch rather than a detailed account of the background and fundamental features of the Danish free school tradition sufficient to tell whether the last 15 years of regulation analysed in the following sections has led to a break with this tradition.

The Danish free school tradition is founded on an opposition against both the domination of the state and the Lutheran-Evangelical state church in the educational sphere. Since the Protestant Reformation (1536), the state and the established church had been closely connected (Danmarkshistorien.dk 2014a, 2014b). In the first part of the nineteenth century, the influential priest, poet, philosopher and politician N.F.S. Grundtvig and the teacher and educationalist Christen Kold, key persons in the free school movement, started criticising the public school system based on a law from 1814 for being authoritarian, dogmatic and ill-equipped to enlighten and empower the population. Grundtvig argued against the close connection between religion and education in the public school and was in favour of removing religion from the curriculum (Korsgaard 2011, 27–34). He and Kold saw the right to establish free schools as an alternative. Schools should be based on dialogue between teacher and student, singing and storytelling, and without the formal strictures of exams, thereby contributing to the national and democratic enlightenment of the 'commoners', transforming them into equal members and citizens of the nation. The free schools ideology was not driven by a defence of a minority identity as such, and both Grundtvig and Kold belonged to the Evangelical-Lutheran Christian majority. However, they favoured a new, more liberal interpretation of the faith emphasising 'the living word' (i.e. the spoken word) over rationally organised doctrine and, crucially, defended a concept of free-mindedness (Danmarkshistorien.dk 2014c). Free-mindedness entails the defence of legally protected rights for all to form and publicly defend their own opinion combined with the right (and obligation) to use all verbal means to criticise false views and beliefs (Bredsdorff and Kjældgaard 2010). The ambition was to create both ideological and pedagogical freedom for the schools through independence from the state and the established church (since 1849 called 'The People's Church').

On his own initiative but with the support of Grundtvig and his circle, Kold established the first free school in 1852, and in 1855, six years after the first Danish constitution, the law on free schools was passed by the Danish Parliament. This law gave parents the right to assume the responsibility for the education of their own children by choosing a non-governmental school (or home-schooling) based on a general duty to educate them rather than a duty to send them to school. However, the law demanded that the private education be equivalent to public school education (Balle 2001, 44). As mentioned in the introduction, these principles concerning the rights and duties in education are now found in article 76 of the current Danish constitution.

The requirement of a public school equivalent education is an open-ended clause enabling the state to specify in a rather detailed manner what non-governmental schools need to do and to control them (Ross 1966, 767–770). In the first eight decades after 1855, the authorities by way of the local school commissions chaired by the local People's Church priest kept free schools on a relatively short leash, requiring them to teach all of the public school subjects, including Christianity studies, and to subject students twice annually to exams to assess whether they achieved the same GPAs as the local public school students (Balle 2001, 43–51). Initially, their ideological freedom and pedagogical freedom were hence rather limited and control was tight. But this began to change from the early 1930s onwards.

First, after pressure from the free school movement and in conjunction with a fortunate constellation of political forces, the monitoring of the schools was in principle turned over to the parents in 1933. After 1933, the ME monitored only written and oral Danish and math as well as Christianity studies through the reports written by the parent-selected external supervisor and priest.[2] The remaining subjects were only parent-supervised. Moreover, schools no longer had to hold exams and give grades. In the late 1970s, the obligation for the free schools to teach every subject required for the public school was also watered down, in part following a similar development for the public school in terms of a looser specification of subjects and academic targets. For example, by 1977, the demand was only that non-governmental schools teach the general subjects (*fagkreds*) of the public school, and these 'naturally would be divided into, including also social sciences, practical-musical and physical education' (Horten-Frida Circular 1977, quoted from Balle 2001, 59). The monitoring of the school only had to include Danish, math and English (the latter added in 1977). In the early 1990s, the parent-selected school supervisor did not even have to be approved by the ME or local authorities. In sum, from the 1930s, the pedagogical freedom of the schools increased significantly over the years, and control was decentralised.

Second, the ideological freedom also increased. In the 1930s, the Minister of Education argued that explicit Nazi sympathies at a particular free school did not disqualify it from receiving state money. The same view applied in the 1970s to schools based on Marxist revolutionary views. This ideological freedom rested on a distinction between 'opinions' and 'actions'. As long as there was no attempt at overthrowing the state by illegal means (violence), the schools should have the right, with state subsidies, to hold points of view that were in strong opposition to the existing political and legal order and against the views of the majority (Korsgaard and Wiborg 2006, 378–379). Formally, the tie between the public school education and the People's Church and the Evangelical-Lutheran faith has been progressively loosened from the late 1930s and with it also the tie between majority religion and non-governmental schools (Kristeligt Dagblad.dk 2014; Danmarkshistorien 2014a). As of 1899, the free schools were able to obtain a state subsidy. It increased over the years and reached its pinnacle in the late 1970s when it amounted to around 85%.

Summing up, the historical development reveals a free school tradition based on free-mindedness and on opposition to state and church dominance in education. As the tradition evolved, the associational freedoms of non-governmental schools increased along the ideological and pedagogical dimensions and in terms of loosened control and increased public funding. In addition to what has been described above, schools also enjoyed a high degree of freedom in the recruitment of staff and students. A defender of the tradition, Balle (2006), sums it up by explicating its five principles of ideological freedom, pedagogical freedom, financial freedom and freedom in the recruitment of both staff and students and argues that it implies minority protection in its prioritisation of the rights of parents over those of the state in the education and upbringing of children:

> The ideological freedom was of course the most fundamental, i.e. the freedom of parents to choose which view of the human being, of life, and of society that should direct their children's upbringing and education, even when those views were in *strong opposition to those of the majority*. The ability to realize this ideological freedom required a high degree of freedom in pedagogy, funding, and staff recruitment. Just as it was necessary to leave it to the schools – and not the public/the state – to decide which children they could admit or expel. These five freedoms against the state were introduced into the legislation regarding the private schools for children and supported by the state. They thereby became a unique and distinguished example of free-mindedness in Danish culture, which were developed by the popular movements by the end of the 19th century. (Balle 2006, 6, translated from Danish, italics added)

According to Balle, the free school tradition consistent with the notion of free-mindedness entails a large degree of associational freedom for schools with an ideological freedom to espouse views which are 'in strong opposition of those of the majority'. As late as 2001, the legislation covering the free schools did not entail any value clause other than that schools must provide public-school-equivalent education. There were no clauses regarding civic education or personality ideals. Over the years, from the 1930s and towards the end of the last millennium, the regulation entailed a decreasing input control in the specification of subjects, curriculum and educational targets; the throughput control in terms of the inspection of school teaching and practices was minimal and carried out by supervisors chosen by the school parents; and the output control in terms of examinations was loose, also considering that it is not obligatory for schools to hold the official final exams. Moreover, schools are not obligated to hire state-certified teachers and can recruit both teachers and students according to their own value base. The schools enjoyed considerable financial freedom, with a public subsidy of around 75% of the average cost of a public school student. However, since the late 1990s, things began to change.

The next section analyses these changes and discusses whether they have altered the Danish free school tradition and the associational freedom of schools fundamentally. The analysis proceeds chronologically and points out the main changes in various dimensions of associational freedom of schools, however, with a special focus on the ideological and pedagogical freedom and the means of control. Not all dimensions were subject of legal changes in the period. The freedom of recruitment was, for example, left untouched. In order to investigate the article's main thesis, the section traces the justifications, i.e. the stated reasons, for making legislative changes in order to tell the extent to which they were based on the concerns about academic quality (competitiveness), integration and the fear of extremism.

## Policy changes

The period of unregulated freedom began to come to an end in the 1990s, when the socialist Tvind school conglomerate was accused of a fraudulent use of state subsidies. This led to legislation requiring schools to be independent units that could not be controlled by other units or transfer money to them. In 1998, in the wake of the Tvind affair, the rules concerning supervision were revised and it became mandatory for schools to teach in Danish in order to receive state subsidies. There was no real opposition to these new rules (Folketinget 1998). The language requirement in part mirrors an increased emphasis on the learning of Danish in the public school as a prerequisite for integration (Holm-Larsen 1999).

In late November 2001, shortly after the 9/11 terrorist attacks, the new Danish People's Party (DPP)-supported centre–right government came to power, having won the election on a strong, 'firm and fair' immigration and integration policy. With two consecutive bills in 2002 and 2005, the centre–right government reduced the ideological freedom of the schools, demanded more documentation for the value of alternative teaching programmes and increased school monitoring.

As part of its 'integration policy package', the new government introduced a bill in 2002 demanding that schools prepare students 'to live in a society with freedom and democracy' (ME 2002). Reducing the ideological freedom of schools, the bill claimed that it had been a presupposition for schools receiving state subsidies that they respected human rights and fundamental freedoms. The bill took the European Convention of Human Rights (ECHR) as its value reference point. Arguably, the bill only demanded that students be given knowledge about the principles of freedom and democracy and not that they were to be equipped with a democratic ethos (thereby still preserving a relatively wide conception of freedom of conscience and belief). The bill also wanted to expand the monitoring of schools to include history/social sciences and the natural sciences. However, in order to create a broad political compromise, the intentions of the original bill were watered down. The explicit reference to the ECHR was removed, and monitoring was only expanded to ensure that the language of instruction was Danish.

In 2005, the government abandoned its previous ambition of reaching a broad political compromise. With the DPP and the SD, it reintroduced expanded monitoring, increased documentation requirements for alternative educational approaches and yet again reduced the ideological freedom of schools receiving state subsidies. The legislative bill refers directly to the OECD PISA results and the ambition to ensure a high academic level in the primary and lower secondary school (ME 2005). The government claimed that the free schools were doing slightly worse than the public schools, and in particular that schools with many ethnic minority children were faring worse. If the schools choose not to follow the educational targets set in the 'Common Goals' for the public school, they must define their own targets and teaching plans for all of the subjects taught in the public school so as to be able to demonstrate how the teaching they provide is equivalent to that of the public school. They must also demonstrate that their teaching leads to the well-rounded development of the individual student, including the 'spiritual, intellectual, musical, physical and social' aspects, a demand reflecting the public school legislation requirement that schooling lead to the 'general education', or *Bildung*, of the individual (ME 2005). The freedom and democracy clause was expanded to its current wording, with direct reference to the integration agenda and fear of political extremism:

> According to their purpose and in all of their work, [the schools] shall prepare the students to live in a society like Denmark, with freedom and democracy, and develop and strengthen the students' knowledge of and respect for fundamental freedoms and human rights, including equality between the sexes. (Law on Free Schools, article 1.2)

In addition to teaching per se, the clause now also covers all activities connected with the school and is made to ensure 'that fundamentalist or extremist actions, which are justified on religious grounds, etc. but which contradict human rights and fundamental freedoms, including gender equality, cannot take place *at or from* a free primary school' (ME 2005, emphasis added).

The legislative bill is not completely unequivocal in relation to the ideological freedom of schools, since it also allows schools 'within the framework of the law' to provide education in line 'with the schools' own convictions and organise the teaching in accordance with those convictions' (ME 2005). This clause was introduced to give the fundamental freedom of the schools appropriate weight when determining whether or not schools fulfil legal requirements. Nonetheless, the bill explicitly reduces freedom further in relation to the 2002 changes since it now directly prohibits schools that want to receive state subsidies from basing themselves on views which contradict gender equality, the principles of Danish democracy and the freedom of religion 'in Denmark or other countries'. Furthermore, schools must teach the theory of evolution, human biology and sex education. Schools that persist with controversial views would arguably be able to do so under the rules of home-schooling – and hence without state subsidies.

From the ministerial guidelines on how to establish whether a school lives up to the freedom and democracy clause, it is clear that schools not only have to provide students with knowledge but also establish a dialogical and democratic educational practice, which combined can 'be traced in the actions and skills of the students' (ME 2011, annex 3). Hence, it indicates that the inculcation of a democratic ethos in students is required and implies a significant reduction of the freedom of conscience and belief within education. The reduction applies in particular to students and to schools and their staff, but also touches upon the freedom of parents to educate their children according to their own worldviews.

In continuation of the introduction of more tests and measurement in the public school, including making the final exams mandatory, the government changed the rules on examinations for free primary schools in 2006 so that they must now actively deselect all of the individual subject exams of the general public final exams rather than being able to pick and choose between exams in different subjects or simply refrain from conducting exams entirely (according to their individual value bases). Individual schools must also declare publicly whether or not they apply the final exams. Moreover, if students have not taken the public school final exams, they are now required to submit to an entrance examination if they want to continue with upper secondary education (*gymnasium*) (ME 2006).

Taken together, the 2002, 2005 and 2006 legislative changes deliberately sought to reduce the ideological freedom of the schools and aimed at increasing input control and (documentation) cost of running alternative teaching programmes and with it the costs of exercising pedagogical freedom. However, not all changes have been in the direction of increased state control and centralisation. In 2010 on the non-governmental school sector's initiative, the monitoring system was revised. The individual schools now appoint a certified inspector or have the municipality appoint one or, alternatively, carry out a 'self-evaluation' according to an ME-approved model (ME 2009b). School associations are contributing to the development of self-evaluation models and the education of inspectors, both of which must be approved by the ME. The 2010 revision implied that the ME's monitoring of academic results should be more based on test results (outcome), and hence allow more flexibility with respect to teaching methods.

The ME's selection for inspections is now based on results (final exams and students' continued education) as well as inspectors' reports and criticism from parents and media. The inspections are generally carried out by examining the schools' curriculum and teaching practices. In addition to the normal inspection efforts, the ME has annual inspection plans with special foci. In 2009, the centre–right government, for example, issued an anti-radicalisation plan and inspected 25 schools to see if they fulfilled the 'freedom and democracy' requirement and whether further legal changes were necessary (Danish Government 2009, 18). The ME also places individual schools on probation (special monitoring) if it believes they are not meeting legal requirements.

Rather than a rigid evaluation model, the ME applies an 'overall evaluation' (*helhedsvurdering*) of whether schools live up to the freedom and democracy clause based on the schools' educational goals, teaching plans and teaching practice, results and overall culture (ME 2009a). The idea is that there are several ways in which the legal requirement can be met. The ME's experience is that problems primarily relate to the level of knowledge among the students – not the inculcation of controversial attitudes – although controversial attitudes theoretically also lead to a negative evaluation (interview with Andersen 2011).

Taken together, the legislative changes over the last 15 years or so have had the effect of reducing the free primary schools' ideological freedom to espouse views which are in 'strong contradiction' to those of the majority if the latter are the basic principles of (Danish) liberal democracy, gender equality and secular modern science. The legislation explicitly requires civic education and the inculcation of a democratic ethos among students. Similarly, it has transferred a personality ideal from the public school legislation about the 'well-rounded development' or *Bildung* of the individual. The legislative changes have also increased the input control of free primary schools in that the educational targets of the Danish state have been more clearly specified, and free schools which do not wish to follow the 'Common Goals' for the public school directly must document how their alternative teaching (at least) achieves the same targets. This arguably diminishes the ability for some schools to exercise their pedagogical freedom because of the documentation costs that this entails and because of the closer specification of the academic targets. Furthermore, the state has introduced structural pressure on the teaching in free primary schools by making the public school final exams the default position, including in relation to access to continued education. The introduction of the public school final exams as the default position also represents a type of increased 'output' control, since it is easier to establish whether non-governmental schools achieve results which are comparable to the public school.

The effort to increase the quality of monitoring, the throughput control, is now primarily carried out by either certified inspectors or based on self-evaluation models. The Danish state does not carry out regular inspections of all non-governmental schools, reacting instead to poor results and criticism from third parties, such as the school-appointed inspectors, parents and the media. Schools can still recruit teachers and students according to their value base and still receive considerable financial support from the state, although the 2014 public subsidies are aimed at reaching a new stable level of 71% of the average cost of a public school student.

As the analysis demonstrates, the reduced associational freedoms of the free schools are based on concerns with academic quality (national competitiveness) and in particular concerns with integration and fears of political and religious extremism, and hence with the realisation of collective goals. However, these concerns overlap with the rights and interests of children in education. The concern is that some children may not develop the competences to participate fully in societal life, as the value bases of some schools 'are so fundamentalist that they *disable the students to function*' in Danish democratic society (ME 2002, emphasis added). Muslim schools were the absolutely overriding concern (interview with Haarder 2013). The introduction of the public school final exam as a default was also partly intended to ensure that some 'immigrant schools did not contribute to the creation of ethnic proletariat suffering from a poisonous combination of ethnic isolation and social exclusion' due to low academic achievement and some parents prioritising religious doctrine over academic achievement (Haarder 2013). Integration and concerns with academic quality were hence linked.

## Evaluation of the policy changes

Legislative changes aimed to circumscribe the associational freedom of free primary schools, in particular along its ideological dimension. The freedom of belief and consciousness was reduced in terms of the ability to espouse views 'in strong opposition' to those of the majority for schools receiving state subsidies. And the (documentation) costs of running alternative teaching programmes including the non-application of the public school final exam were also increased, thus arguably delimiting the pedagogical freedom. There is therefore textual basis in the legislative bills for concluding that the Danish free school tradition has been changed at a fundamental level. However, there is a sense in which the nature of a tradition can only be adequately judged by those who practice it and in which freedom is relative to the ends that you (think you) should be able to pursue. So in order to gauge whether those who practice the tradition have found their freedom reduced or changed, all the chairmen of the Danish school associations (except a minor one representing only 14 German minority schools out of a total of 537 schools, please refer to Appendix 1) were interviewed along with the chairman of 10,000 free primary school teachers. The chairmen were interviewed in their capacity of chairmen, i.e. as formally representing the members of their organisations in political matters. Their responses reflected their representative functions, but also the experiences and complaints of individual members (schools and teachers) as well as their own experiences, in the majority of cases, as school directors. The interviews were semi-structured and open-ended and concerned the main legislative changes analysed above, in particular those relating to the freedom and democracy clause, the requirement to document teaching programmes, the introduction of public school final exams as default, the latest revisions of the monitoring system as well as the general health of the free school tradition. The interviews also led to the identification of additional things perceived to affect the freedom and diversity of schools, notably the demands of parents. Of course, the interviews do not have the kind of statistical representativeness that a survey of the individual schools would yield, but they still give us a good indication of how the recent years' legislatives are interpreted by the sector in relation to their associational freedom and the tradition.

From the interviews, it is not clear whether all school associations see school freedom as reduced. This very much depends on whether they find legislation on civic education to be unnecessary state regulation and/or that parents should be fully trusted to take the interests of their own children seriously – and more so than the state. In general, the less ideologically charged associations do not see the civic education requirement and more comprehensively defined academic standards as an encroachment on their members' freedom. The freedom and democracy clause neither introduces uncertainty in the legislation nor does it represent an illegitimate distrust of schools/parents on the part of the state, but is only a fair requirement considering the amount of money the state gives to non-governmental schools (Ernst, Danish Private School Association (DPSA) and Jensen, Association of Catholic Schools in Denmark (ACSD)). Moreover, the introduction of exams and close description of the educational targets in relation to the public school 'Common Goals' does not generally represent a problem for these schools, since they have traditionally applied the public school final exam and followed the public school curriculum. Nor do they constitute an undue expense on schools with alternative programmes in terms of documentation work. For each of these associations, the responsibility of what they see as a possible tendency towards reduced diversity among schools primarily lies with the unwillingness and lack of courage of schools to utilise the actual degrees of freedom in the law. In their eyes, the 'Danish Free School Tradition' is generally intact.

Common to all organisations is that they are generally satisfied with the recent revisions to the monitoring system. They think that certified inspectors increase the quality of inspections and reports, and that the self-evaluation models carry great potential for self-improvement. Some of them point out that a monitoring system based more on 'output' than 'throughput', which might give even more flexibility regarding teaching methods, could create perverse incentives for schools to deselect students with limited academic potential.

However, the Free School Teachers' Union (FSTU), the Free School Association (FSA), the Small School Association (SSA) and Association of Christian Free Schools (ACFS) are slightly more critical of the legislative developments. Some of them recognise the freedom and democracy clause as reducing the freedom of the schools as compared with the relatively high trust of the past in parents as the guardians of their children's rights and tolerance towards, for example, revolutionary and conservative Christian views (Pedersen (FSTU), Lilliendal (FSA), and Larsen (SSA)). Some of the SSA members and smaller FSA schools endure increased costs in the documentation of how alternative programmes are equivalent to the public school's Common Goals, which has led to a pragmatically induced reduction in the diversity of the schools and their teaching programmes (Larsen (SSA) and Lilliendal (FSA)). Together with Bjerregaard (ACFS) whose members all follow the public school's Common Goals, see the aggregated effect of individual legislative initiatives as reducing the schools' associational freedom. However, not everyone sees the impetus towards less diversity solely coming from the legal requirements. Along with the DPSA and ACSD, they see a lot of the pressure coming from parents who demand teaching programmes and subject definitions similar to the public school – and not least the application of the public school final exam. Most interviews clearly reveal the perception of a split between parents and schools despite the fact that many school board members are often elected parents. As one interviewee put it, schools and parents are no longer conceptually understood together as a 'congregation', but rather as two separate entities (Larsen (SSA)). This is partly due to the manner in which the ME holds school boards accountable and partly due to the fact that parents are currently more preoccupied with academic achievements than the transmission of particular religious, philosophical or political convictions.

Pedersen (FSTU) alone sees the civic education requirement as a lack of trust in free schools and parents' guardian rights as such. And everyone agrees that respecting the constitution, the law and freedom and democracy is a presupposition for running a free school in Denmark, but many of them think that the administration of the law in terms of ME inspections of Muslim schools, as in connection with the 2009 anti-radicalisation plan, evinced a high and generally completely unjustified distrust in Muslim schools, which has left the schools uncertain about how to come across as democratic and freedom-respecting (Lilliendal (FSA), Larsen (SSA), Bjerregaard (ACFS), and in part Ernst (DPSA)).

Muslim schools, main targets for several of the legislative changes, are members of the FSA and the DPSA and do not have their own association and formal representation. However, the experience of distrust was partly confirmed by two interviews carried out in 2009 with two directors of Muslim schools who revealed a high level of uncertainty and felt that Muslim schools and their students were almost deliberately placed under a general suspicion of being potential radicals and terrorists (Kjærgaard and Larsen 2010, 68–75). In a later interview from 2013 with a certified inspector working at a Muslim school in Copenhagen and inspecting others, this impression is only partly confirmed, although schools are clearly very conscious about signalling that they live up to the civic education requirement and take very few 'risks' in terms of alternative teaching programmes that might stick out and call for inspection (Jensen 2013). Moreover, Jensen explains how the freedom and democracy requirement is not necessarily perceived as an externally imposed ideological restriction on the religious freedom of schools. At The Islamic Arabic Private School, it thus guides the cooperation between school and parents, since the school has a diversity of Muslims represented who disagree internally about doctrine and its practical consequences. Interviews with persons working at three different schools do not yield representativeness in the strict statistical sense but can provide an indication of how policy changes have been received by Muslim schools.

The FSTU, the SSA, FSA and the ACFS are less sanguine about the intactness of the Danish free school tradition. Pedersen (FSTU) claims that there is not much free-mindedness left, but also questions whether there ever was a lot it; Larsen (SSA) complains that the new generation of politicians has no deep understanding of the free school tradition and the principles of education in the Danish constitution. Bjerregaard (ACFS) finds that the tradition is a little 'worn around the edges', and overall that 'one forgets that it is healthy that we live in the fatherland of Grundtvig, where we can experiment with things and where freedom is allowed to flourish'.

## Conclusion

The article has demonstrated a reduction through legislative changes of the associational freedoms of the free primary schools in Denmark to espouse views which are in 'strong opposition' to those of the majority, defined as the principles of Danish liberal democracy, gender equality and modern science, and that it has increased the documentation costs for schools wanting to run alternative teaching programmes that they are equivalent to public school education. The changes have been motivated by concerns about integration, radicalism, in particular among Muslim immigrants, and a general concern, in light of national competitiveness, with the quality of Danish education, including 'non-governmental sector education'. The development largely mirrors the development in public school policy.

The legislative bills give textual basis for concluding that the Danish free school tradition developing from the 1930s and founded on a notion of free-mindedness has been fundamentally changed since schools based on views contradicting basic principles of the Danish state can no longer receive public subsidies. The state demands loyalty and a democratic ethos in return for money and has consequently limited the freedom of conscience and belief. The ideological freedom of the schools has been reduced and the costs of exercising pedagogical freedom in terms of running alternative teaching programmes have increased. However, not all changes have been in the direction of less freedom. While input control through documentation and to some extent output control through more focus on outcome has been increased, the monitoring structure has been decentralised with the introduction of certified inspectors and not least self-evaluation models.

That said, the conclusion regarding the reduction in ideological freedom is moderated somewhat by the interviews with school sector representatives who all agree that a self-evident presupposition for running a school in Denmark is that it respects the law, the constitution and freedom and democracy. Those who are most critical of the legislative changes do not so much argue against the civic education requirement in itself, but are more concerned with the aggregate effect of a series of legislative and administrative changes which – along with parents as critical customers threatening to vote with their feet – pressure schools into becoming more similar to the public school. Hence, their criticism is more directed against the state regulation of the educational sphere than against the 'ideological limitation' set by the freedom and democracy clause. They fear that the education principles in the Danish constitution have been forgotten.

They also read the changes as induced by concerns with academic quality (in light of globalisation) and in particular what they see as a political overreaction against Muslim schools. Additionally, they see changes as driven by administrative and political control logic according to which similar requirements issued to similar entities (i.e. schools) are much easier to administer and track from the state level.

The analysis also demonstrates that Danish free primary schools retain comparatively large degrees of associational freedom despite increased 'value' and input control. Formally, schools can still define and run alternative teaching programmes, deselect the public school final exam, recruit students and teachers according to their value base, and the (throughput) control is still primarily based on a decentralised system of parent-appointed inspectors or, indeed, self-evaluation models. Interviewees are generally very satisfied with the latest revision of the monitoring system, and although there could be concerns with the arbitrary selection for ministerial inspection, school sector representatives do not appear to find that the legal requirements entail a level of legal uncertainty that in itself leads to the underutilisation of the schools' freedom.

**Notes**
1. The free schools were not the only non-governmental schools. In Copenhagen people had been free to choose between public schools and home-schooling controlled by authorities. In the provincial towns and on the countryside the authorities could before 1855 *grant permission* that the school duty was met in alternative ways, e.g. by way of private schools and home-schooling (Ross 1966, 766). From the middle of the 19th century, both public and

private 'real schools' were established which taught practical subjects, modern languages, geography, math and natural sciences to the sons (and daughters) of the bourgeois estate who had to enter public service and commercial life and therefore did not need 'classical education'. These schools focused on academic achievement and the passing of publicly defined exams and less on (ideological) freedom from state and church (Larsen 2010).

2. After 1933, the priest could be from a 'free congregation' within the People's Church aligned with the school's own understanding of the Evangelical-Lutheran faith.

## References

Andersen, Anders. 2011. Former Consultant in ME, Responsible for Inspection. Interview by Tore Vincents Olsen, 21 June, Copenhagen. Digital Recording.
Bader, V. M. 2007. *Secularism or Democracy?* Amsterdam: Amsterdam University Press.
Balle, T. 2001. "'Stå mål med' – Om det offentliges krav til indholdet af den private børneundervisning 1814–2001." *Uddannelseshistorie* 35: 38–69.
Balle, T. 2006. "En historisk belysning." *Undervisningsministeriets Tidsskrift for Uddannelse* 9: 3–8.
Berg-Sørensen, A. 2006. "Religion i det offentlige rum? En rundtur i de danske sekularismer." *Kritik* 182: 30–38.
Bredsdorff, T., and L. H. Kjældgaard. 2010. *Tolerance – Eller hvordan man lærer at leve med dem man hader*. Copenhagen: Gyldendal A/S.
Christoffersen, L. 2010. "State, Church and Religion in Denmark." In *Law & Religion in the 21st Century: Nordic Perspectives*, edited by L. Christoffersen and S. Andersen, 145–162. Copenhagen: DJØF Publishing.
Danish Government. 2009. *En fælles og tryg fremtid. Handlingsplan om forebyggelse af ekstremistiske holdninger og radikalisering blandt unge*. Copenhagen: Danish Government. http://www.nyidanmark.dk/NR/rdonlyres/4443E64E-3DEA-49B2-8E19-B4380D52F1D3/0/handlingsplan_radikalisering_2009.pdf
Danmarkshistorien.dk. 2014a. "Lov Om Folkeskolen, 18. Maj 1937'." http://danmarkshistorien.dk/leksikon-og-kilder/vis/materiale/lov-om-folkeskolen-18-maj-1937/
Danmarkshistorien.dk. 2014b. "Skole og undervisning 1814-2010." http://danmarkshistorien.dk/leksikon-og-kilder/vis/materiale/skole-og-undervisning-1814-2010/
Danmarkshistorien.dk. 2014c. "Grundtvigs Kristendomssyn." http://danmarkshistorien.dk/leksikon-og-kilder/vis/materiale/grundtvigs-kristendomssyn/
Folketinget. 1998. *Parliamentary Readings Regarding Legislative Bill L 25 submitted to Parliament 26 March 1998, Folketinget*. http://webarkiv.ft.dk/?/Samling/19972/lovforslag_oversigtsformat/L25.htm
Haarder, Bertel. 2013. Former Minister of Education, (2005–2010, 1982–1993), and Integration (2001–2005). Interview by Tore Vincents Olsen, 15 November, Copenhagen. Digital Recording.
Holm-Larsen, S. 1999. "Skolen i årets løb." *Uddannelseshistorie* 33: 143–164.
Holm-Larsen, S. 2006. "Uddannelserne i årets løb." *Uddannelseshistorie* 40: 100–135.
Horten-Frida Circular. 1977. Cirkulæreskrivelse om lov om friskoler og private grundskoler mv. af 23 august 1977, signed by Head of Office, Frida Horten.
Jensen, K. 2010. *Citizenship Education in Denmark, CIVITURN Workpackage on Education*. Aarhus: Department of Political Science, Aarhus University.
Jensen, Peter. 2013. Certified Inspector Working at The Islamic Arabic Private School. Interview by Tore Vincents Olsen, 25 November, Copenhagen. Digital Recording.
Kjærgaard, K., and M. Ø. Larsen. 2010. "På vej mod en fælles og tryg fremtid? Et governmentality-perspektiv på anti-radikalisering." MA Thesis. Aarhus: Department of Political Science, Aarhus Universitet.
Korsgaard, O. 2010. "Samfundets trosbekendelse." *Politik* 13 (1): 44–52.

Korsgaard, O. 2011. "Grundtvig's Philosophy of Enlightenment and Education." In *The School for Life: N.F.S. Grundtvig on Education for the People*, edited by E. Broadbridge, 13–35. Aarhus: Aarhus University Press.
Korsgaard, O., and S. Wiborg. 2006. "Grundtvig: The Key to Danish Education?" *Scandinavian Journal of Educational Research* 50 (3): 361–382.
Kristeligt Dagblad.dk. 2014. Temaside: Kristendomskundskab. http://www.kristeligt-dagblad.dk/kristendomskundskab#section_10579
Larsen, C. ed. 2010. *Realskolen gennem 200 år, vols 1 +2*. Copenhagen: Danmarks Privatskoleforeningen.
Lindekilde, L., and M. Sedgwick. 2012. *Impact of Counter-terrorism on Communities: Denmark Background Report*. Institute for Strategic Dialogue. http://www.strategicdialogue.org/Country_report_Denmark_AD_FW.pdf
Ministry of Education. 2002. *Legislative Bill no L 163 2001/2, 2. Assembly, Submitted to Parliament 13 March 2002*. Copenhagen: Folketinget. http://webarkiv.ft.dk/?/samling/20012/menu/00000002.htm
Ministry of Education. 2005. *Legislative Bill no LF 105 2004/2, Submitted to Parliament 23 February 2005*. Copenhagen: Folketinget. http://www.ft.dk/samling/20042/lovforslag/L105/index.htm
Ministry of Education. 2006. *Legislative Bill no L 185, Submitted to Parliament 28 March 2006*. Copenhagen: Folketinget. http://www.ft.dk/samling/20051/lovforslag/l185/bilag/13/index.htm#nav
Ministry of Education. 2009a. *Indikatorbaseret model for tilsynet med frihed og folkestyre*. Copenhagen: Ministry of Education. http://www.ktst.dk/frie%20skoler/~/media/Styrelsen/Friskoleomraadet/Indikatorbaseret%20model%20for%20tilsynet%20med%20frihed%20og%20folkestyre.ashx
Ministry of Education. 2009b. *Legislative Bill no L 217, Submitted to Parliament 18 June 2009*. Copenhagen: Folketinget. http://www.ft.dk/samling/20081/lovforslag/L217/som_fremsat.htm#dok
Ministry of Education. 2011. *Departmental Order on Special Monitoring of Free Schools, BEK no 1172 of 12/12/2011*. Copenhagen: Retsinformation. https://www.retsinformation.dk/Forms/R0710.aspx?id=139653
Minstry of Education. 2014. *Statistik om folkeskolen og frie skoler*. Copenhagen: Ministry of Education. http://www.uvm.dk/Service/Statistik/Statistik-om-folkeskolen-og-frie-skoler
Mouritsen, P., and T. V. Olsen. 2013. "Denmark Between Liberalism and Nationalism." *Ethnic and Racial Studies* 36 (4): 691–710.
Olsen, T. V. 2011. "Danish Political Culture: Fair Conditions for Inclusion of Immigrants?" *Scandinavian Political Studies* 34 (4): 269–286.
Pedersen, O. K. 2011a. *Konkurrencestaten*. Copenhagen: Hans Reitzels.
Pedersen, O. K. 2011b. "Folkeskolen og politisk kultur." *Politik* 14 (2): 11–18.
Ross, A. 1966. *Dansk statsforfatningsret, Vol 2*. Copenhagen: Nyt Nordisk Forlag.
Torfing, J. 2004. *Det stille sporskifte i velfærdsstaten: en diskursteoretisk beslutningsprocesanalyse*. Aarhus: Aarhus University Press.

**Appendix 1.** Overview of school sector organisations and interviewees

| Organisation | Background | No. of members | Interviewee |
|---|---|---|---|
| The Free School Association (FSA) | The heir of the free school movement based on the thoughts of Grundtvig and Kold | 275 schools (32,000 students) | Chairman Ebbe Lilliendal (23.6.2011) |
| Denmark's Private School Association (DPSA) | Organising traditional private schools, many former private 'real schools' (see note 1) | 153 schools (50,000 students) | Chairman Kurt Ernst (18.11.2013) |
| Small School Association (SSA) | Based on progressive pedagogy (reform pedagogy) | 61 schools (8800 students) | Chairman Søren Larsen (13.12.2013) |
| Association of Christian Free Schools (ACFS) | Typically associated with conservative Evangelical movements and congregations | 35 schools (6000 students) | Chairman Thorkild Bjerregaard (14.11.2013) |
| Association of Catholic Schools in Denmark (ACSD) | Closely connected to the Catholic Church in Denmark | 21 schools (8600 students) | Chairman Dan Jensen (18.11.2013). |
| Association of German minority schools in Denmark | Schools teaching German minority in German | 14 schools (1400 students) | Not interviewed |
| Free School Teachers' Union (FSTU) | Representing teachers in all free primary schools in Denmark | 10,184 teachers | Now former chairman Arne Pedersen (22.6.2011) |

Note: Numbers are derived from organisation homepages. Officially, there are a total of 537 free primary schools with a total of 104,740 students compared to 1318 public schools with 561,553 students (2012). Another 26,433 students (predominantly 9th and 10th graders) are at private, publicly subsidised boarding schools (*efterskoler*), and the remaining 12,843 are placed in schools and programmes for children with special needs. There are a total of 708,569 students in Grades 0–10.
Source: ME (2014).

# Non-governmental religious schools in Germany – increasing demand by decreasing religiosity?

Annette Scheunpflug

*Institute of Education, University of Bamberg, Bamberg, Germany*

> This paper addresses the situation of non-governmental religious schools in Germany. The available empirical data demonstrate an increasing demand for these schools in recent decades. In this paper, possible causes of this development are discussed. First, the given constitutional framework for religion in governmental and non-governmental schools is presented. The particularity of the German school system comes into view: not only the churches but also the state – as an expression of its neutrality towards religion – maintains religious schools; furthermore, denominational religious instruction is also given in governmental non-religious schools. Second, the phenomenon of religious school selection will be considered: in which educational domains are non-governmental religious schools increasing? Where are they decreasing? Third, hypotheses explaining these developments – such as the special educational profiles of non-governmental religious schools, the wish for social distinction, avoiding problems of governmental schools, and better performance – are discussed.

## 1. Introduction

In Germany, non-governmental Christian religious schools[1] are experiencing an increase in demand. In general, these schools have waiting lists for enrolment, accepting only one-third of all applicants. The number of religious primary schools has doubled in the last 10 years, especially in the former socialist Eastern states. What might be the reason for this development in a society where more than 30% of the population do not belong to any religion? In this paper, possible answers will be discussed, reflecting parental choice, the performance of non-governmental religious schools, and their contribution to school segregation.

First, to understand the specific situation of governmental and non-governmental schools as well as the situation of religious schools, I examine the legal status of religion and of non-governmental schools in Germany. Second, I take a closer look at non-governmental religious schools by providing a general overview of these types of schools, demonstrating that it is not the demand for non-governmental religious school system in general which is increasing, but for special types of schools. Third, I discuss different hypotheses for choosing non-governmental religious schools. Finally, I summarise the empirical findings.

## 2. Context: the legal status of religion and education in Germany

The legal status of religion in both governmental and non-governmental schools has a considerable impact on the German school system. Germany, the country where the Lutheran reformation in 1517 took place, has through its history incorporated a system of balance and cooperation between churches and state (see Kalyvas 1996; Gould 1999; Monsma and Soper 2009, 172–178; for an historical overview). This cooperation was mainly built on the understanding of two dominant denominations, which for centuries had functioned according to '*cuius regio, eius religio*' (= the religion of the ruler is to be the established religion of a region or a state), as enshrined in the Augsburg religious peace treaty of 1555 and the Treaty of Westphalia of 1648. In 1918, when Germany transformed into a democratic system and established a new constitution, church and state were officially separated. The majority of schools at this time were either Protestant or Catholic. Higher, selective secondary schools – 'Gymnasien' – were not generally denominational and were only attended by a small proportion of the school-aged population. During the early part of the twentieth century, the right to found non-government schools also was ensured. However, during the Nazi era, these schools were officially 'secularised' and the majority of non-governmental religious schools were closed down, especially the Jewish ones.

Later, in the German Constitution of 1949 ['Grundgesetz', GG] in the Western part of Germany, the legal status of non-governmental religious schools was reconstituted and specified. Meanwhile, in the former German Democratic Republic (lasting until 1989), religious schools were not allowed, and there was strong disapproval of all religious activities and institutions (Cordell 1990; Mau 2005). Accordingly, in the new federal states, non-governmental religious education only started in 1990. However, with internal migration in Germany after World War II, labour migration after 1960 and especially with reunification (due to the fact that the most secularised population lives in the new federal states), the former system came under increasing pressure to adapt.

The situation of non-governmental religious schools of today is shaped by several factors. First, the GG frames a fundamental understanding of religion in regards to governmental education as well as of non-governmental education. This leads to a situation where, with respect to religion, three types of schools coexist in some parts of Germany: governmental schools, governmental religious schools, and non-governmental religious schools, which I describe later. As I will show, recent developments in Germany mean that there are new tensions for non-governmental religious schools.

### 2.1. *The constitutional framework of religion and education: free exercise of religion*

To analyse the framework of non-governmental religious schools, first the relation between state and education, as articulated in the constitution, has to be taken into consideration.

#### 2.1.1. *The relation between religion and state: free exercise of religion in a secularised state*

Germany, at least in its self-understanding, is a secular state with the free exercise of religion (GG Art.4). The free exercise of religion is seen 'as a basic, fundamental right', which 'is rooted in the twin emphases on religious liberty as a positive right and the principle of neutrality' (Monsma and Soper 2009, 178/179). Robbers states: 'The German law mirrors this public relevance of religion, and it provides specific structures for the manifestations of religion. Freedom of religion as well as institutional guarantees form the basis on which religious life can develop' (Robbers 2010, 20). This right 'obliges the state to provide the necessary space for the person to positively live a life in accordance with his or her religion' (Robbers 2010, 93). The freedom of religion is seen as a positive right which 'implies an obligation on the part of the state to create a social order in which it is possible for the religious personality to develop and flourish conveniently and easily' (Kommers 1997, 461). In other words, the religious neutrality of the secularised state leads to an understanding of state–church relations requiring the state 'to make room for or to accommodate those, who wish to live a religious life' (Monsma and Soper 2009 204). This understanding is deeply rooted in German history (see Kalyvas 1996; Gould 1999).

However, this understanding does not mean that the free exercise of religion is unlimited. In cases where the freedom of religion infringes on human dignity, personal health, safety, the protection of animals, environmental issues, or basic rights, a balancing and weighing process must take place, as is evident in the respective rulings of the Federal Constitutional Court. Therefore, religious values are forced to compromise and be balanced with other values. In practice, this leads to a strong cooperation between state and religions, especially regarding religious education in all types of schools in Germany.

### 2.1.2. *Religious education and the freedom of religion in schools*

This understanding of positive freedom of religion means that the religiously neutral state has to open possibilities for religious and non-religious expression in schools. Therefore, in most federal states, religious education in governmental schools is not given as secular instruction about different religions, but as one-faith-based religious education. In 14 federal states[2], religious education is taught in governmental schools by authorities of the religions themselves; this is mostly Protestant and Catholic religious education, though in some regions, Islamic, Orthodox, Jewish, and Buddhist religious education are also offered (see de Wall 2012, 173). de Wall explains:

> The most important and characteristic feature of religious instruction in German state schools is its *Konfessionalität* or "denominational character". In religious instruction, students are not only given information about religion or the various denominations and their doctrines and practices but, as the Federal Constitutional Court puts it, religion is seen as being a "denominational commitment" (BVerfGE 74, 252). (de Wall 2012, 173)

That means that a governmental school should offer religious education according to the religion of the students (for the exceptions in some federal states, see de Wall 2012). Agnostic students or students who opt out of religious education are obliged to attend a religiously neutral 'Ethics instruction' instead (see de Wall 2012, 172). Religious education is part of the state curriculum and is given by the religious bodies themselves as a '*res mixta*' between religious bodies and state. As these requirements were established during a time of relative religious homogeneity, this system is now coming under considerable strain, especially in some parts of the larger cities given the increase of religious heterogeneity via migration in the last decades (see the following section).

Governmental schools can provide certain religious services in schools (see Robbers 2010, 642). For example, in some federal states, prayers in the morning, interfaith religious ceremonies, Christmas services, or services for first day at school are common. Students also can demand a place to pray during breaks. No student can be forced to participate in religious activities, even if the majority in the school participate. No student or teacher is obligated to take part, so in principle anyone can opt out.

In 1979, the Federal Constitutional Court of Germany explained how these activities at governmental schools are rooted in positive religious freedom in the so-called 'school prayer case':

> To be sure, the state must balance this affirmative freedom to worship [ ... ] by permitting school prayer with the negative freedom of confession of other parents and pupils opposed to school prayer. Basically, [schools] may achieve this balance by guaranteeing that participation be voluntary for pupils and teachers. (BVerfGE 1979 52 223; translated by Kommers 1997)

Religious freedom is interpreted in a way such that religion may be expressed in the public sphere of a governmental school not only in religious education but through prayers, services, etc. Students have to tolerate the religion of others, but may not be forced to subscribe to a religion in which they do not believe. In this sense, governmental schools in Germany may be seen as interdenominational and interreligious religious schools, allowing religion to be publicly practiced in school. Because the secular neutral state has to create space for religion in the public sphere, a strong cooperation results, where 'religion' does not enjoy a privileged status of non-governmental religious schools, but is simply a characteristic of the government school system itself. This is visible with regard to religious education, the foundation of both the majority of non-religious governmental schools as well as religious schools.

The main difference between governmental schools and non-governmental religious schools is essentially the fact that non-governmental religious schools in general offer space only for one religion or denomination, and students do not have the right to opt out of this specific religious education. Of course, a non-governmental religious school may strengthen religion in the school profile. Similarly, if parents want to have religious education, prayers, and services at school for their child, it is not necessary to enrol the child in a non-governmental religious school because in the majority of federal states religion is taught at governmental non-religious schools too.

## 2.2. *The constitutional framework of non-governmental schooling: state control and school choice without limitations by family income*

The second precondition of the understanding of non-governmental religious education in Germany is the fact of the restrictive position towards non-governmental education. Schooling in Germany is an issue of federal states (*Länder*). Each of the 16 federal states has its own school system, and so it is difficult to speak about *the* German school system. When it comes to non-governmental schools, a strong indicator of regulation is the fact that the fundamental understanding of non-governmental schools is based not on the federal state level but in the German constitution (GG Art 7). First of all, all non-governmental schools that deliver German examinations are restricted in terms of tuition, as they are not allowed to economically discriminate by tuition fees (that means, in 2014, the maximum level of tuitions does not exceed €140 per month). In consequence, federal states subsidise between 60% and 90% of the costs of a school (see Bohne and Stoltenberg 2001, 245).[3] The Federal Constitutional Court has argued: 'Only when [non-governmental schooling] is fundamentally available to all citizens without regard to their financial situation can the [constitutionally] protected educational freedom actually be realized and claimed on an equal basis by all parents and students' (Glenn 2012, 218; BVerG 74, 40).

Second, non-governmental schools at the primary school and the lower academic levels section of the tracking school system [*Volksschule* or *Hauptschule*] are only approved if they show religious reasons or explore pedagogical innovation for the governmental school system. The fact that non-governmental schools at the primary and lower secondary levels need to offer exploration of pedagogical innovation for the governmental educational system forces non-governmental schools to bring an additional value to the school system. The pedagogical function plays an important role for obtaining permission and funding and the permission is not easy to achieve. Establishing a non-governmental school can be done by anybody. Non-governmental religious schools may be run by parishes, churches, monasteries, diaconal bodies, foundations, or parents who consider themselves as religious.

In general, the public subsidies for non-governmental schools imply a wide range of regulations similar to governmental schools (such as teachers being obliged to have a state-approved examination, teachers' salaries, building standards, state inspections, use of the federal state curriculum, and exclusive use of state approved textbooks). This leads to substantial state influence on non-government schools. Teachers at non-governmental religious schools may be civil servants of the state (and 'loaned' to the non-governmental school) or hired by the school. In the former case, the school can only refuse to accept a paid teacher, but not scrutinise his or her moral or religious convictions (e.g. with respect to homosexuality or divorce). In the latter case, religion is a factor of selection but not in a way that conflicts with the constitution.

## 2.3. *Governmental and non-governmental religious schools*

The established church–state relations, the positive freedom of religion, the relatively restrictive terms to establish non-governmental schools – in particular in the case of primary education – as well as the reciprocal financing by the state and the restriction on tuition fees demonstrate that religion in the school system exists in three different forms, of which only one represents a non-governmental religious education.

### 2.3.1. *Governmental schools*

As already mentioned, in 13 of 16 federal states, governmental schools are seen as schools rooted in the Christian culture (*Christliche Gemeinschaftsschule*), and they have to provide faith-based religious education. Students can opt out of religious education and take an 'Ethics class'. In these federal states, religion has to be offered in school so that students can 'express' their religion in school if they want to. This system has developed over a longer historical time span for the two Christian denominations. These legal possibilities are put into practice differently in various regions. There are areas in Germany where school prayer, worship services at the start of school, and high numbers of pupils in religious lessons are a matter of course. There are other regions where the majority of students withdraw from religious lessons, and a spiritual life at school is nearly non-existent. Differences are mainly due to the regional differences in religious affiliation.

## 2.3.2 *Governmental religious schools*

A further consequence of the specific way in which freedom of religion is understood by German law (and by history; Glenn 2012, 219–221; Böhm-Kasper 2007; Landtag Nordrhein-Westfalen 2013) is the fact that in two federal states, there are denomination-based primary schools and low tracking secondary schools operating as governmental religious schools. This is the case in North Rhine-Westphalia (NRW), the federal state with the highest population of all German states, and in Lower Saxony.

Presently, in NRW, there are about 80 governmental Protestant schools, 1000 governmental Catholic schools and 1 governmental Jewish school (out of a total of 3000 state primary schools; this means that one-third of all governmental schools are Catholic schools), and 44 Catholic and 5 Protestant state can be considered as lower secondary schools[4] (*Hauptschule*) (out of a total of 680 schools). In Lower Saxony, there are 7 Protestant and 128 Catholic governmental primary schools (from a total of 1760 governmental primary schools). To establish such a school, a democratic decision by parents must be passed (Art 129/1 School Law of Lower Saxony). This decision can be reviewed on a regular basis.

Until about 1990, governmental denominational schools had to comprise about 60% of students of the given denomination; today, this is no longer the case. This means, to take an improbable example, that it would be possible for a population of 100% agnostic parents to opt for their children's school to become a Catholic school. In governmental religious schools, all students are admitted without any regard to their religion, but their religious education is offered only in the respective denomination and is obligatory for all students. Parents have to declare that they respect the denominational base of the school and agree with the corresponding religious education. However, it is not necessary that the parents or the children live according to the standards or (in the case of Catholic schools) the dogma of the religion. However, instruction should mainly be carried out by teachers who belong to the specific denomination.

## 2.3.3. *Non-governmental religious schools*

The majority of non-governmental religious schools are Catholic or Protestant schools (see Sections 3 of this paper). The Jewish Community runs nine primary schools (partly very small) and two higher secondary schools (lit. 'Gymnasium') (Zentralrat der Juden in Deutschland 2013). The one existing Muslim primary school in Berlin has about 150 students and has won some awards for its integrating, tolerant profile and interreligious focus.

The control of non-governmental religious schools by the state as well as the constitutional embedding of the freedom of religion in the human rights leads to a mainstreaming of religion, balancing the autonomy of religions with all the other basic rights. It is illegal in non-governmental religious schools to omit the teaching of evolution (as this is part of the curriculum), or not to teach swimming based on religious reasons (see BVerwG 6 C 25.12).

However, teachers who are hired by governmental and non-governmental religious schools can be chosen based on the framework of the religion in regard to membership and personal life. In general, schools are not tolerant with respect to membership (as the funding from the state is related to teachers being members of a religion, esp. church) but are tolerant with regard to personal matters, that is, in most of the religious schools, divorce, or homosexuality would not be a matter of discussion.

When it comes to students, the constitution protects all personal rights: for example, a religious school would not be allowed to expel a homosexual student, or even to put pressure on the student (though admittedly there is a grey area of hidden pressure in this regard, which is difficult to control).

### 2.4. *Recent developments*

As the religious landscape is becoming more and more heterogeneous and secularisation is progressing, the historically entrenched form of cooperation between (Christian) religions and the state in education is coming under pressure.

The balance between religious freedom and other constitutional values has led to various discussions and court decisions related to expressions of religious identity in the last decade.

One case involved the presence of a crucifix in the classroom. Since 1949, a Bavarian law requires a crucifix to be displayed in every classroom of a governmental school. In 1995, agnostic parents went to the Federal Constitutional Court and the Court decided that non-believing students are not able to 'remove themselves from its [= the crucifix's] presence and message' (see BVerGE 93, 1), and therefore a cross needs to be removed in the event that a particular student in a particular classroom complains. The idea was not to change the practice as this law is rooted in a cultural heritage but instead to provide flexibility in case there is a complaint.

Another case concerned the question of whether women in governmental non-religious schools were allowed to wear Muslim headscarves, or hijabs, as these symbols would not only touch on religious issues but also broader considerations of recognition because they are sometimes believed to symbolise the unequal rights of women. The Federal Constitutional Court argued that headscarves can be only forbidden if there is a local law prohibiting religious garments for teachers of all religions, and all religions have to be treated equally (see Robbers 2005). This has led to a situation where different federal states have taken different – and even contradictory – decisions, that is, Berlin no longer allowing teachers to wear symbols of their faith, including the cross, or others such as Bavaria banning headscarves for Muslim teachers but allowing crosses as a symbol of a part of Germany's cultural tradition.

Yet another ongoing issue concerns whether it remains easier to set up a religious school as opposed to a non-governmental secular school. As mentioned earlier, founding a non-governmental primary school requires special standards in regards to the pedagogical orientation. If parents wish to establish a primary or lower secondary school, the foundation of religious non-governmental schools may be seen as favourable. Particular pedagogies (such as those promoted in Steiner or Montessori schools) are very difficult to implement under the current rules of governance; hence many believe that attempts to establish a school on religious grounds will be more likely to succeed. Because state subsidies are not granted during the first three years of establishing a school, and no money can be raised through higher tuition, a backup organisation or a sponsor is needed when founding a school. Furthermore, because the churches over the centuries built up foundations for these issues, it remains much easier for parents to establish a non-governmental religious school than a non-governmental secular school (see the discussion of this practice by Bader 2007, 282; Glenn 2012, 215).

At the same time, the system of denominational faith-based religious education in schools is being tested as the religious diversity in Germany continues to increase. For example, it is relatively easy for a school to organise religious classes for Protestant and Catholic instruction but difficult or impossible for other religions. To offer religious instruction as a subject, religions have to be organised as bodies 'by public law' (*Körperschaft des öffentlichen Rechts*); this means being organised in a formal structure with an official and traceable membership. This causes problems for religions that are not organised in such forms, as is the case with Islam. Hence Muslims have criticised the German state for forcing them to change into a 'church' (Aries 2011). Because Islam does not have an organisational structure with a central body, German authorities are claiming they have problems in organising Islamic religious education at schools, and Islamic authorities also do not feel that their input is respected (see Robbers 2005; de Wall 2012).

A final issue on the agenda is public funding. The public funding of schools varies between the federal states and the types of schools, ranging from 60% to 90%. Non-governmental schools criticise the lack of transparency in funding and the constant shortages. In 2013, the court of Saxonia challenged the parliament of the federal state to increase the funding of non-governmental schools, as funding had been reduced in an attempt to cause an increase in the population of students enrolling in government schools (see Sächsischer Verfassungsgerichtshof 2013 Vf. 25-II-12).

## 3. Types of non-governmental religious schools between charity and elite education – increasing demand in special sectors

The description of the legal background of non-governmental religious schools demonstrates that the state itself offers religious education and religious schools on the basis of an understanding of religious freedom. This kind of openness gives the state the possibility of controlling non-governmental religions schools by legal and financial regulations. This leads to the fact that, in general, the percentage of non-governmental schools in Germany is low (see the contribution of Maussen and Bader in this volume). However, the number of non-governmental religious schools is increasing. When reflecting on the increase in demand of non-governmental religious schools, it is first important to discuss the increase itself and then to analyse the reasons for the increased demand. Germany has a multi-track school system, differing from one federal state to another. In general, after Grade 4 (or 6), parents have to decide which type of school the child will attend – ranging from schools serving children with special needs, resulting in a very low qualification, or the way to 'Gymnasium', required for university admission. The general increase demands further scrutiny: which types of non-governmental religious schools attract the special interest of parents and which types are increasing?

### 3.1. *The overall notion of non-governmental religious schools*

As religion is not excluded from education in the state system, non-governmental religious schools represent only a tiny portion of the entire German school system. In 2010, less than about 5.2% of schools were non-governmental religious schools – compared to the situation in other countries, where non-governmental religious schools are very common (see the introduction of Maussen and Bader to this volume).

Table 1. Non-governmental religious schools per type of school and Christian denomination in Germany.

| | Protestant[a] | Catholic[b] | Sum of both confessions | in % of this school type in Germany[c] | in % of this school type in 2002[c] |
|---|---|---|---|---|---|
| Primary schools | 162 | 77 | 239 | 1.5 | 1.0 |
| 'Hauptschulen' (lower secondary schools) | 20 | 24 | 44 | 1.3 | 1.4 |
| 'Realschulen' (middle secondary schools) | 47 | 144 | 191 | 7.6 | 7.0 |
| 'Gymnasien' (higher secondary schools) | 92 | 215 | 307 | 9.9 | 9.2 |
| Multi-tracking schools | 47 | 34 | 81 | 2.5 | 1.9 |
| Secondary evening schools | 0 | 24 | 24 | 7.5 | 8.6 |
| Vocational schools | 596 | 22 | 818 | 9.2 | 6.7 |
| Schools for students with special needs | 170 | 150 | 320 | 9.8 | 11.1 |
| In total | 1.134 | 890 | 2.024 | 5.7 | 4.11 |

[a]Statistic of EKD (2009).
[b]Statista (2010).
[c]Statistisches Bundesamt (2014).

### 3.2. *Types of non-governmental religious schools*

Non-governmental religious schools are unevenly distributed over the different types of schools. Compared to the number of state-dependent schools, there are few primary schools (just 1.5% of all primary schools) as well as few schools in the lower secondary level (*Hauptschule*) (1.3% of all lower secondary schools) (Table 1). This reflects the restricted possibilities of establishing primary- and lower secondary-level non-governmental schools in general, which is granted by the constitution.

In secondary education, for non-governmental religious schools, the main focus is on *higher secondary schools* (lit. 'Gymnasium') visited by about 36% of the German students (see Autorengruppe Bildungsberichterstattung 2010, 62). About 9% of these schools are non-governmental religious schools. For middle secondary schools, about 7% are non-governmental religious schools and about 2.5% are multi-tracking schools (Table 1).

Apart from the higher secondary schools, there are two other types of non-governmental religious schools that comprise more than 9% of the total number of schools: vocational schools and schools serving pupils with special needs (Table 1). In vocational schools, the main focus for non-governmental religious schools is on geriatric and children care, social work, and health. In some federal states, for example, Bavaria, the state does not run any schools in some of these sectors and has completely abandoned this education to the social welfare agencies of the churches.

### 3.3. *Increase and decline of non-governmental religious schools*

Between 2002 and 2010, there was an *increase* of non-governmental religious schools from about 4.1% to 5.7%. In every track, with the exception of schools with special needs, the numbers have gone up. There are important increases in the number of Protestant schools in the primary sector from 93 (2002) to 162 (in 2007), and from 56 to 105 in the new member states. Vocational schools, especially in the geriatric sector, increased from 502 to 596 (see Statistic of EKD 2009). Furthermore, in recent years, inclusion has played an important role in mixing pupils, particularly given that schools serving pupils with special needs are falling out of favour. Indeed, this sector has dramatically declined over the last several years. Table 1 provides an overview of the number and overall percentages of non-government Christian schools per school type[5].

Non-governmental religious schools play an important role in the higher secondary schools, in the vocational sector, and schools with special needs. The increasing overall demand is related to the increase of Protestant primary schools, multi-tracking schools, and vocational schools. These trends are discussed in the following section.

## 4. Why an increasing demand?

The complaint of Holtappels and Rösner from 1986 about 'the deficit of knowledge about private-depending schools' (Holtappels and Rösner 1986, 235, Translation A. S.) in Germany is still relevant today. Meanwhile, there is a dearth of research on non-governmental religious schools in Germany. What little empirical research is available I use below. Yet because information is scarce, findings are tentative and should be seen more as hypotheses than as robust evidence (also see Merry 2015). As religious instruction and a spiritual life are offered by governmental schools as well, this first-hand argument to visit a non-governmental religious school for religious reasons loses its plausibility.

### 4.1. *First hypothesis: Parental choice for religious homogeneity?*

In some Western federal states, schools are fairly homogeneous because non-governmental religious schools are forced by the state to have a minimum of 80% of students from the respective denomination (i.e. Lower Saxony, Schleswig-Holstein, Bavaria, Baden-Württemberg); if they fail to meet this requirement, then they lose their funding. Conversely, in the Eastern federal states, only 20% of the students must belong to the respective denomination (i.e. Saxony, Thuringia). Bonchino-Demmler (2010) demonstrated in her study of Thuringia and Saxony-Anhalt that religion is an aspect of admission in only a small percentage of schools. Standfest, Köller, and Scheunpflug demonstrated in a non-representative case study in the eastern part of Germany that more than 40% of students of non-governmental religious schools were officially atheist, or not belonging to any kind of religion (Standfest, Köller, and Scheunpflug 2005, 87f.). Another case study in a lower secondary Protestant private school in western Germany indicated that 13% of students are Muslim (Standfest, Köller, and Scheunpflug 2005, 120). There is one private-Protestant school in NRW whose profile is to promote religious encounters between Christians and Muslims, in which about 40% of the students are Muslim.

With respect to teachers in non-governmental religious schools, there are few empirical studies focussing on their religiosity. Even if the state claims that teachers have to be members of the church, recent studies have shown a membership of 80% (Bonchio-Demmler 2010, 192) and even 60% (Pirner 2008, 33) in non-governmental religious schools. Pirner (2008) verified in his study that the religiosity of teachers in non-governmental religious schools corresponds to the average of the population. Holl (2011; Pirner, Scheunpflug, and Holl 2010) outlined in her study that even teachers in this sector who claim to be religious do not have the competence to talk about or to link their religion explicitly to the profile of their schools. Only teachers with clear fundamentalist convictions were able to express their faith.

Taking these findings into consideration, religious homogeneity may be a reason for parental choice in regard to non-governmental religious schools, especially in regions where the state insists on only allowing students with the specific denominational background. However, non-governmental religious schools tend to have higher religious plurality than expected, so that 'religious literacy' then becomes a matter of concern (Schreiner 2008). Religious homogeneity may be a reason for school choice but does not appear to be a dominant one.

### 4.2. *Second hypothesis: Parental choice for social and cultural distinction?*

Non-governmental religious schools may be attractive to parents because they offer opportunities for social and cultural distinction. However, a major worry about non-governmental religious schools is their selectivity by social status, except for vocational education and schools for students with special needs. In the German case, discouraging selectivity is one of the reasons that school fees are capped by the constitution.

However, there are empirical findings indicating that non-governmental confessional schools are slightly selective as this concerns the educational and socioeconomic status of parents (Standfest et al. 2004), especially the lower secondary school (Standfest, Köller, and Scheunpflug 2005, 154). It seems that especially parents with higher educational backgrounds (not necessarily with high socioeconomic status) are interested in non-governmental religious schools, and parents with less than excellent performing children having problems in reaching the higher secondary school 'Gymnasium' tend to choose a non-governmental religious school. This shows a parental choice based on the educational background of parents. And perhaps these data are linked to the understanding of religion itself: the relation to reading competence is very important for the self-understanding of Protestants. Wößmann and Becker showed that from the Reformation to 1816, being Protestant led to higher literacy rates and therefore higher economic developments (Wößmann and Becker 2010). Finally, Scheunpflug (2013) demonstrated a significant difference between Protestant and atheist parents in terms of sending their child to non-governmental Protestant schools, based on the amount of books at home, whether anyone played a musical instrument or did handcrafts at home (following some categories of a distinctive Protestant culture in Max Weber's sense). All of this suggests that some cultural influences of parental choice are linked to religious background.

Yet another factor influencing parental choice may have to do with *migration*. Unfortunately, there is only a scarce amount of data on this topic (Standfest, Köller, and Scheunpflug 2005). In non-governmental Protestant schools, the proportion of Protestant Russian and especially Protestant Transylvanian Saxons from Romania (having a strong education interest) is very high. Non-governmental religious schools may have the same migration rate as state schools, but with a higher percentage of migrants where parents have strong educational aspirations, partly rooted in their religious backgrounds or minority experience. For the Western parts of Germany schools, where many migrants are seen as 'problematic', this may be an important reason for parental choice, but this does not explain the increase of non-governmental religious schools in the Eastern part of Germany where the level of migration is very low.

### 4.3. Third hypothesis: Better performance of non-governmental religious schools?

There is an ongoing international debate on the performance of non-governmental schools due to the market situation or their special values (Glenn 2012, 224). Non-governmental religious schools in Germany aspire to be role models for quality education; they aim to be 'better schools' inspired by Christian anthropology (Schweitzer 1993, 127; Storim 2000, 9). But are they really better schools? There are different ways that we might analyse this; using the available data, I will reflect on academic achievement, equity, and the profile of the school.

In regard to *academic achievement*, in 2000 and 2005, the academic performance of non-governmental religious schools was comparable or slightly better than that of state run schools (Standfest, Köller, and Scheunpflug 2005). In lower and middle secondary schools, the academic achievement in reading and mathematics was better compared to governmental schools. Controlling for sex and social background, there was still a difference of 14 points in reading. At higher secondary schools, however, no difference in academic achievement could be seen when controlled for sex and social background (for similar findings Dronkers and Hemsing 2005; Dronkers and Avram 2009).

Another issue of quality is the *decoupling of academic achievement and social background*. Do non-governmental religious schools contribute as much to equity as they claim to do (EKD 2010; Frank and Hallwirth 2010)? PISA 2000 has shown that in Germany this correlation was quite strong. In the same PISA-sample for governmental schools, the explained variation of academic achievement in mathematics by social background was 16% by an average achievement of 484 points; for non-governmental religious schools, the explained variation was 10%, with an average academic achievement of 553 points (Scheunpflug, Köller, and Standfest 2006; Scheunpflug 2011). These differences could not be traced to a higher percentage of private lessons or class repetition. In these schools, a better combination of higher average achievement and less coupling with social background may be assumed with caution (as in PISA 2000, non-governmental religious schools were not representatively sampled). Standfest and others demonstrated, however, that in general, the potential of students in regard to cognitive and social background is not yet being attained (Standfest, Köller, and Scheunpflug 2005, 69–71). Non-governmental religious schools claim to provide better support, acknowledgment of the individuality, community, and engagement in society. Standfest, Köller, and Scheunpflug (2005) showed that these values were visible in their different confessional expressions (individual support on the Protestant and community on the Catholic side), even in the perception of the learning climate by the students.

Non-governmental religious schools have more possibilities of profiling and addressing students with special educational needs or particular interests or profiles in comparison to the centralistic model of schooling in the German states. This means that schools with such profiles are often religious schools, for example, a school for circus and show children (Schule für Circuskinder) or schools for gifted students. The school for excellence in winter sports (achieving 10 medals by students or former students in the Olympic Winter Games in Sochi 2014) is a Protestant school – on the one hand, serving the high-performance athletic students and, on the other hand, having a profile for children with serious asthmatic problems (CJD-Schule Berchtesgarden). There are several non-governmental religious schools serving famous boys' choirs (as the Dresdner Kreuzchor or the Windsbacher Knabenchor).

Even if the performance of non-governmental religious schools is not better than that of governmental schools, the stronger profile, the positive publicity of some famous non-religious schools, and the lack of empirical data may help to explain why many parents see better chances for their child by enrolling them in a non-governmental religious school.

### 4.4. Fourth hypothesis: Increase of non-governmental schools as a reaction to problems of governmental schools?

The fourth chain of reasoning is related to the fact that the attractiveness of non-governmental religious schools is also related to challenges the governmental school system has to face. There is some evidence that this could partly explain the increasing demand of some sections of non-governmental religious schools in Germany. Founding non-governmental religious schools as a response to challenges in the state system is not a new phenomenon. In the last centuries, for instance, founding schools for girls was an important motivation in the Catholic private school sector, still visible today as the churches are basically the only ones still operating single-sex schools. The absence of state provision for students with special needs was in the last century and the post-war period an important motivation for setting up non-governmental religious schools.

In the eastern states, due to demographic decline, in recent years the state has closed several primary schools for financial reasons. Between 1990 and 2003, for example, 149 governmental primary schools in Brandenburg were closed down, 25% of the total number (Fröhlich 2012). The reaction of some parents was to reopen the closed schools as non-governmental religious schools, not wanting their children to travel (which might be more than 30 km), asking for support from one of the churches. The increase in primary education in non-governmental religious schools may be linked to this fact.

In addition, Berlin-Brandenburg is the only federal state in which governmental primary school lasts 6 years and the tracking system starts in Grade 7. Non-governmental religious schools are allowed to start tracking after Grade 5. Especially parents choosing the higher-level secondary school 'Gymnasium' or parents planning to move between federal states choose non-governmental religious schools for this reason (see BVerwG 6 C 6.95; see Wiarda 2005).

Furthermore, it may be relevant that the percentage of non-tracking comprehensive schools in the non-governmental religious sector is increasing and this may be attractive for parents who do not value the tracking system, fearing a social decline for their children (especially if their children will not attend the higher-level secondary school 'Gymnasium'). In these states, where comprehensive governmental schools are not very common (i.e. in Bavaria), non-governmental religious comprehensive schools are constantly over-subscribed.

A final reason for the increase of non-governmental religious schools is the fact that in some federal states, governmental schools are no longer available. As mentioned previously, there are hardly any vocational schools for education or elderly care besides the non-governmental religious schools because the state has decided to discontinue schooling in this sector (i.e. in Bavaria, vocational schools for social workers *Fachakademien für Erzieher und Sozialpädagogik*).

## 4.5. Summary: a multi-causal effect, calling for more research

These reflections show that a mono-causal reason for the attractiveness of non-governmental religious schools is not apparent. Instead, we can observe a complex interplay of factors. As the state restricts what non-governmental religious schools are able to do, there is only a light socio-economic selectivity because additional financing by parental tuitions is constitutionally restricted. The fact that the state is trying to limit the heterogeneity of students may be more important for explaining school homogeneity than parental choice, but of course it may contribute to a certain attractiveness of these schools. The fact remains that non-governmental religious schools have the image of being better schools. There is some evidence to support this assumption, even if the empirical evidence for it is weak. Additionally, in some sectors, the state has problems with governmental schools, which immediately leads to an increase of non-governmental religious schools. These findings all require stronger empirical support but they already suggest that there are no mono-causal reasons for the increasing demand of non-governmental religious schools, not being related to an increase in religiosity.

## 5. The cooperation between the state and non-governmental religious schools – a model under pressure?

Historically, in Germany, a centralised school system developed on a federal level, maintaining closed and regulated relations to the established religions, especially the Christian confessions. Accordingly, religious communities have an assigned place in state schools, being responsible for religious education in cooperation with the state. Furthermore, they have the right to establish non-governmental religious schools, which are funded by the state. Hence religious variety is accepted in schools and religious freedom continues to exist. At the same time, the state leaves no doubt that both educational and religious organisations have to be constrained by the constitution. In this sense, religions are 'domesticated' by the state in their duty to comply with common constitutional law. Social cohesion and inclusion of the citizens are important tasks of schooling, and confessional schools are seen as partners in this task. This may be the major reason why the market share of non-governmental religious schools in Germany is relatively small. Indeed, the balance between the state and its religions, allowing a positive freedom of religions in school, is coming under pressure by *secularisation, a growing atheism and religious pluralisation.*

Increasingly one hears calls for the state to neglect religions and for subsidies to be cut for religious services to society (i.e. hospitals, schools, and broadcasting; see Schmidt-Salomon 2006). There are some federal parliaments, especially in eastern federal states, where there have even been some attempts to cut funding for non-governmental religious schools through an interpretation of the neutrality of state as complete disengagement with religion in all of its forms. In 2013, the Constitutional Court in Saxony decided against the Parliament that the cut in financing non-governmental religious schools was against the constitution and had to be revised. The previous understanding of the cosy relationship between the state and religion is no longer taken for granted. Religious plurality leads to the situation where it is more difficult for the state to organise its relations to the different stakeholders and the plurality of religions in schools. This may lead to a certain neglect of religions in schools in general, or to pressure between denominations for more cooperation; it also may lead to greater public demand for more interfaith cooperation. On the other hand, we may expect to see a demand for more religious segregation, a very likely consequence of an increasing number of non-governmental religious schools (see Merry 2015).

The precarious balance between the state and religion also increasingly is coming under pressure because of a widely assumed association of religion with intolerance instead of freedom and enlightenment. In recent years, in the public discourse, the impression developed due to the force of images by mass media after September 11 is that religion is synonymous with intolerance, while non-religious thinking is believed to promote liberality and tolerance. In fact, many Europeans have been fostering this understanding of the relation between religion and education for a long time (Schreiner 2012).

Equity in education is important, and, for the moment, non-governmental religious schools appear to contribute more to equity than to selectivity. However, this may change when funding is decreasing and parental choice increasingly is becoming a matter of income. Indeed, these conditions are more likely to yield greater levels of social selectivity.

The German marriage between religion and the state concerns an institutionally shaped religion, that is, an organisational structure, membership, church law, and theology. As I have shown, some of the 'new religions', especially Islam, do not operate using the same organisational structures. Consequently, Muslims complain about being forced by law to become 'church-like'. On the other hand, for the German state, it is a challenge to communicate with a body for which it is not clear, based on German law, with whom one is communicating, and precisely how many persons this organisation is alleged to represent (see Monsma and Soper 2009; de Wall 2012).

It remains to be seen whether the current relationship between the German state and religion will be flexible and elastic enough to facilitate solutions to these challenges and to absorb the diversity of religions in the German school system.

So far, non-governmental religious schools are not part of any large-scale assessments; this means that the academic performance of their students remains largely hidden from view. This is not only a challenge in regard of an evidence-based policy, but a lack of research opportunities as well. Integrating non-governmental schools in these kinds of assessment would not only allow knowing more about social selectivity, self-segregation, migration background, and academic performance but would in addition give the opportunity to learn more on the influence of religion in regard to educational processes. Here, much less is known than in many other domains of socialisation and education.

There is little knowledge about the differences in every day school-life between governmental schools and non-governmental religious schools in Germany. Does religion play a role? Does it play a distinctive role in the different type of schools (governmental schools, governmental-religious schools, and non-governmental religious schools)?

The discourse on non-governmental religious schools as well as on governmental religious schools in Germany needs more attention in order to show how this country – beyond constitutional and legal arguments – deals with fundamental tensions or conflicts between the right of religion, personal autonomy, the right of non-discrimination, equal educational opportunities (see Bader, Alidadi, and Vermeulen 2013), and the monitoring of the educational system.

It remains unclear to what extent the different federal states fulfil their obligation to finance non-governmental religious schools. Further research needs to be done to bring transparency into the debate, to explore the different percentages of funding, and to reflect issues of equity, for example, between school types or religions in this regard.

## Acknowledgements
I would like to thank the editors of this volume for helpful comments and suggestions.

## Notes
1. In this article, the terminology of Maussen and Bader and is used in order to distinguish between governmental and non-governmental schools. (Maussen and Bader this volume; Bader and Maussen 2012.) The German terminology distinguishes between public confessional schools (= governmental schools, rooted in the Christian culture), denominational schools (being either protestant or catholic), and private religious schools (related to Christian, Islamic, or Jewish religion) (see, for German-English translations, Glenn 2012).
2. In Hamburg, religious education is not given for different religions; in Berlin-Brandenburg, there is no faith-based religious education but L-E-R [lit. Lebensgestaltung, Ethik, Religion = Life Shaping, Ethics, Religious Knowledge], a non-confessional neutral instruction on religion, and in Bremen, religious education is not a faith-based instruction and does not have a denominational commitment (Bremer Klausel; see de Wall 2012).
3. In the case of some schools, such as international schools not running with the German exams and curricula, schools running in accordance with foreign states, etc., the situation differs, but these special cases of non-governmental schooling, concerning very few non-governmental providers, are not discussed in this paper (see Hornberg 2010).
4. Accordingly the lower secondary schools are not selective.
5. For more information on non-governmental religious schools (see Comenius-Institut 2008, 2012, 78–88).

## References
Aries, W. A. 2011. "Imame in Deutschland: Besteht die Gefahr einer "Verkirchlichung" im Gemeinschaftsleben? [Imams in Germany. Is there the danger of getting a church in the organization]." *Islamische Zeitung*, January 6.
Autorengruppe Bildungsberichterstattung. 2010. *Bildung in Deutschland 2010 [Education in Germany 2010]*. Bielefeld: W. Bertelsmann Verlag.
Bader, V. 2007. *Secularism or Democracy? Associational Governance of Religious Diversity*. Amsterdam: Amsterdam University Press.
Bader, V., K. Alidadi, and F. Vermeulen. 2013. "Religious Diversity and Reasonable Accommodation in the Workplace in Six European Countries: An Introduction." *International Journal of Discrimination and the Law* 13 (2–3): 54–82. http://jdi.sagepub.com/cgi/content/abstract/1358229113493691v1
Bader, V., and M. Maussen. 2012. "Religious Schools and Tolerance." In *Tolerance and Cultural Diversity in Schools*. Comparative report, edited by M. Maussen and V. Bader, 87–107. Accept-Pluralism, Working paper, 2012/01. http://cadmus.eui.eu/handle/1814/20955
Böhm-Kasper, O. 2007. "Warum wählen Eltern für ihre Kinder lieber konfessionelle Grundschulen? [Why choose parents governmental religious private schools?] Überprüfung anhand aktueller empirischer Daten." *Schulverwaltung Nordrhein-Westfalen* 18: 278–280.
Bohne, J., and A. Stoltenberg, eds. 2001. *Zukunft gewinnen. Evangelische Schulgründungen in den östlichen Bundesländern in den Jahren 1996–2001 [Foundations of Protestant schools 1989–1994]*. Göttingen: Vandenhoek & Ruprecht.

Bonchino-Demmler, D. 2010. *Evangelische Schulen in freier Trägerschaft in Mitteldeutschland. Eine Bestandsaufnahme zum Schuljahr 2008/2009. Survey im Auftrag des Dezernates Bildung im Landeskirchenamt und des Evangelischen Schulwerkes der Evangelischen Kirchen in Mitteldeutschland.* [Protestant schools in free ownership in middle-Germany. A survey]. Jena: Edition Paideia.

BVerfGE. 1979. Entscheidungen des Bundesverfassungsgerichts [Decisions of The Federal Constitutional Court]. 124 vols. Tübingen: Mohr.

Comenius-Institut für evangelische Erziehungswissenschaft, ed. 2008. *Evangelische Bildungsberichterstattung. Machbarkeitsstudie.* [Protestant educational report. Feasibility study]. Münster: Comenius Institut.

Comenius-Institut für evangelische Erziehungswissenschaft, ed. 2012. *Evangelischer Bildungsbericht 2012.* [Report on Protestant Educational]. Münster: Comenius Institut.

Cordell, K. 1990. "The Role of the Evangelical Church in the GDR." *Government and Opposition* 25 (1): 48–59.

Dronkers, J., and S. Avram. 2009. "Choice and Effectiveness of Private and Public Schools in Six Countries. A Reanalysis of three PISA Data Sets." *Zeitschrift für Pädagogik* 55 (6): 895–909.

Dronkers, J., and W. Hemsing. 2005. "Differences in Educational Attainment and Religious Socialization of Ex-Pupils from Grammar Schools with Public, Catholic, Protestant, and Private Backgrounds in the German State of Nordrhein-Westfalen during the 1970s and 1980s." *International Journal of Educational Policy, Research, & Practice* 5 (4): 73–93.

EKD (Evangelische Kirche in Deutschland). 2009. Schulstatistik. Accessed February 1, 2014. http://www.evangelische-schulen-in-deutschland.de/aktuelles/48-statistik-evangelischer-schulen

EKD (Evangelische Kirche in Deutschland). 2010. [3. Tagung der 11. Synode]. "Niemand darf verloren gehen!". Evangelisches Plädoyer für mehr Bildungsgerechtigkeit ["No one should be lost". A Protestant Plea for Educational Justice]. epd Dokumentation 49/2010, Frankfurt: Gemeinschaftswerk der evangelischen Publizistik.

Frank, J., and U. Hallwirth, eds. 2010. *Heterogenität bejahen. Bildungsgerechtigkeit als Auftrag und Herausforderung evangelischer Schulen.* [Approving heterogenity. Educational justice as demand and challenge for protestant schools] Schule in evangelischer Trägerschaft. Vol. 12, Münster: Waxmann.

Fröhlich, A. 2012. "Neue Welle von Schulschließungen droht. [New wave of closing down schools is threatening]." *Neue Potsdamer Zeitung*, August 2.

Glenn, C. L. 2012. "Germany." In *Balancing Freedom, Autonomy and Accountability in Education*, Vol. 2, edited by C. L. Glenn and J. de Groof, 209–228. Nijmegen: Wolf Legal Publishers.

Gould, A. C. 1999. *Origins of Liberal Dominance: State, Church and Party in Nineteenth-Century Europe.* Ann Arbor: University of Michigan Press.

Holl, A. 2011. *Orientierungen von Lehrerinnen und Lehrern an Schulen in evangelischer Trägerschaft. Eine qualitativ-rekonstruktive Studie.* [Orientations of teachers at Protestant schools]. Schule in evangelischer Trägerschaft, Vol. 13. Münster: Waxmann.

Holtappels, H.-G., and E. Rösner. 1986. "Privatschulen – Expansion auf Staatskosten? [Private schools – expansion being paid by the state?]." In *Jahrbuch der Schulentwicklung*, [Yearbook of school development] vol. 4, edited by H.-G. Rolff, K. Klemm, and K.-J. Tillmann, 211–235. Weinheim: Beltz.

Hornberg, S. 2010. *Schule im Prozess der Internationalisierung von Bildung [Schools in process of internalisation].* Münster: Waxmann.

Kalyvas, S. N. 1996. *The Rise of Christian Democracy in Europe.* Ithaca, NY: Cornell University Press.

Kommers, D. P. 1997. *The Constitutional Jurisprudence of the Federal Republic of Germany.* 2nd. ed. Durham, NC: Duke University Press.

Landtag Nordrhein-Westfalen. 2013. *Kleine Anfrage 1232; Drucksache 163925: Nachfragen zu öffentlichen Bekenntnisschulen* [brief inquiery of the Parliament: questions in regard to governmental religious schools]. Düsseldorf: Landtag Nordrhein-Westfalen.

Mau, R. 2005. *Der Protestantismus im Osten Deutschlands (1945–1990).* [Protestantism in the East of Germany] Kirchengeschichte in Einzeldarstellungen IV/3. Leipzig: Evangelische Verlagsanstalt.

Merry, M. S. 2015. "The Conundrum of Religious Schools in Twenty-first Century Europe." *Comparative Education* 51 (1): 133–156.

Monsma, S. V., and J. C. Soper. 2009. *The challenge of Pluralism: Church and State in Five Democracies.* 2nd rev ed. Lanham: Rowman & Littlefield.

Pirner, M. L. 2008. *Christliche Pädagogik. Grundsatzüberlegungen, empirische Befunde und konzeptionelle Leitlinien.* [Christian Pedagogics. Foundations, empirical knowledge and conceptual debates]. Stuttgart: Kohlhammer.

Pirner, M. L., A. Scheunpflug, and A. Holl. 2010. "Lehrkräfte an Schulen in christlicher Trägerschaft im deutschen Sprachraum. Zum Stand der empirischen Forschung. [Teachers in christian schools in Germany. A review on the empirical research]." *Theo-Web. Zeitschrift für Religionspädagogik* 9 (1): 193–209.

Robbers, G. 2005. "The Permissible Scope of Legal Limitations on Religious Freedom." *Emory International Law Review* 19: 865–882.

Robbers, G. 2010. "Germany. Religion." In *International Encyclopaedia of Laws*, edited by R. Torfs. Alphen aan den Rijn, NL: Kluwer Law International.

Sächsischer Verfassungsgerichtshof. 2013. "Urteil zur Privatschulfinanzierung [Judgment toward financing of private schools]" 15.11.2013 Vf. 25-II-12.

Scheunpflug, A. 2011. "Anspruch und Wirklichkeit evangelischer Schulen. [Ideal and reality of Protestant schools]." In *Protestantische Schulkulturen*, edited by M. Kumlehn and T. Klie, 405–419. Stuttgart: Kohlhammer.

Scheunpflug, A. 2013. "Die Kultur des Protestantismus und die Bildung – eine empirische Spurensuche [Culture of Protestantism and Education – empirical traces]." In *Bildung als protestantisches Modell*, edited by R. Koerrenz, 97–114. Paderborn: Schöningh.

Scheunpflug, A., O. Köller, and C. Standfest. 2006. "Schulen in konfessioneller Trägerschaft. Ein Beitrag zur Bildungsgerechtigkeit? [Confessional schools, a contribution to educational justice?]." In *Zur Gerechtigkeit im Bildungssystem*, edited by D. Fischer and V. Elsenbast, 173–180. Waxmann: Münster.

Schmidt-Salomon, M. 2006. *Manifesto of Evolutionary Humansim. Plea for an Alternative Mainstream Culture.* 2nd ed. Aschaffenburg: Alibri.

Schreiner, M. ed. 2008. *Religious literacy und evangelische Schulen.* [Religious literacy and protesant schools] Schule in Evangelischer Trägerschaft, Vol. 9, Münster: Waxmann.

Schreiner, P. 2012. *Religion im Kontext einer Europäisierung von Bildung. Eine Rekonstruktion europäischer Diskurse und Entwicklungen aus protestantischer Perspektive.* [A reconstruction of European Discourses on Religion from a Protestant Perspective] Religious Diversity and Education in Europe, Vol. 22, Münster: Waxmann.

Schweitzer, F. 1993. "Ziele und Aufgaben für eine Hauptschule in evangelischer Trägerschaft. [Objectives of protestant schools on the lower academic track]." *Korrespondenzblatt evangelischer Schulen und Heime*, 34. Jg., H. 5: 122–132.

Standfest, C., O. Köller, and A. Scheunpflug. 2005. *Leben – Lernen – Glauben. Zur Qualität evangelischer Schulen. Eine empirische Untersuchung über die Leistungsfähigkeit von Schulen in evangelischer Trägerschaft.* [An empirical study on the performance of Protestant schools] Schule in Evangelischer Trägerschaft, Vol. 5. Münster u.a: Waxmann.

Standfest, C., O. Köller, A. Scheunpflug, and M. Weiß. 2004. "Profil und Erträge von evangelischen und katholischen Schulen. Befunde aus Sekundäranalysen der PISA-Daten. [Profile and performance in Protestant and Catholic schools. Findings from a PISA analysis]." *Zeitschrift für Erziehungswissenschaft* 7 (3): 359–379.

Statista. 2010. Katholische Schulen in der Bundesrepublik Deutschland. Accessed February 1, 2014. http://de.statista.com/

Statistisches Bundesamt. 2014. *Schulen* [Statistic on schools] Fachserie 11 Reihe 2 – Schuljahr 2012/2013. Wiesbaden: Statistisches Bundesamt.

Storim, W. ed. 2000. *Bildung und Erziehung in christlicher Verantwortung. Zum theologischen und pädagogischen Profil evangelischer Schulen.* [Education in Christian responsibility. The theological and pedagogical profile of Protestant schools]. Schriftenreihe der Evangelischen Schulstiftung in Bayern. Nürnberg: Evangelische Schulstiftung.

de Wall, H. 2012. "Religious Education in a Religiously Neutral State: The German Model." In *Law, Religious Freedoms and Education in Europe*, edited by M. Hunter-Henin, 171–182. Farnham: Ashgate.
Wößmann, L., and S. Becker. 2010. "The Effect of Protestantism on Education before the Industrialization: Evidence from 1816 Prussia." *Economics Letters* 34 (2): 133–147.
Wiarda, J.-M. 2005. "Schulkampf in Berlin. Unter den Mittelstandsfamilien der Hauptstadt tobt ein erbitterter Wettbewerb um die raren Gymnasialplätze für Fünftklässler. [Competition among middle-class families on the rare places in higher secondary schools for grade 5 in the capital]." *Die Zeit*, March 10.
Zentralrat der Juden in Deutschland. 2013. "Jüdische Bildung in Deutschland. [Jewish education in Germany]." Accessed December 28, 2013. http://www.zentralratdjuden.de/

# The national management of public and Catholic schools in France: moving from a loosely coupled towards an integrated system?

Xavier Pons[a], Agnès van Zanten[b] and Sylvie Da Costa[c]

[a]Largotec, UPEC, OSC Sciences Po, Créteil, France; [b]OSC, CNRS-Sciences Po, Paris, France; [c]OSC, Sciences Po, Paris, France

> In this article, we analyse changes in the contemporary management of private Catholic schools under State contract in France since the 1980s. Writing from a 'policy sociology' perspective, we use data from previous studies on policy and on public and private schools as well as from an ongoing research project comparing policies of accountability in France and in Quebec. After presenting an outline of the constitutional, legal and institutional context in which public and religious schools operate, we show that the introduction of new public management approaches and instruments in the field of education has not exerted a significant influence either on the public management of State-controlled private schools or on the coupling between the public and the private sector. The management of Catholic schools is still mainly based, on the one hand, on regulation through inputs and limited intervention by public authorities and, on the other hand, on a complex system of internal moral controls by the private authorities themselves. However, although the management of public and private schools remains loosely coupled, some moves towards a closer interaction between the authorities in charge of both systems have taken place in the last decade.

## Introduction

A growing body of research now stresses the increasing privatisation of school systems in various parts of the world (Whitty and Power 2000; Ball 2007). Be it 'endogenous' (through the introduction of quasi-markets, new public management (NPM) or accountability policies) or 'exogenous' (through various forms of contracting, partnerships or international capital building), these processes frequently redefine the links between private schools, including private faith schools, and political authorities (Ball and Youdell 2007). In many OECD countries, these trends are indeed leading governments to implement both new policies favouring private sector supply of education and various instruments to control and monitor its activity (Mons 2011). A central issue is therefore that of the tension between respecting and encouraging the autonomy of the private (religious) sector and of private schools and increasing public scrutiny of and intervention in their functioning (Glenn and Groof 2002).

The aim of this article is to bring new data and interpretations to this issue by focusing on a specific national case study: France. France is an interesting case for the study of this tension for three reasons. Historically, the strong implication of the State in the field of education brought about the institutionalisation of a secular Republican school created to a large extent in opposition to religious congregations (Lelièvre 1990). Ideologically, many civil servants, teachers from the public sector and common citizens show a strong attachment – at least in discourse – to public services and strongly contest privatisation and neoliberalism, notably in education (Laval et al. 2011). At the same time, parents and citizens have also demonstrated against attempts to reunify public and private schools and brought about the resignation of a Minister of education who made such a proposal under the first Socialist government of François Mitterrand (Prost 1993). There is also presently a growing political and scientific concern about the contribution of private schools to a 'ghettoisation at the top' of the French education system due to their increasing attractiveness and social selectivity (Merle 2012). This concern is in turn leading some observers to criticise the limited supervision of Catholic schools under State contracts.

We focus in this article on changes in the contemporary management of private Catholic schools under State contract in France since the 1980s using data and new information collected through interviews and a case study,[1] and writing from a 'policy sociology' perspective (Ozga 1987; Ball 2006). These schools represent about 95% of State-subsidised private schools and in 2011–2012 they hosted about 97.2% of the pupils registered in a private school (MEN-DEPP 2012). The importance of this State-subsidised private sector and its specific form of institutionalisation, examined below, are two factors that contribute to make its comparison with the public sector an interesting object of study. Our leading questions are the following: To what extent is there a central State management of Catholic schools and what are its main characteristics? Has this management been affected by the introduction of NPM principles and techniques in the public sector and become more similar to the management of public schools? To what extent is there a specific internal management of private Catholic schools and how does it relate to public management? And finally, is there a movement towards greater integration of the two systems or do both systems remain loosely coupled?

Except for some recent accounts of the relationship between the State and private education provided by high civil servants (Toulemonde 2009) or by researchers, mainly through historical approaches (Poucet 2001, 2011; Verneuil 2011), these questions have attracted very little attention in France as evidenced by their virtual absence from a recent review of research on private education (Poucet 2012). Studies on private education deal with three topics that are not directly related to its management: parental switching of children from public to private schools and vice versa, especially in big cities and the motives and impact of their choices (Ballion 1980, 1991; Héran 1996; Langouet and Léger 1997; van Zanten 2009; Merle 2010, 2011), the comparison of pupils' success and school careers in public and private schools (Ben Ayed 2000; Tavan 2004) and, more exceptionally, the current transformations of non-Catholic faith schools, for instance Jewish schools (Cohen 2011).

In the following pages, we first present an outline of the legal and institutional context in which private Catholic schools operate. This outline clearly highlights the growing 'public character' of Catholic schools in France even if this trend is not hegemonic.[2] In a second section we show that the introduction of NPM approaches and instruments – including a focus on outcomes rather than inputs and the introduction of projects, contracts and evaluations – in the field of education has not until now exerted a significant influence either on the public management of State-controlled private schools or on the coupling between the public and the private sector. This management, based on regulation through inputs and little direct intervention, has allowed to a large extent private authorities to develop their own modes of formal and informal regulation and contributed to the persistence of a loosely coupled system of management of private and public schools despite some minor recent changes towards a closer interaction.

**The growing public character of French Catholic schools**

The first official texts – the Education Act of 1806 and the Education Decree of 1808 – that founded the French contemporary school system did not mention Catholic schools specifically (Poucet 2011). The subsequent imposition by the political leaders of the Third Republic of a system of public education through the secularisation of teaching and curriculum (Education Act of 1882), the secularisation of education staff (education Act of 1886) and the official separation of the Church and the State (Act of 1905) were to a large extent decisions taken against religious congregations and were accompanied by major social conflicts. These conflicts have sometimes been revived by mass demonstrations against various reform projects concerning private education, for instance those of 1984 and 1994,[3] at least in the national imaginary. Nevertheless, the Debré Act of 1959 established a durable political balance between both sides (Toulemonde 2009, 253). The maintenance, but also the evolution, of this balance have progressively driven Catholic schools to become more 'public' at two levels. On the one hand, the Act underlined their contribution to the public service and, on the other, it constrained their autonomy by increasing the degree of formal State regulation.

*The durability of a soft compromise: the Debré Act (1959)*

The Constitution of 1958 defining the current French 5th Republic asserts two founding principles in education. The first one is secularism (*laïcité*), also mentioned in the article L. 141-1 of the French code of education: 'the Nation guarantees equal access of children and adults to instruction, training and culture: the organisation of a free and secular education at every level is a State duty'. This principle implies the secular nature of teaching, curriculum, staff and school premises and the optional character of religious teaching in private schools. But it also requires that the State is neutral towards religion and that public education must not be developed at the expense of religious instruction, hence for instance the obligation for the State to keep one day free during the week for parents who would like to provide their children with religious instruction.

The second principle is educational freedom leading to the protection of alternative forms of education such as private education, but also home schooling. Article L. 151-3 of the French code of education therefore states that primary and secondary schools can be public or private, the former being financed by the State and local political authorities whereas particular actors or associations support the latter.

The Debré Act of 1959 – which is still the legal reference despite several attempts to reform it – tried to reconcile these two partially contradictory principles in three ways. First, it (re)asserts the founding principles while slightly reformulating them: the State must provide an education to all children according to their aptitudes 'with equal respect for all beliefs'. It must respect freedom of religious practice and religious instruction (*liberté des cultes et de l'instruction religieuse*) among pupils attending public schools (art. L. 141-2) and it must preserve the educational freedom of private schools abiding official norms (art. L.151-1). Second, the Act introduces the possibility for private schools to sign a contract with the State. There are two kinds of contracts: the 'simple contract' and the 'association contract'. Their characteristics are synthesised in Table 1.

These contracts imply that private schools have to comply with specific State requirements (for instance the obligation to accommodate all kind of pupils, not only those who have the same religion, or the possibility for each teacher to be inspected by State inspection bodies) but also that their 'specific character' (*caractère propre*) must be preserved. Private schools that sign a contract can therefore organise and manage various activities according to their religious orientations, but only if these activities do not affect the transmission of the national and secular curriculum. Finally, the legal framework of the Debré Act also stipulates that the State does not recognise private education as such but only a variety of private schools whose activity is framed by specific contracts and official texts.

Retrospectively, the Debré Act seems to have been quite successful in favouring the maintenance and development of the private sector. About 13% of pupils in primary education in France and 21% in secondary education have been registered each year in a private school since the beginning of the 1990s. The proportion of pupils using the private sector is even much higher if pupils' movements from one sector to another are taken into account as two pupils out of five (belonging to almost 50% of families) spend at least one year in a private school (Langouet and Léger 1997). Given that about 95% of private schools under State contract are Catholic (Toulemonde 2009, 254) and that there has been in France a long process of secularization of social life, some observers have argued that this Act has prevented the otherwise fatal decline of French Catholic schools (Poucet 2011). For instance, despite secularization, the number of secondary private schools has remained stable (around 3500) since 2000

Table 1. Two kinds of contracts for private schools.

|  | Simple contract | Association contract |
|---|---|---|
| Conditions required | The school has been in operation for at least five years<br>Teachers have the required qualifications<br>The number of pupils is sufficient (there exists a 'recognised education need')<br>Buildings are appropriate | |
| Scope | Primary education only | Primary and secondary education |
| Status of teachers | The school recruits teachers with the same level of qualification as their public counterparts on the basis of a private contract, but paid by the State | Teachers, with the same level of qualification as their public counterparts, are either civil servants ('*maîtres titulaires de la fonction publique*') or State contract teachers |
| Curriculum | The school must comply with 80% of the national curriculum | Total respect of the national curriculum and associated requirements (hours of teaching, examinations, inspections, etc.) |
| Funders | Parents and schools raise and manage budgets. Municipalities are not obliged to provide financial support to schools | Same organisation as in the public sector |

(MEN-DEPP 2012). However, at the same time, the Debré Act and the modifications that were introduced later to it, as well as other factors addressed in the following sections, have progressively increased the 'public character' of Catholic schools.

## *Catholic schools increasingly 'public-dependent'*

The growing public character of private schools takes various forms. It is first visible in the number of pupils' attending private schools under contract with the State. Since the 1980s, the average proportion of primary and secondary education pupils registered in private schools under State contract has been above 90% (97.2% in 2011–2012). The association contract is far more widespread although it imposes more constraints on private schools.[4] It is dominant in secondary education but also, to a lesser extent, in primary education. According to the French association of education administrators (AFAE), only one-third of private education pupils are registered in schools with a simple contract.

Another key factor is the substantial and fast decline of religious staff among teachers in Catholic schools since 1950. As noted by Jacqueline Lalouette (in Poucet 2011), in 1952, nearly all of the 50,000 teachers in Catholic schools were priests or nuns. In 1973–1974, 87.1% of the 100,000 teachers were lay teachers.[5] This author also points out that this change has led Catholic authorities to regularly question the motives of teachers who choose to teach in Catholic schools. These motives tend to become more diverse and less related to religion and ideology (for instance, avoiding an official appointment in a disadvantaged public school, being sure to be recruited locally, working in a more 'humane' organization, etc.). She also reports Catholic authorities' difficulties to find teachers who meet their expectations concerning Catholic education. Furthermore, the Lang-Couplet agreements enacted in 1992 for primary education and in 1993 for secondary education have, among other things, transferred to the State the obligation to train private schools teachers and modified their recruitment by State-subsidised private schools. Headteachers in private schools, who still have the final say concerning the appointment of teachers, must now choose among a list of candidates who succeeded at a competitive national examination (*concours*), very similar to the one taken by students preparing to teach in the public sector (Verneuil in Poucet 2011).[6]

Also, State-subsidised private schools must comply with a series of requirements guaranteeing the transmission of a secular curriculum. According to the high central inspector Toulemonde (2009), even schools under simple contract rarely take the liberty that they were given to comply with only 80% of the national curriculum to develop their own curriculum since it would be a risk to disadvantage pupils in their school career. Catholic and other faith schools have indeed the possibility to provide curricular and extracurricular activities allowing for the expression of their 'specific character' (*caractère propre*) but these activities must be implemented in addition to the transmission of this national curriculum. In addition to this, this 'catch-all' notion, which was not precisely defined in the Debré Act, is supposed to integrate different dimensions, not only the religious and spiritual ones, and in fact forced Catholic authorities to more clearly define their educational project. If some Catholic texts underlined the 'Gospel spirit'[7] and the 'Christian conception of reality' that must prevail in schools in the 1960s and the 1970s (Lalouette in Poucet 2011, 88–89), the status of the French Catholic education adopted in 1992[8] emphasises the fact that Catholic education pursues two main goals (teaching for the Nation and society and teaching Catholic faith) and that its educational project integrates 'all noble causes' and takes into account the diversity of cultures beyond the fundamental reference to the Gospel. The last status adopted in April 2013 confirms Catholic education's mission of serving the 'general interest' by reasserting the need to meet this goal through a specific and original curricular provision.[9] All of these elements contribute to a growing formal separation between teaching and religious activities.

It is also important to note that the possibility to refer to their 'specific character' was perceived by Catholic schools, at least since the 1970s, as an opportunity to provide and market alternative educational models. This was done through the blending in their educational projects of their original Catholic mission with other dimensions and the creation of new market niches responding to different parental demands concerning school results, pedagogy and discipline (Ballion 1981; Prost 1981; van Zanten 2009; Costa and van Zanten in Poucet 2011).

A fourth important factor is related to funding, which is increasingly public even if registration fees for parents may be high. Under the association contract, funding is almost the same as in the public sector: the State-subsidises teachers, curriculum, organization of diplomas, etc. and local political authorities have in charge the school premises, classroom equipment and school meals. The funding by local authorities often allows private schools to pay the salaries of non-teaching members of staff. Under the simple contract, in principle municipalities are not obliged to fund private primary school but this is decreasingly the case. In primary education, municipalities must even pay for pupils who want to study in a private school outside the city (Toulemonde 2009).

Finally, as shown by various studies, the motives of parents who choose private Catholic schools are decreasingly religious[10] (except for Catholic families who attend Church regularly) and increasingly diversified. The search for a better quality as measured by school results plays a central role (globally, private schools tend to outperform public schools although this is to a large extent due to their selectiveness) (Ballion 1981; Langouet and Léger 1997). Parents, however, also tend to think that private education proposes more diversified educational provision and more opportunities for an education 'patterned' to the needs and tastes of each child, allowing pupils to develop and express their personality and forming all-round subjects (van Zanten 2009).

**Does the state only 'pay and withdraw'?**

Has this increasing public character led the State to renew its management of Catholic schools? And if this is the case, what are the main features of this new State management? Does it contribute to bridge the gap between private and public education? To answer these questions, we use data from an on-going *NewAGE* research study, which compare policies of accountability in France and in Québec. In this project, we analyse the implementation of NPM procedures and of new policies of accountability in education in France that has taken place under the generic slogan of 'outcomes-based management' (*pilotage par les résultats*) since the 1980s and its possible impact on State-subsidised private schools. Here, we use these data with two purposes: understanding the traditional management of Catholic education in France and appreciating the possible changes introduced by this 'outcomes-based management', both on private education and on its connection with public education.

## The permanence of a traditional and loosely coupled management

Our initial work in this project highlighted two main features of the national management of Catholic schools.

The first is the importance still given by the Ministry and the representatives of Catholic education to a particular type of management which combines a strong focus on regulation through inputs (and irregular *ex post* control through the inspection of teachers), a highly politicised management of 'hot issues' directly by the Minister's cabinet and very limited attempts to exert regular administrative control and scrutiny of private schools. The persistence of this type of management was visible in two specific data sets that we selected and analysed to explore the introduction of NPM[11] as well as in the interviews we have conducted with high civil servants from the central administration of the Ministry (especially within the department in charge of financial issues, the *Direction des affaires financières* (DAF)). Three main features must be underlined. First, most managerial meetings between the ministry and private education representatives consist in deciding each year the amount of public funds devoted to private education and distributed to the various education regional territories and to teachers' managerial staff. Very few mechanisms of control intervene beyond the verification that teachers are indeed recruited and their possible inspection in classrooms. Second, the amount of this public funding is generally decided according to a tacit budgetary rule (the '80%/20%' rule[12]), which is reproduced each year and is part of a strong implicit consensus among participants. This rule allows the ministry to limit the development of private education but provides at the same time a stable and predictable framework within which Catholic authorities can handle the complex internal organisation of Catholic education. Third, the offices within the Ministry of education devoted to private education are small units and their main function is to translate and apply decisions taken in public education onto private education, especially as this concerns staff management. If they may be associated to some NPM processes, such as the contract process between the central administration and the *academies* mentioned below, the main budgetary decisions are taken in parallel to these processes according to the aforementioned rules. This has continued to be the case after 2006 and the implementation of a new law, the LOLF, which makes it mandatory for all public services to measure their performance.[13]

The analysis of the official circulars that are published at the beginning of each school year (*circulaires de rentrée*) and which are key official texts providing directives for the organization of the educational system in the French institutional context, also shows that there is still an important disjunction between the State management of public and private education. These circulars very seldom mention private education. A statistical textual study of one data set gathering circulars for the period 1998–2012 showed that State contract private schools were quoted only seven times, either to indicate that a particular action also concerned private education or to invite private schools to comply with national regulation through various stylistic processes (for instance the use of the future tense in expressions such as 'private schools will conform to', etc.). In both cases, quotations do not refer to new managerial initiatives but to more general educational issues such as the implementation of new options or the provision of educative support and tutoring.

## A low impact of state new managerial initiatives

The progressive implementation by the State of a new 'outcomes-based management' does not seem to have modified this regulation regime. For instance, private education is seldom mentioned in traditional professional and institutional journals[14] that present and discuss changes in the public management of education although high civil servants and advisers of ministers in various cabinets have frequently publicly declared that some initiatives in private education (for instance, the development of projects and contracts or the notion of 'educational community'; put forward in the Education Act of 1989), motivated political leaders and policy-makers to ask for the introduction of changes in the public sector.[15]

Furthermore, our on-going study on a specific and emblematic new managerial tool – contracts established since 1998 between the central administration of the ministry and its regional authorities (*rectorats*) – reveals that considerations about private education are integrated in the process at a very general level but that the specific features of the private sector are not taken into account in actual practice. For instance, as far as the three regional educational territories studied in the *NewAGE* project are concerned (the *academies* of Créteil, Lyon and Versailles), the recent documents at the basis of the yearly managerial dialogue process (*dialogue de gestion*) between the central and regional administrations as well as the four-year contracts signed between the two parties only evoke private education as general contextual data (through indicators on the number of private schools) or through statistical indicators aggregating both private and public education (like the percentage of pupils passing national exams). Private education is neither referred to specifically – with respect for instance to targeted indicators, specific measures or particular objectives – nor compared to public education, even in regional territories with a high proportion of private schools such as the *académie* of Lyon.

This absence of references to private schools is also noticeable in the texts and public discourses devoted to NPM and 'outcomes-based management' that have proliferated since the end of the 1970s. While it is logical to suppose that these new forms of management have therefore not had any significant impact on the national management of private schools and have not contributed to a closer integration of private and public education, it is important to point out the gap between public management discourse and action in public education itself. As shown by several research studies on the transformations of regulation and governance of the French (public) education system, the introduction of NPM has been more rhetorical than real (Maroy 2006). It has given birth to an inflation of incantatory discourses, to many articles and public interventions by professionals and high civil servants, but also to an ambiguous institutionalisation of new managerial tools which are in fact rarely linked to high institutional stakes (Pons 2010). In fact, the traditional mode of regulation of the French education system is still strongly based on three main pillars: a neo-corporatist mode of decision-making based on the interaction between State officials and teacher union representatives, a strong, centralised, bureaucratic administration and the importance given to the charisma and ethos of both decision-makers and teachers (van Zanten 2008).

The limited diffusion of NPM in public education does not seem to favour its transfer to private education. A further reason that might explain why public authorities have not been very keen on extending it to the private sector has to do with the fact that a focus on outcomes tends to enhance the already better reputation of private schools with respect to public schools. This is so because some of the specific features of private schools make them appear more effective than they actually are. Because private schools can select their pupils, and because parents who choose the private sector and pay for private schools have higher expectations for their children, it is easier for private schools to perform better than public schools on league tables and other types of accountability instruments. However, although a regulation based on outcomes might increase competition between public and private schools, it is important to point out that it is difficult to assess the exact impact of each sector as many pupils now move from the public to the private sector and vice versa, and their results reflect these mixed trajectories.

A more sophisticated analysis of the limited impact of NPM on private schools must nevertheless also take into account the internal regulation of private education, which is quite impervious to the top-down and bureaucratic mode of regulation and introduction of reforms in the public sector. Historically, 'Catholic education' is an umbrella term to designate a wide variety of schools with a strong tradition of independence and whose head teachers enjoy considerable autonomy. According to the institutional status of the school, the latter are appointed either by a representative of a specific religious congregation or by the head of the diocese, both acting under the authority of the bishop. Schools, and private education in general, have a strong tradition of self-government. State representatives and high civil servants are not encouraged to supervise them, especially not during periods of actual or potential conflict. Indeed, several times in history the State has decided in favour of private schools' autonomy rather than the regulatory initiatives of local civil servants (Poucet 2011).

Due to this strong tradition, even very limited attempts by State officials to introduce management tools at the national and local levels tend therefore to be seen by private authorities and schools as a form of illegitimate State overstepping over the autonomy of the private sector. In addition to that, it is important to note that State efforts to diffuse new modes of management into the Catholic sector also have to contend with an increasingly complex distribution of responsibilities within Catholic education and with the emergence of new instances. This complexity is due to the fact that the decentralisation of the French education system since 1980s, which has had a strong impact on Catholic schools under State association contract, and the growing imperative to manage staff has led Catholic educational authorities to create organisations at various levels, with specific mandates[16] including the development of specific management devices.[17]

Moreover, it is important to underscore that while the strength of bureaucracy in the public sector both facilitates the introduction of top-down reforms and limits their impact by absorbing them into a common mould (van Zanten 2012), the dominant mode of regulation in the private sector, which is very different, leads their representatives both to be wary of and to have a more negative view of the impact of bureaucratic and NPM tools developed by national State officials. The power relations within the private sector are not, as in the public sector, strongly conditioned by legal principles and instruments. Indeed the legal foundation of the internal organisation of Catholic education is still weak, since it has no status in French administrative law (Toulemonde in Poucet 2011, 128). The authority of the General Secretary of Catholic education at the national level and that of Diocese's Directors at the level of each department is essentially moral. In addition to that the micropolitics of the private sector do not have, as in the public sector, a clear hierarchical basis: the private national authorities have no direct power on decisions taken by the Dioceses and the latter cannot directly control the activities of schools. The cohesion and effectiveness of the system are strongly dependent on the moral commitment of different actors, which is obtained through selection and socialization processes but also through the exertion of moral pressures to reduce resistance or deviance and create consensus at every institutional level. The Catholic authorities, who have always tried to protect this implicit and value-laden mode of coordination from what they perceived as the negative impact of State bureaucracy, also believe that NPM tools will also contribute to its erosion. On their side, public authorities feel that this mode of regulation does not provide a solid foundation for a government-based accountability and a State-driven form of NPM.

The fact that Catholic education authorities and public authorities are confronted with similar problems concerning the governance and reform of large educational systems seems nevertheless to be giving way to similar efforts to develop more sophisticated management tools. These tools however still differ in their conception and even more in their use due to their embeddedness in different regulation frameworks. The interviews we have conducted at the General Secretary of Catholic Education and at several Dioceses also show a growing level of dialogue with public officials concerning national policy decisions on key areas such as teacher training or the school curriculum. This dialogue does not however favour homogeneity but rather the strengthening of a specific type of loose coupling, whereas greater openness to school reform is associated with a strong determination to preserve and when possible enhance the specific features of Catholic private schools.

## Conclusion

### *Interpreting institutional reproduction*

In this article, we have shown that despite the growing public character of private schools and the progressive implementation in public education of a specific government-based accountability and State-driven form of NPM, the national management of French Catholic schools has evolved very little since the beginning of the 1980s. Regulation of this sector is still based on inputs (financial and human resources, regulatory texts on the provision of education) and on a weak, targeted and politicised *ex post* control. To quote Poucet (2011, 38) who was describing the situation in the 1970s, to a large extent, 'the State [still] pays and withdraws'. Based on a series of tacit and low constraining rules, this management system leads to a loosely coupled model of organisation of public and private schools and to a voluntary reciprocal ignorance of the complexity of each system.

Why is this management still in place despite the fact that it limits the State's capacity to regulate educational processes and results? Although our ongoing research study might help us provide a more complex explanation, it is clear that the existing arrangements and compromises are viewed by State and Catholic national representatives and policy-makers alike as a 'satisficing' global strategy (Simon 1952). Since an optimal consensual agreement is difficult to conceive and even more difficult to put into practice, this strategy is seen as at least protecting against excesses such as the liberalisation of the education system and fierce competition between private and public schools as well as against burning political struggles that might favour radical and unilateral stances and get out of their control, that both types of authorities morally condemn and that would erode their actual power.

In addition to that, the degree of institutionalisation of existing arrangements and compromises is such that it seems that only a very powerful exogenous shock, one capable of redefining system needs, will be able to alter it significantly (Mahoney 2000). However, since the Debré Act of 1959, although successfully embedding private education into the ideological and regulatory foundations of the French school, has left open the question of its concrete modes of organisation and management, changes in the social and policy context have brought and will continue to give birth to evolutionary and incremental changes (Campbell 2004; Streek and Thelen 2005) that might progressively alter the general institutional framework (Lindbom 1959).

**Notes**

1. We use data from previous studies on choice of private schools and on the internal dynamics of private schools (van Zanten 2009; van Zanten and Costa in Poucet 2011) as well as from an ongoing research project comparing policies of accountability in the public and private sectors in France and in Quebec. This last project is based on interviews, in the public and private sectors, with national policy-makers, high civil servants, administrative staff in schools and parents, as well as on the analysis of several data sets of public documents (official texts, press dispatches, professional and institutional reviews) and on a case study of the implementation of a new contract programme between the central administration of the ministry of education and regional and local educational authorities.
2. 'Public' and 'public character' refer here to the notion of 'public service' and its conception in France, where it traditionally designates both a set of activities and organisations under political authorities' responsibility, a legal status with its own obligations and privileges and a strong source of legitimacy since public service is supposed to materialise and guarantee the 'general interest' (Chevallier 2003). Education in France is mainly provided by the State, local political authorities and some associations with a public service mission. The distinction public/private used here is similar to that of Bader and Maussen (2012, 92) who distinguish governmental and non-governmental schools, even if our presentation also stresses the empirical limits of such distinctions.
3. On June 24, 1984, opponents to the socialist project of creation of a unified secular public service of education, including private education, organized a mass demonstration to preserve pluralism and educational freedom. On January 16, 1994, on the contrary, it was the turn of those opposed to the deregulation of the development of private education to demonstrate in the streets against a bill project to eliminate the article 69 of the Falloux Act (1850) which limited the financial support of secondary private schools by the State and local political authorities (cities, *départements*, regions). In both cases, these demonstrations, widely covered by the media, were the final outcomes of political dynamics where radical stances prevailed on moderate ones and led the government to abandon its initial project (Robert 2010).
4. The latter have less autonomy in the coverage of the national curriculum and they cannot recruit (and dismiss) teachers as easily as when they are hired on a private contract as in a private school under simple State contract.
5. The trend is the same for other categories, even if the proportions are lower. For instance, in 1974, already 51% of headteachers of private schools were lay headteachers. From 1994, the leader of the General Secretary of catholic education (SGEC) is a lay person (Toulemonde 2009).
6. Two separate *concours* have been maintained, but the subjects, the exercises and the composition of the jury are very similar.
7. *Vatican II, Gravissimum educationis momentum*, 28th October 1965.
8. Conférence des évêques de France, *Statut de l'enseignement catholique*, 14 mai 1992.
9. Conférence des évêques de France, *Statut de l'enseignement catholique*, 18 avril 2013.
10. Antoine Prost (1981) was one of the first scholars to point out that a symmetric process could be observed concerning public education with a decreasing loyalty of some families toward public services.
11. The first data set comprises 958 dispatches published since 1998 by AEF, a press agency that specialises in education issues. AEF was created in 1998. It offers its clients a continuous, synthetic and factual stream of information concerning the implementation of reforms in the educational system and the evolution of national public debate in the area of compulsory and higher education. (See www.aef.info). The second one comprises the 300 official texts (circulars, decrees, *arrêtés* etc.) published on private education since 1987 and listed

by the French Ministry of education on a specific on-line database called Mentor (See http://www.education.gouv.fr/pid285/le-bulletin-officiel.html).
12. This rule is not mentioned in any official text but according to our interviewees, it has been tacitly and loyally reproduced for decades. It consists in giving to private education 20% of the budget devoted to public education. Thus the formula '80%/20%' is misleading. Private education is not given 20% of the global budget of the State devoted to education, but 20% of the budget devoted to public education, that is to say between 17% and 18% of the global State budget.
13. The LOLF (*Loi organique relative aux Lois de finances*) was voted in 2001 by Parliament and enforced in 2006. It reorganises the budget of the State, its structure and its process in 'missions' with a focus on policies rather than ministries. Each mission includes several programmes in which various actions are targeted, with detailed objectives and various indicators. According to this law, the budget given to the missions by the Parliament directly depends on the capacity of the State to meet its goals as they are mentioned and measured in the programmes. The Parliament has in theory the right, within the same mission, to move budgets from a programme to another according to results. The head of each programme (which is not the minister) can do the same within the same programme between different kinds of actions. In primary and secondary education, the mission *enseignement scolaire* includes six programmes. Programme 139 is devoted to private education. If other programmes like those for primary public education (programme 140) or secondary public education (programme 141) are led by the head of an important central administrative department (the DGESCO), programme 139 is under the responsibility of the head of the department devoted to financial issues (DAF). If this choice is consistent with the structure of the programme (99% of the programme corresponds to staff salaries), it is also a sign of the weak integration of private education in State management strategies. Contrary to other programmes, which gave birth to a translation at the regional level of academies and therefore to a strategic discussion between the central administration and regional education representatives (*recteurs* in particular), programme 139 was still managed nationally by the head of the DAF until the year 2012. From that date, and in compliance with the lessons of an experimentation launched in 2006, the management of the programme was transferred at the regional education level of the *rectorats*.
14. We analysed all the contributions on the 'outcomes based management' published in the following journals: *L'éducation* (1968–1980), *Courrier de l'éducation* (1975–1981), *L'éducation Hebdo* (1980–1982), *Cahiers de l'Éducation nationale* (1982–1986), *Les amis de Sèvres* (1949–1988), *Éducation et pédagogies* (1989–1993), *Revue internationale d'éducation* (1994–2012), *Administration et éducation* (1979–2012), *Éducation et management* (1989–2009), *Nouveaux regards* (1994–2012).
15. See for instance Toulemonde (in Poucet 2011, 123).
16. For instance, the CAEC (*Comités académiques de l'enseignement catholique*), i.e. committees which gather the representatives of various unions and authorities, were created in 1985 and are supposed to be the interlocutors of the State for the regional management of teachers. In 1992, in a context of a decreasing influence of religious congregations on the appointment of head teachers, the episcopacy created a specific body for these appointments, the diocese council of supervision ('*conseil diocésain de tutelle*') (Toulemonde 2009).
17. Like the observatory *Solfege* which aim is to organise teachers' management (Toulemonde 2009).

## References

Bader, Veit, and Marcel Maussen, eds. 2012. "Tolerance and Cultural Diversity in Schools. Comparative Report." ACCEPT Pluralisme Working Paper 02/2012. Florence: European University Institute Robert Schuman Centre for Advanced Studies.
Ball, Stephen. 2006. *Education Policy and Social Class. The Selected Works of Stephen Ball*. London: Routledge.
Ball, Stephen. 2007. *Education Plc: Private Sector Involvement in Public Sector Education*. London: Routledge.
Ball, Stephen, and Deborah Youdell. 2007. *Hidden Privatisation in Public Education*. London: Institute of education.
Ballion, Robert. 1980. "L'enseignement privé: une école 'sur mesure'?" *Revue française de sociologie* XXI (2): 203–231.
Ballion, Robert. 1981. *Les consommateurs d'école*. Paris: Stock.
Ballion, Robert. 1991. *La bonne école. Évaluation et choix du collège et du lycée*. Paris: Hatier.
Ben Ayed, Choukri. 2000. "Familles populaires de l'enseignement public et privé: caractéristiques secondaires et réalités locales." *Éducation et sociétés* 5 (1): 81–91.
Campbell, John. 2004. *Institutional Change and Globalization*. Princeton: Princeton University Press.
Chevallier, Jacques. 2003. *Le service public*. Paris: PUF.
Cohen, Martine. 2011. "De l'école juive … aux écoles juives. Première approche sociologique." In *L'État et l'enseignement privé*, edited by Bruno Poucet, 237–261. Rennes: PUR.
Glenn, Charles, and Jan de Groof. 2002. *Finding the Right Balance. Freedom, Autonomy and Accountability in Education*. Vol. I. Utrecht: Lemma Publishiers.
Héran, François. 1996. "École publique, école privée: qui peut choisir?" *Économie et statistique*, no. 293: 17–39.
Langouet, Gérard, and André Léger. 1997. *Le choix des familles*. Paris: Fabert.
Laval, Christian, Francis Vergne, Pierre Clément, and Guy Dreux. 2011. *La nouvelle école capitaliste*. Paris: La Découverte.
Lelièvre, Claude. 1990. *Histoire des institutions scolaires*. Paris: Hachette.
Lindbom, Chales E. 1959. "The Science of 'Muddling Through'." *Public Administration Review* 19 (2): 79–88.
Mahoney, James. 2000. "Path Dependence in Historical Sociology." *Theory and Society* 29 (4): 507–548.
Maroy, C. 2006. *École, régulation, marché*. Paris: PUF.
MEN-DEPP. 2012. *Repères et références statistiques*. Paris: MEN-DEPP.
Merle, Pierre. 2010. "Structure et dynamique de la ségrégation sociale dans les collèges parisiens." *Revue Française de Pédagogie*, no. 170: 73–86.

Merle, Pierre. 2011. "Concurrence et spécialisation des établissements scolaires. Une modélisation de la transformation du recrutement social des secteurs d'enseignement public et privé." *Revue française de sociologie* 52 (1): 133–169.

Merle, Pierre. 2012. *La ségrégation scolaire*. Paris: La Découverte.

Mons, N. 2011. "Privatisation sous haute surveillance étatique: une comparaison international." In *Où va l'éducation entre public et privé?* edited by Yves Dutercq, 19–35. Bruxelles: De Boeck.

Ozga, J. 1987. "Studying education policy makers through the lives of policy makers." In *Changing Policies, Changing Teachers*, edited by Stephen Walker and Len Barton, 138–150. Milton Keynes: Open University Press.

Pons, Xavier. 2010. *Evaluer l'action éducative*. Paris: PUF.

Poucet, Bruno. 2001. *La loi Debré, paradoxes de l'État éducateur?* Amiens: CRDP.

Poucet, Bruno. (Dir.). 2011. *L'État et l'enseignement privé*. Rennes: PUR.

Poucet, Bruno. 2012. *L'enseignement privé en France*. Paris: PUF.

Prost, Antoine. 1981. *Histoire générale de l'enseignement et de l'éducation en France, tome IV: L'école et la famille dans une société en mutation*. Paris: Nouvelle Librairie de France.

Prost, Antoine. 1993. "La tornade qui emporta Alain Savary." In *Education, société et politiques: une histoire de l'enseignement en France de 1945 à nos jours*, edited by Antoine Prost, 169–187. Paris: Le Seuil.

Robert, André. 2010. *L'école de 1945 à nos jours*. Rennes: Presses universitaires de Rennes.

Simon, Herbert. 1952. *Models of Bounded Rationality. Economic Analysis and Public Policy*. Cambridge: MIT Press.

Streeck, Wolfang, and Kathleen Thelen. 2005. *Beyond Continuity: Institutional Change in Advanced Political Economies*. Oxford: Oxford University Press.

Tavan, Chloé. 2004. "Ecole publique, école privée: comparaison des trajectoires et de la réussite scolaire." *Revue Française de Sociologie* 45 (1): 133–165.

Toulemonde, Bernard. 2009. "L'enseignement privé." In *Le système éducatif en France*, edited by Bernard Toulemonde, 253–268. Paris: La Documentation française.

Verneuil, Y. 2011. "Les accords Lang-Couplet (1992–1993): une histoire écrite à l'avance?" *Histoire de l'éducation*, no. 131: 51–87.

Weick, Karl. 1976. "Educational Organizations as Loosely Coupled Systems." *Administrative Science Quarterly* 21 (1): 1–19.

Whitty, Geoff, and Sally Power. 2000. "Marketization and Privatization in Public Education." *International Journal of Education Development* 20 (2): 3–107.

van Zanten, Agnès. 2008. "Régulation et rôle de la connaissance en éducation en France: du monopole à l'externalisation de l'expertise?" *Sociologie et sociétés* 40 (1): 69–92.

van Zanten, Agnès. 2009. *Choisir son école*. Paris: PUF.

van Zanten, Agnès. 2012. *Les politiques d'éducation*. Paris: PUF.

# Religion and education in Ireland: growing diversity – or losing faith in the system?

Nathalie Rougier and Iseult Honohan

*School of Politics and International Relations, University College Dublin, Dublin, Ireland*

> This paper examines the evolution of the state-supported denominational education system in Ireland in the context of increasing social diversity, and considers the capacity for incremental change in a system of institutional pluralism hitherto dominated by a single religion. In particular, we examine challenges to the historical arrangements emerging in two recent contentious issues: cuts in special funding for Protestant secondary schools and proposed diversification of the patronage of primary schools, revealing pressures on the dominant role of the Catholic Church and on the privileged place of religion in education. We identify a shift towards a more varied pluralism, or greater 'diversity of schools', in which multi- or non-denominational schools now feature more prominently, rather than towards either a secular system or privileged recognition of religious schools. These developments entail a change in the historical balance of religious equality and freedoms: from leaning more towards collective religious freedom and equality among religions, to tilting more towards individual religious freedom and non-discrimination. Yet the limited possibilities of incremental change are suggested by delays in changes of patronage, and the emerging balance displays continuing tensions between individual and collective freedom, clustered around 'diversity in schools': the integration of religion in the curriculum, religious instruction in the school day, and the accommodation of children and teachers of other beliefs in religious schools.

## 1. Introduction

Whether or not the state should support religious schools is a contested issue. Equal citizenship, individual freedom, and social cohesion are sometimes seen as requiring a common state secular education for all children. On another view, equal recognition for religious minorities dictates support for separate religious schools. But it can be argued that state funding for religious schools may support religious freedom, both individual and collective, and equality of educational provision for all citizens of whatever religious beliefs. Thus, Bader, on the basis of a conception of justice as even-handedness, contrasted to justice as neutrality, has argued that a state-supported pluralist system of schools is more appropriate than *either* a secular system based on the idea of neutrality *or* the absolute accommodation of religious groups in education (Bader 2007, 266).[1] This approach acknowledges that every system of education strikes a particular balance between individual religious liberty and non-discrimination, on the one hand, and collective religious freedom, on the other, as well as other concerns such as social cohesion and the need for civic education. Which of these concerns are most salient will vary with different social and political contexts, and different ways of striking the balance may be appropriate in different contexts. Bader argues further that this institutional pluralist approach gives minorities some autonomy, encourages cohesion, and is more flexible than other systems as it can 'allow piecemeal, incremental changes instead of full-scale system change' (Bader 2007, 288).

Here we examine the evolution of Ireland's religiously segmented system of education. Unique in Europe, this has been one in which schools, almost wholly owned and managed by religious bodies, predominantly the Catholic Church, but also Protestant and other religious minorities, are mainly funded by the state. While respecting both collective and individual religious freedom in principle, the system of education has historically leaned more towards collective religious freedom. In the last 25 years, this institutional settlement has, however, allowed the accommodation of new religious and non-religious groups. Increasing diversity of religious belief has been accompanied by further pluralisation of state-supported education rather than moves towards either secularisation or absolute accommodation of religious groups.

In order to assess the evolution of the system of state-supported religious schools in Ireland and the particular balances in operation, we examine the two most controversial issues concerning the system that have arisen in recent years: cuts in special funding for Protestant secondary schools in 2008, and a 2011–2012 consultation process on diversifying the management of primary schools.

These raised issues of both collective religious freedom and equality – special supports for minority religious schools and the predominance of the Catholic Church in primary schooling – and individual religious freedom – the denominational character of schools, the integration of religious instruction in the curriculum, and the way in which children (and teachers) of other beliefs are, or are not, accommodated in religious schools, especially where there is denominational religious instruction in school.

The way in which these issues have been addressed confirms a continuing tendency towards the pluralisation of schools, with a shift from a segmented religious pluralism towards a more varied pluralism, in which multi-denominational or non-denominational schools now feature more prominently. While arguments for a secular system have been receiving more public articulation than hitherto, more significant is an increasing focus on protecting individual religious freedom within schools, or, in the current discourse, accommodating diversity *within* schools as well as accommodating diversity *of* schools.

The system may thus seem to be allowing the kind of incremental change that Bader suggests institutional pluralism makes possible. The balance currently emerging still supports collective freedom while addressing some concerns of individual freedom, with continuing tensions where the reconciliation of collective and individual freedom is proving more intractable.

## 2. State support for religious schools in Ireland

The context in which these issues arise is a society which, although the majority of the population has been Roman Catholic for centuries, has had significant religious minorities, mainly Protestants, along with a small community of Jews. It has become more religiously diverse over the past 20 years, as the proportion of immigrants increased from 3% of the population in 1993 to 12% in 2011. A wider variety of Protestant denominations and significant numbers of members of other religions are present, including Orthodox Churches and Islam. In addition, 6% of the population in the 2011 Census described themselves as atheists and agnostics, or stated 'No religion' – five times more than that in 1991 (CSO 2012). A worldwide 2012 Red C survey found that the percentage of Irish people declaring themselves to be 'a religious person' had plummeted from 69% in 2005 to 47%, and that Ireland had the seventh highest proportion of atheists of the 57 countries surveyed (McGarry 2012). This increasing diversity has posed certain challenges for schools and for the nature and structure of the Irish education system (Devine 2005; Smyth et al. 2009; Gilligan et al. 2010).

The structure of the education system in the Republic of Ireland is unique among European countries: since the foundation of the state, almost all schools have been religious; 96% of primary schools, and a large proportion of secondary schools, are still denominational. The financing and administration of the education system are highly centralised in the Department of Education, including curricula; regulations for the recognition, management, resourcing, and staffing of schools; and negotiation of teachers' salaries. Yet, the provision and management of education are almost entirely devolved to other, largely private, bodies, so that there is virtually no strictly public state education in Ireland. The typical Irish school is neither strictly public, nor strictly private, but a hybrid. On the categorisation proposed by Maussen and Bader, Irish primary schools can be classified as 'non-governmental' (i.e. 'owned and run by (central or local) religious organisations or associations whether (partly or fully) publicly financed or not' (Maussen and Bader 2012). Secondary schools are more diverse: many are non-governmental in this sense, but there are also 'governmental schools' (i.e. 'owned and financed by (a flexible combination of) governmental (federal, state, municipal) authorities') (Maussen and Bader 2012). In recent years, all, including 'non-governmental', schools have been subject to increasing scrutiny with respect to pupil–teacher ratios, additional funding sources, and other areas.

The Irish education system rests on two main pieces of legislation: the Irish Constitution (1937) and the Education Act (1998a). The Constitution laid the basis for a system of schools that are religiously diverse, privately established, and state supported. It defines the family as 'the primary and natural educator of the child' (Art 42.1), and gives parents the right to provide for their child's religious education. In addition, it stipulates that 'The State shall not oblige parents in violation of their conscience and lawful preference to send their children to schools established by the State, or to any particular type of school designated by the State' (Art 42.3).

On the state's positive role, the Constitution lays down that:

> ... the State shall provide for free primary education and shall endeavour to supplement and give reasonable aid to private and corporate educational initiative, and, when the public good requires it, provide other educational facilities or institutions with due regard, however, for the rights of parents, especially in the matter of religious and moral formation. (Art. 42.4).

It should be noted that the formulation 'provide for' replaced the 'right to free primary education' stated in the previous Free State Constitution; in defining the state's role as supplementary, this represented a concern to limit the potential economic implications for the State, as well as deference to the Catholic Church.

The Irish Constitution has a clearly religious character, influenced by Catholic social thinking of the early twentieth century. Thus, rather than any strict separation of Church and state, as in the French republican model, the Catholic Church and certain named religions were originally (until 1972) given a clear status in the state.

But Article 44.2 stipulates that the state cannot endow any religion, and provides for non-discrimination among religious schools and individual freedom of religion: the State 'shall not discriminate between schools under the management of different religious denominations' and 'shall not affect a child's right to attend a state funded school without attending religious instruction at that school' (44.2.4°). It also provides that '[e]very religious denomination shall have the right to manage its own affairs, own, acquire and administer property, movable and immovable, and maintain institutions for religious or charitable purposes' (44.2.5°).

These latter provisions in particular were relied upon in various contexts to support the right of minority religious communities to have their own schools. They also allowed schools to select their pupils and teachers on the basis of their religious beliefs. Thus, the Employment Equality Act of 1998 (Government of Ireland 1998b) and the Equal Status Act of 2000 (Government of Ireland 2000) both give specific exemptions to schools, allowing them to give preference, in employment and admission, respectively, to teachers and pupils of their religion or ethos, confirming the primary emphasis on collective relative to individual religious freedom.[2]

In the last 20 years, several aspects of the education system have become controversial, and have led to pressure on the existing system of support for religious schools. Not only are there greater numbers of different faiths and non-believers, but also many parents seek for their children an education that is either not denominational or not religious at all. This not only partly reflects a greater tolerance towards other religions and a belief in the importance of integration, but also reflects the erosion of the authority of the Catholic Church in Ireland due, most significantly, to its handling of allegations of sexual abuse by priests and in institutions run by religious orders. Thus, significant debates have emerged about the way in which education can be provided in a way that treats equally those of different or no religious beliefs, and that fosters tolerance among children. Issues have arisen concerning the structure of the educational system, in particular the support for denominational schools and the predominance of Catholic schools, the role of religion in the curriculum, and the treatment of children and teachers of other beliefs in religious schools.

## 3. The reduction of special provisions for Protestant secondary schools

In 2008, the Irish government reduced the long-standing special funding provision for Protestant secondary schools; this represented a shift from special accommodation of a minority religion towards more formal equal treatment among religious schools. Protestantism was established in Ireland as part of a British colonising process, but 'Irish independence placed Southern Protestants in the position that for centuries they had struggled to avoid: becoming a minority in a Catholic-dominated state' (Ruane and Todd 2009). After the foundation of the State in 1922, Protestants declined from 7.4% of the population and, even with a slight recovery with recent immigration, constituted just over 5% of the population by 2006.[3] Nonetheless, Protestants generally continued to have a higher than average social and economic status. Along with the primacy of the majority Catholic ethos, the Constitution originally also recognised named Protestant denominations and, from the foundation of the State, in addition to the constitutional provision of freedom of religion, their primary schools were supported, and they were accorded certain special accommodations at the secondary level.

In particular, Protestant schools enjoyed special treatment when 'free' secondary education was introduced in 1967. Prior to this move to fund existing denominational schools, there was little direct state involvement in second-level education. Some comprehensive and community schools were also established then (Coolahan 1981; Glendenning 1999), so that there are now three main sectors in second-level education: voluntary secondary schools; vocational schools and community colleges; and community and comprehensive schools. Here the first category can broadly be considered 'non-governmental', while the second and third are 'governmental'.[4]

Protestant secondary schools mainly fall into the voluntary sector of schools, which are privately owned and managed, while teachers' salaries are paid by the state. Voluntary schools are run by trusts (often religious communities), boards of governors, or individuals. Since the 1960s, most do not charge fees, but participate in the free secondary education scheme, through which they receive per capita grants towards running costs. A minority of 'fee-paying' schools receive no per capita grant, although the State pays the teachers' salaries. There are thus no strictly private or independent secondary schools in Ireland.

In the 1960s, all schools had to choose whether to remain private and 'fee paying', or become 'free', and receive a per capita grant. As the Protestant population is geographically scattered, many Protestant pupils needed to attend boarding schools. A special accommodation treated Protestant schools as part of the free education scheme, while still being allowed to charge fees. The per capita payment to Catholic 'free' schools became a 'block grant', along with certain ancillary grants. This special arrangement acknowledged the role of these schools in maintaining an education for Protestants according to their religious ethos.

In 2008, the Minister for Education, in the context of a series of budgetary cuts, removed special ancillary grants for fee-paying Protestant schools and increased their pupil–teacher ratio, thus striking at their treatment as 'free schools' (though leaving their 'block grant'). The decision was widely criticised by the Protestant community, and generated a significant media and political debate.

The move was ostensibly driven by the requirements of formal equality, but it led to a debate about the kind of accommodation needed to support collective religious freedom and equality, as well as the importance of providing for greater diversity. It is noteworthy that the change was not motivated by an aim to reduce the presence of denominational schools, or any concern about their impact on integration, since Protestant schools were seen as providing a needed diversity rather than presenting a threat of fragmentation.

A number of significant issues were at stake in these developments. The first was discrimination. The Minister for Education, Batt O'Keeffe, cited advice from the Attorney General that 'to continue the grant that was available would be unconstitutional because it was being given to the Protestant denomination and being refused to the Catholic denomination' (McGarry 2009). He further argued that the retention of the block grant meant that the State was continuing to uphold Protestants' 'right to have their children educated within their denominational ethos'.[5] Against this, the Protestant community also invoked the principle of non-discrimination in Article 44.2.4° of the Constitution; the Church of Ireland Archbishop of Dublin, Dr John Neill, argued that the move was discriminatory towards students who wished to be educated in the Protestant ethos and that the cuts could entirely wipe out the Republic's Protestant schools (Irish Examiner 2009).

Special grants for Protestant schools could be seen as anomalous support for a relatively wealthy existing elite. But in rural Ireland sending children to a school of one's ethos means sending them to boarding school, and Protestant schools take in many boarders from low income families whose fees are paid by the state, and so are not comparable to Catholic fee-paying schools. Opponents of the cuts also argued that Protestants had made adjustments: merging schools (whose numbers had declined from 43 in 1965 to 26 in 2008), and welcoming pupils of diverse faiths and socio-economic backgrounds, and that the grants enabled them to be more inclusive (Committee on Management for Protestant Secondary Schools 2009).

Thus, these schools may be seen as promoting the goal of diversity – not only for Protestants but also more widely – in an otherwise overwhelmingly Catholic education system. This view was expressed, perhaps surprisingly, by the Catholic Archbishop of Dublin, Diarmuid Martin, who stated: 'I believe there is a public interest in guaranteeing the right of the Protestant community to education ... without the Protestant communities and without their schools, I believe Ireland today, or pluralism in Ireland, would be poorer' (RTE 2009). Others outside the Catholic Church, such as Senator Ivana Bacik, argued for the added value of Protestant schools in promoting diversity and offering an alternative in the Irish education system for parents of no religion, in the absence of any non-denominational schools at the secondary level. She stated that 'Currently, Protestant schools offer less inculcation in religious doctrine than most Catholic schools. [ ... ] in many Protestant schools there is a wider diversity of class backgrounds than in their Catholic fee paying counterparts'.[6] Thus, the support for Protestant schools was based on their contribution not only to collective religious freedom and equality, but also to individual religious freedom.

The issue at stake went beyond the specific funding cuts to broader concerns: the equality of Protestants and other minorities, and the value of diversity. Irish commentators and policy-makers have in recent years generally agreed in principle that increasing diversity of beliefs and practices has been a positive contribution to Irish society. Thus, rather than emphasising the problems that diversity might bring, public discourse has stressed the need to respect diversity, while encouraging interaction among members of different religions and cultures.

For the State, however, non-discrimination, or formal equality of state funding for education was considered to fulfil the requirement of equal treatment among religious groups. In 2009, the Education Minister repeatedly emphasised that maintaining the block grant for Protestant schools clearly indicated the 'importance the Government attaches to ensuring that students can attend schools that reflect their denominational ethos',[7] and in 2011, his successor, Ruairi Quinn, reiterated the Constitution-based argument on discrimination.

This development and the debate surrounding it raised issues of collective religious freedom, equality between religious groups, and recognition of minority religions. It revealed a change in the commitment to collective religious freedom, making more tenuous the footing of any special accommodation. Removing funding from Protestant schools represented a shift from a form of provision that could be seen as essential to effective equality and collective religious freedom of the Protestant minority. It also clarified that, although the education system is one which supports minorities and religious schools, the policy is not one of unconditional recognition or absolute accommodation. This is borne out also by the fact that, while several multi-denominational secondary schools have now been approved, proposals for a Muslim secondary school have not.

The impact of these ongoing developments is still uncertain, however. Since the 2008 funding cuts, three Church of Ireland secondary schools have entered the free education system. With increasing scrutiny of all aspects of education budgets, up to eight

Catholic and Protestant fee-charging schools have indicated an interest in a similar move (McGuire 2013; RTE 2013a, 2013b; Humphreys 2014).

## 4. Diversifying the patronage of primary schools

The issue of individual freedom arose more centrally in the consultation process on diversifying the management of primary schools that was initiated by the government in 2008. This process had potentially a more far-reaching impact than the changes in Protestant school funding.

Primary education has an almost entirely 'non-governmental' structure, which combines state funding with management by a range of non-state institutions, and in which almost all the costs of primary, or 'national', schools, including teachers' salaries, are funded by the State.[8] The system of management, or *patronage*, originated in the nineteenth century, although the original intention was to create a non-denominational, integrated system with separate religious instruction; this failed, due to opposition from a range of religious denominations, and the system that emerged was primarily denominational (Drudy and Lynch 1993; Devine, Kenny, and MacNeela 2004). Patrons include churches and, more recently, limited companies for multi-denominational and all-Irish schools. The patron's educational philosophy is reflected in the distinctive character or 'ethos' of the school.

The vast majority (96%) of national schools are denominational parish schools; almost 90% are Catholic, but there are also a significant number of schools owned and managed by the largest Protestant denomination, the Church of Ireland, and smaller numbers of Presbyterian, Methodist, Jewish, Quaker, and, recently, Muslim schools. *Gaelscoileanna* (Irish-medium schools), expanding late in the twentieth century, can be denominational, multi-denominational, or inter-denominational. Multi-denominational schools, often opened to meet parental demand, and accepting children from all religious backgrounds, developed from the late 1970s, and are now one of the fastest growing primary school sectors. Most multi-denominational schools are under the patronage of Educate Together, a limited non-profit company. These schools do not include religious instruction or observance during school hours, although they facilitate this on school premises outside school hours.

The system of state support for religious primary schools, and the constitutional basis on which it developed, has accommodated the establishment of separate primary schools for minority religions with little or no controversy, thus more easily than in some other European countries. Until recently the religiously segregated structure of the education system was not seen as really problematic. However, as the population has become more diverse, the issue of religious schools has given rise to growing debates. These raise issues of discrimination in access to schooling for those of beliefs other than Catholic, and questions of individual religious liberty within schools.

There is a shortage of schools in areas of high population growth, and there is a limited choice of schools in general (Mawhinney 2006, 2007). Catholic schools give priority in admission to children of Catholic families. Some parents have their children baptised specifically to ensure they can gain entry to a school of any kind. But non-Catholic children may be left without any school place. This raises serious problems of discrimination.[9] To address this, in 2008, in response to pressures in areas with considerable numbers of immigrants, where children could not get places in existing local schools, the Minister for Education took the step of endorsing a new kind of (governmental) school, the 'Community National School', managed by a local authority, Vocational Education Committee. By early 2014, there were eight such schools in operation.

Yet, particularly outside major urban areas, parents often have no choice but to send their children to the local Catholic or Protestant school. Individual religious freedom is not protected when children have little option but to attend these schools, as doctrinal religion is taught there both through timetabled religious education classes and in the 'integrated curriculum'. Based on a holistic conception of education, the integrated curriculum was introduced in 1971. It was interpreted to mean that religion is not restricted to particular classes, but is integrated with other subjects throughout the school day. According to Rule 68 of the *Rules for National Schools*, religion is central:

> Of all the parts of a school curriculum Religious Instruction is by far the most important ... Religious Instruction is, therefore, a fundamental part of the school course, and a religious spirit should inform and vivify the whole work of the school. (DES 1965, 1971).

This is still central to Catholic and Church of Ireland schools, which *can* and *must* teach the integrated curriculum (Mawhinney 2007). In theory, a student can be exempted from any subject that is contrary to the conscience of the parent or student, a practice referred to as the 'opt-out clause'. However, in an integrated curriculum, 'opting-out' is not effective. In multi-denominational schools, a broad ethical education programme is taught in place of religion. The new Community National Schools have a multifaith religious programme, accommodating all religious faiths, but posing problems for parents who do not want a religious education of any kind for their children.

To address the first issue, the lack of diversity in schools, and the problem of individual religious freedom that is entailed, a series of proposals to diversify schools has been made.

In 2008, in a remarkable initiative, the Catholic Archbishop of Dublin, Dr. Diarmuid Martin, called for an 'open and honest debate on the future of the school system' and stated that he was prepared to 'divest some schools of their Catholic patronage to allow other patrons to take over where demand exists' (RTE 2008). Subsequently, he identified that this could be up to half the Catholic schools. A 2010 *Irish Times*/Ipsos, MRBI poll revealed that a majority of people (61%) believed that the Catholic Church should give up its control of the primary school system; 28% said it should maintain its position; and 11% had no opinion (Collins 2010).

In 2011, the Minister for Education, Ruairi Quinn, established a *Forum on Patronage and Pluralism in the Primary Sector*. An Advisory Group was appointed to convene the Forum and to collect submissions on how best to establish the demand for diversity of patronage, to manage the transfer of patronage, and to accommodate diversity where just one or two schools serve a community. The Group's report, published in April 2012, noted the increased demand for multi-denominational, non-denominational, and Irish language schools, and recommended diversifying the patronage of the existing stock of schools in areas where the population is stable. It advised realising this in phases, through adopting a catchment approach and taking account of the preferences of parents (Coolahan, Hussey, and Kilfeather 2012). In June 2012, the Minister for Education broadly accepted the recommendations and requested that the process should start immediately.

The report proposed examining patronage in 47 areas with potential demand for a diversity of school types. A pilot survey of five areas indicated sufficient demand for some changes in each of these. Educate Together – the multi-denominational patron – received the highest level of both first and combined preferences in each area. Further surveys indicated sufficient parental demand in 23 areas to support immediate change: for an Irish language school in one area, for Educate Together schools in 20 areas, and for Community National Schools in two other towns.[10] In the remaining 15 areas, there was not sufficient support to ensure the viability of a school of different patronage (DES 2013a).

Among the many issues that emerged in the Forum, three can be singled out: diversity of schools, the role of parental choice, and the possibility of secularising schools.

### 4.1. *Diversity of schools*

The first concern was the need for schools to represent the new religious *diversity* of the population, including those of no religious beliefs. At the launch of the Forum, Minister Quinn noted

> We have now a much more diverse population than we had even two decades ago ... In addition, many people's views about the place of religion in society and in their own lives have undergone profound change. The patronage of our schools needs to reflect those changes. (DES 2011).

This was also acknowledged by some Catholic Church leaders. Even before Archbishop Martin's interventions, the Irish Bishop's Conference 2007 document *Catholic Primary Schools, A Policy Provision into the Future* made it clear that 'As the Catholic Church accepts there should be choice and diversity within a national education system, it believes that parents who desire schools under different patronage should, where possible, be facilitated in accessing them' (Irish Catholic Bishops' Conference 2007, 6).

Official and professional bodies have also called for a re-organisation of patronage to mirror the changes in society. The Irish Human Rights Commission's 2011 report *Religion and Education: A Human Rights Perspective* made 13 recommendations to Government, in particular to increase the diversity of school types to accommodate the diversity of religious and non-religious convictions, thus allowing Ireland to meet its human rights obligations (IHRC 2011). International agencies, including the Committee on the Elimination of Racial Discrimination (CERD) in 2005 and 2011, and the Council of Europe in 2008, recommended that Ireland meet the demand for non-denominational and multi-denominational schools. In 2008, the committee on the International Covenant on Civil and Political Rights (ICCPR) emphasised the need for the state to address the 'integrated curriculum' and to increase the diversity of primary schools. While these statements were mentioned during the Forum, the debate was, however, conducted mainly in domestic terms.

### 4.2. *Parental choice*

Perhaps the most pervasive issue arising was that of parental choice. As Hyland (1996) notes, the emphasis on parental choice and parental input in the 1937 Constitution, and thus the 'subsidiary role' of the State in providing 'for' education, in itself reflects Roman Catholic teaching and has resonated through the Irish education system.

In the discussions of patronage, parental choice was emphasised by *all* participants, whether representing the Catholic Church or contesting its educational hegemony. At the publication of the Forum's report, the Minister reiterated that 'Parental choice should be our main concern' (DES 2012). Perhaps surprisingly, the constitutional basis of this right was not often cited, as if it went without saying.

The actual responses of parents were interpreted in various ways. Some saw these as supporting immediate change in existing school patronage, while Catholic school representatives queried the size and representativeness of the response in this direction. The Education Minister attempted to reassure supporters of Catholic education, emphasising its positive contribution. But he also deplored 'scaremongering' by some Catholic schools, whose representatives sometimes claimed that expressing a desire for any other form of patronage would lead to a 'unilateral handover' of Catholic schools to non-Catholic patrons (Holden 2013b). The debates on patronage demonstrated that Catholicism in Ireland is far from a 'monolithic entity', but includes both Archbishop Martin's open approach to divesting Catholic schools and others, including the Catholic School Partnership's more defensive attitude.

Some did contest the emphasis on parental choice. In a contribution to the Forum, two legal academics, Eoin Daly and Tom Hickey, argued that 'The debate should instead hinge on the cardinal values of religious liberty and equality, not on "parental choice" or on "diversity"', which could never be fully realised in any case (Daly and Hickey 2011).[11] Yet, the term 'choice' as used in these debates is, arguably, somewhat ambiguous. It could be understood either as individual religious freedom of parents, or as a more libertarian sense of market choice. In our view, it was primarily a stand-in for individual religious liberty – as the primary aim of those seeking change was that children should not have to attend denominational schools at odds with their beliefs. Apart from including Irish language schools, it did not appear to imply a wider principle of parental choice of schools with respect, for example, to alternative curricula or levels of state involvement.

It is true, however, that, while collective freedom of religion may be supported through a broader system of institutional pluralism, and a greater diversity of schools may give some increased support for individual religious freedom, the necessarily limited range of schools in many areas of low population means that providing for individual freedom of religion is more problematical in these contexts.

### 4.3. *Secularisation of schools*

From this observation, Daly and Hickey argued that a common secular school system or a 'universal model of non-denominational education' (Daly 2011) would provide a greater degree of religious liberty. They argued for a move

> to a discourse on the construction of a common, non-sectarian school, as a republican project within which the ideal of equal religious liberty can be realised independently of the power relations between different religious and non-religious factions within Irish society. (Daly and Hickey 2011).

It may be noted that this republican-inspired argument was still primarily concerned with problems of individual freedom and equality rather than securing civic education or social cohesion, which have not been a significant issue in Irish, in contrast to international, debates on religious schools.

Following the Forum's Report, Bishop Leo O'Reilly, who, like Archbishop Martin, had earlier acknowledged a need for more plurality, but warned against a rush to put primary schools under secular control and expressed a concern at a turn towards the potential secularisation of schools, stated: 'It's a position that essentially suggests freedom of religion is freedom from religion. That's a crucial distinction and worrying in itself' (Ryan 2012).

But the route of secularising the primary system was not widely advanced, and the possibility was downplayed by the Forum's Chair, John Coolahan, since the place of religious schools is secured in the Constitution, and cannot be changed without a referendum, which would appear unlikely to be passed at this point in Ireland (personal interview, 31 May 2011). Rather than secularisation, the possibility of supporting individual liberty through more parental involvement in the management of schools was raised in the Forum's report. It suggested the inclusion of a new section in the Education Act that would make boards of management 'accountable to the parent body, while upholding the characteristic spirit of the school, for also upholding the constitutional rights of parents and children with regard to denominational religious education/faith formation' (Coolahan, Hussey, and Kilfeather 2012, 79).

### 4.4. *From diversity of schools to diversity within schools*

Since diversity of schools alone cannot guarantee individual religious freedom, the Forum brought to the fore other challenges in addition to the debate on the structure of schools for which it was designed. Rather than common secular schools, the focus was on accommodating diversity *within* as well as diversity *of* schools. These challenges concerned the integrated curriculum and the time allocated to religious education; the proposed introduction of 'ethics programmes' in all schools; and the accommodation in denominational schools of pupils of other beliefs.

The Advisory Group's report recommended that doctrinal instruction, in particular sacramental preparation, should not intrude on the time allocated for the general curriculum. This reflects in part a growing concern about a relative decline in the attainment of Irish pupils in literacy and numeracy in the PISA evaluation system. The OECD's *Education at a Glance* indicated that Ireland and Israel spend considerably more time than other OECD countries on religious instruction in schools (OECD 2013). In an Irish National Teachers' Organisation (INTO) survey, over 70% of teachers reported spending more than the allocated 2.5 hours a week on religious instruction. In addition, while 90% of teachers work in a denominational school, overall only 49% of those surveyed reported teaching religion 'willingly' (Holden 2013a). The current Education Minister has repeatedly suggested reducing the time given to religious education in school (RTE 2011; Holden 2013b; O'Brien 2014). The vice-chair of the Catholic Primary Schools Managers has indicated that his organisation would have considerable difficulties if sacramental preparation were to be entirely removed from the school (Holden 2013a).

In addition, the Advisory Group recommended a review of the *Rules for National Schools*, in particular Rule 68, requiring the integration of religion throughout the school day, which poses an obstacle to individual religious freedom; they stated that 'Rule 68 should be deleted as soon as possible' and that schools should be made aware of the human rights requirements of national and international law. Thus, the primary curriculum 'should be revised to ensure that, while the general curriculum remains integrated, provision is made for denominational religious education/faith formation to be taught as a discrete subject' (Coolahan, Hussey, and Kilfeather 2012, 81). The broad acceptance by the Minister of the Forum's recommendations sparked concern among Catholic stakeholders in this matter. For example, Fr Michael Drumm, head of the Catholic Schools Partnership, suggested that Rule 68 'could be rephrased, but not deleted', arguing it was 'about values such as charity, justice and truth' (Donnelly 2012).

The Advisory Group expressed particular concern for children who 'opt out' of religious education classes in denominational schools but receive no instruction in religious beliefs or ethics. They recommended Education about Religion and Beliefs (ERB) and Ethics programmes for all pupils, and the Minister announced his intention to explore such programmes for *all* schools to supplement faith formation.

The 2013 INTO survey cited earlier in the paper indicated that there are some pupils of other beliefs in 80% of Church-linked schools. With respect to these, the report recommended that, in addition to matters of formal religious education, denominational schools should be more inclusive, should develop policies on religious and cultural celebrations and displays, and aim in general to be more respectful and inclusive of the beliefs and culture of all pupils. The Minister announced a consultation on how to promote greater inclusiveness in all primary schools: 'Together, we need to examine how we can take account of the ethos and traditions of existing schools, while respecting the rights of those of different traditions (DES 2013c)'. While 'Guidelines for Catholic schools on how best to integrate students of other faiths' had been issued for Catholic secondary schools in 2010 (Mullally 2010), none exist at the primary level (Holden 2013b). In its initial response to the surveys of parental preferences in 2013, the Catholic School Partnership announced a project to help schools develop their capacity for dealing with children of all faiths and none, while continuing to 'roll out a *Process for understanding, supporting and taking ownership of the characteristic spirit in a Catholic school*' (CSP 2013).

Finally, with respect to issues of teachers' rights to individual freedom and non-discrimination, the Advisory Group, outside its formal recommendations, suggested examining the provision in the Employment Equality Act 1998 that allowed schools to give preference in employment to teachers of their religion or ethos, which, it noted, could put pressure on teachers to 'engage in dissimulation practices' to gain an appointment in certain schools (Coolahan, Hussey, and Kilfeather 2012, 99). More recently, Mawhinney has argued further that, through providing exemptions from equality legislation for religious organisations, 'the Irish State is disregarding its responsibility to protect the right to non-discrimination, the right to education and the right to freedom of religion of those who do not adhere to the ethos of these religious service providers' (2012, 622). These raise issues of accommodating religious beliefs in employment, parallel to those that have become increasingly prevalent internationally. An approach based on justice as 'even-handedness' would suggest that, in such cases, reasonable accommodations of teachers should be provided for (Bader, Alidadi, and Vermeulen 2013). This would become more feasible if religious education ceases to be integrated through the entire school day. But it would continue to present difficulties for those religious perspectives that adopt a holistic religious approach to education in school.

At the launch of the Forum, the Education Minister optimistically stated: 'I see the objective for this forum as being a very simple one. As a society, the patronage of our primary schools should reflect the diversity within our population' (DES 2011). In practice, things have not been so simple. By April 2014, just two schools – one Church of Ireland and one Catholic – had been divested, as discussions over which schools would be transferred continued to encounter obstacles (MacDonald 2014).

## 5. Conclusions

We have seen that Ireland faces growing questioning of the denominational system of schools, with respect to its functioning and practices, and the constitutional and legal instruments on which it is based. The two cases considered here highlight major issues in education concerning both the *status of religious schools* and the *place of religion in schools*. It is notable, in comparison with international debates, that these concern indigenous rather than immigrant religious schools. In Ireland, there have not been significant issues either with respect to the establishment of Muslim primary schools, or about the wider curriculum in these schools; following the nationally laid down, curriculum is a requirement for a school's recognition. In addition, neither the need for civic education nor social cohesion has featured prominently in arguments about religious schools.

These developments suggest nonetheless that a more profound reconsideration of the place, role, and future of religion in the Irish education system may be in the making, and that religion may be losing some ground – at least its apparently invulnerable position – in the area of education. Is there a loss of faith in the system? The traditionally established way of providing for religious freedom and equality through religiously segmented pluralism is currently under pressure. The cuts to Protestant school funding, while occurring in an economic context requiring cuts across the board, put the special position of Protestant schools into the limelight, and, on the basis of non-discrimination arguments, limited special accommodation for a religious minority. The non-recognition of a proposed Muslim secondary school further testifies to the fact that religious and educational equality are not seen as systematically requiring accommodation. On the other hand, the proposed changes in the patronage of primary schools show a significant openness towards religious and non-religious diversity, but with the character of a more varied pluralism, through expanding multi-denominational schools, rather than of a systematically secular education system.

It could be argued that the place of religion and religious schools is less secure – in so far as the assured predominance of denominational education has ended. While some, like Archbishop Martin, interpret such evolution as an opportunity for the Catholic Church to renew itself and reconsider its place and role in education, with a smaller and stronger Catholic school system, it also extends to call for a reduction of the place of religion in schools.

Thus, the character of the educational system in Ireland is evolving from its original form of institutional pluralism dominated by a single religion. This broadly supported collective religious freedom for minority as well as majority religions, but was less protective of individual freedom. The system has now extended to include further diversity, which suggests some capacity to facilitate incremental change. Yet achieving a satisfactory balance between individual and collective freedom has not proved easy. Collective religious freedom is still supported in the recognition of schools across an increasingly wide range of religious and other beliefs. But special accommodation for religious minorities has been reduced, which may make their status more tenuous. The planned – but not yet realised – diversification of patronage promises, if it succeeds within a reasonable time scale, to support greater individual religious freedom for some. But this has clear limits, especially in places with only a few schools. Thus, the specific tensions in the balance between collective and individual freedom emerge in a cluster of issues: the integrated curriculum, religious (or ethical) instruction in school, and ways of including pupils and teachers of other beliefs in religious schools.

## Notes

1. On 'justice as even handedness', see also Carens (2000, 8–14).
2. Section 37 of the Employment Equality Act states that: A religious, educational or medical institution which is under the direction or control of a body established for religious purposes or whose objectives include the provision of services in an environment which promotes certain religious values shall not be taken to discriminate against a person for the purposes of this Part or *Part II* if – (a) it gives more favourable treatment, on the religion ground, to an employee or a prospective employee over that person where it is reasonable to do so in order to maintain the religious ethos of the institution or (*b*) it takes action which is reasonably necessary to prevent an employee or a prospective employee from undermining the religious ethos of the institution. Section 7(3) of the Equal Status Act states that: An educational establishment does not discriminate under sub-section (2) by reason only that – (c) where the establishment is a school providing primary or post-primary education to students and the objective of the school is to provide education in an environment which promotes certain religious values, it admits persons of a particular religious denomination in preference to others or it refuses to admit as a student a person who is not of that denomination and, in the case of a refusal, it is proved that the refusal is essential to maintain the ethos of the school.
3. The 2011 census revealed growth in some Protestant denominations and continuing decline in others.
4. Vocational schools and community colleges, owned by the local vocational education committees (VECs), with boards of management including VEC, parents, teachers, and community representatives, are largely state funded. Community and comprehensive schools were established to provide a broad curriculum for all the young people in a community, often amalgamating existing voluntary secondary and vocational schools; these are financed entirely by the State and managed by boards of management that include local interests and religious representatives.
5. Dáil Éireann (2008), Vol. 669, No. 4, 4 December 2008.
6. Seanad Eireann (2009), Vol. 197, No. 5, 8 October 2009.
7. Dáil Éireann (2009), Vol. 676, No. 6, 5 March 2009.
8. For the history of the Irish Education system, see Coolahan (1981).
9. There are additional concerns, outside the scope of this article, that certain schools, denominational and non-denominational, are sought by some parents because they have a lower proportion of special needs and Traveller children, and that the religious school system is socially discriminatory.
10. Of the 38 areas, 30 already included *gaelscoileanna*; parental demand for primary education through Irish in these areas was close to existing provision.
11. For elaboration, see Daly (2009, 2012).

## References

Bader, V. 2007. *Secularism or Democracy? Associational Governance of Religious Diversity*. Amsterdam: Amsterdam University Press.
Bader, V., K. Alidadi, and F. Vermeulen. 2013. "Religious diversity and reasonable accommodation in the workplace in six European countries: An introduction." *International Journal of Discrimination and the Law* 13 (2–3): 54–82.
Bunreacht na hÉireann. 1937. *The Irish Constitution*. Dublin: The Stationery Office.
Carens, J. 2000. *Culture, Citizenship and Community: a Contextual Exploration of Justice as Evenhandedness*. Oxford: Oxford University Press.
CSP (Catholic Schools Partnership). 2013. "Response to the Reports from the Department of Education and Skills on Surveys of Parental Preferences in 43 areas." April 13, 2013.
CSO (Central Statistics Office). 2012. *This is Ireland – Highlights from Census 2011, Part 1*. Dublin: The Stationery Office.
CERD. 2005. "Concluding observations of the Committee on the Elimination of Racial Discrimination – Ireland." Committee on the Elimination of Racial Discrimination, CERD/C/IRL/CO/2, April 4, 2005.

CERD. 2011. "Concluding observations of the Committee on the Elimination of Racial Discrimination – Ireland." Committee on the Elimination of Racial Discrimination, CERD/C/IRL/CO/3–4, March 10, 2011.

Collins, S. 2010. "Catholic Church should give up control of primary schools." *Irish Times*, January 25.

Committee on Management for Protestant Secondary Schools. 2009. "Response to the McCarthy Report (An Bord Snip)." Committee on Management for Protestant Secondary Schools, August 2009.

Coolahan, J. 1981. *A History of Irish Education*. Dublin: Institute of Public Administration.

Coolahan, J., C. Hussey, and F. Kilfeather. 2012. "The Forum on Patronage and Pluralism in the Primary Sector – Report of the Forum's Advisory Group." April 2012.

Council of Europe. 2008. "Report by The Commissioner for Human Rights on his visit to Ireland, CommDH(2008)9." Strasbourg: Council of Europe, November 26–30, 2007.

Dáil Éireann Debate. 2008. Vol. 669, No. 4, *Written Answers – Departmental Funding*, December 4.

Dáil Éireann Debate. 2009. Vol. 676, No. 6, *Written answers – Grant Payments*, March 5.

Daly, E. 2009. "Religious freedom as a function of power relations: dubious claims on pluralism in the denominational schools debate." *Irish Educational Studies* 28 (3): 235–251.

Daly, E. 2011. "Citizens should have access to non-sectarian public schools." *Irish Times*, May 26.

Daly, E. 2012. *Religion, Law and the Irish State. The Constitutional Framework in Context*. Dublin: Clarus Press.

Daly, E., and T. Hickey. 2011. "Submission to the Forum on Patronage and Pluralism in the Primary Sector." June 6, 2011.

DES. 1965. *Rules for National Schools under the Department of Education*. Dublin: The Stationery Office.

DES. 1971. *Primary School Curriculum, Teacher's Handbook, Part I*. Dublin: Department of Education.

DES. 2011. "Launch of Forum on Patronage and Pluralism in the Primary Sector – Department of Education and Skills," Speech by Mr Ruairi Quinn TD, Minister for Education and Skills, April 19, 2011.

DES. 2012. "Minister Quinn publishes the report of the Advisory Group to the Forum on Patronage and Pluralism in the Primary Sector." Department of Education and Sills, Press release, April 10, 2012.

DES. 2013a. *Report on the surveys regarding parental preferences on primary school patronage*. Dublin: Department of Education & Skills.

DES. 2013c. "Minister Quinn addresses the Catholic Primary School Management Association's Annual Conference." Department of Education and Skills, Speeches, April 12, 2013.

Devine, D. 2005. "Welcome to the Celtic Tiger? Teacher responses to immigration and increasing ethnic diversity in Irish schools." *International Studies in Sociology of Education* 15 (1): 49–70.

Devine, D., M. Kenny, and E. MacNeela. 2004. "Experiencing Racism in the primary school – Children's perspectives." In *Primary Voices – Equality, Diversity and Childhood in Irish Primary Schools*, edited by J. Deegan, D. Devine, and A. Lodge, 183–205. Dublin: Institute of Public Administration.

Donnelly, K. 2012. "Bishops oppose axeing class religion rule." *Irish Independent*, April 11.

Drudy, S., and K. Lynch. 1993. *Schools and society in Ireland*. Dublin: Gill and Macmillan.

Gilligan, R., P. Curry, J. McGrath, D. Murphy, M. Ní Raghallaigh, M. Rogers, J. Scholtz, and A. Gilligan Quinn. 2010. *In the Front Line of Integration: Young people managing migration to Ireland*. Dublin: Children's Research Centre, Trinity College.

Glendenning, D. 1999. *Education and the Law*. Dublin: Butterworths.

Government of Ireland. 1998a. *Education Act 1998*. Dublin: Office of the Attorney General.

Government of Ireland. 1998b. *Employment Equality Act, 1998*. Dublin: Office of the Attorney General.

Government of Ireland. 2000. *Equal Status Act. Irish Statute Book*. Dublin: Office of the Attorney General.

Holden, L. 2013a. "Only 49% willingly teach religion in schools." *Irish Times*, March 1.

Holden, L. 2013b. "Quinn questions amount of school time spent on religious education." *Irish Times*, April 13.

Humphreys, J. 2014. "Landmark Protestant cathedral school scrap fees." *Irish Times*, May 16.

Hyland, A. 1996. "Multi-Denominational Schools in the Republic of Ireland 1975–1995." Paper delivered at a conference education and religion organised by C.R.E.L.A. at the University of Nice. 21–22 June 1996.

ICCPR. 2008. "Consideration of reports submitted by states parties under article 40 of the covenant – Concluding observations of the Human Rights Committee, Ireland." International covenant on civil and political rights, CCPR/C/IRL/CO/3, July 30, 2008.

IHRC. 2011. *Religion & Education: A Human Rights Perspective*. Dublin: Irish Human Rights Commission.

Irish Catholic Bishops' Conference. 2007. *Catholic Primary Schools, A Policy Provision into the Future*. Dublin: Veritas.

Irish Examiner. 2009. "Archbishop: Cutbacks could wipe out Protestant schools." *Irish Examiner*, October 20.

MacDonald, S. 2014. "Local politicians 'delaying divesting of Catholic schools'." *Irish Independent*, February 10.

Maussen, M., and V. Bader. 2012. *Tolerance and Cultural Diversity in Schools: Comparative report*. Florence: European University Institute.

Mawhinney, A. 2006. "The opt-out clause: imperfect protection for the right to freedom of religion in schools." *Education Law Journal* 7 (2): 102–115.

Mawhinney, A. 2007. "Freedom of religion in the Irish primary school system: a failure to protect human rights?" *Legal Studies* 27 (3): 379–403.

Mawhinney, A. 2012. "A discriminating education system: religious admission policies in Irish schools and international human rights law." *International Journal of Children's Rights* 20 (4): 603–623.

McGarry, P. 2009. "O'Keeffe to discuss cuts' impact on Protestants." *Irish Times*, October 21.

McGarry, P. 2012. "Survey finds Ireland second only to Vietnam in loss of religious sentiment." *Irish Times*, August 8.

McGuire, P. 2013. "The end of the private school?" *Irish Times*, April 16.

Mullally, A. 2010. *Guidelines on the Inclusion of Students of Other Faiths in Catholic Secondary Schools*. Dublin: JMB/AMCSS Secretariat.

O'Brien, T. 2014. "Primary teachers should use religious class time to teach maths, says Quinn." *Irish Times*, January 25.

OECD. 2013. *Education at a Glance 2013: OECD Indicators*. OECD Publishing. http://dx.doi.org/10.1787/eag-2013-en.

RTE. 2008. "Archbishop calls for open schools debate." *RTE News*, January 6.

RTE. 2009. "Protestant schools to meet Minister for Education." *RTE Morning Ireland*, October 21.

RTE. 2011. "Quinn wants sacraments out of school time." *RTE News*, April 1.

RTE. 2013a. "State to pay for teachers at Kilkenny College." *RTE News*, February 22.

RTE. 2013b. "Protestant fee-paying schools eye Kilkenny College move." *RTE News*, February 22.

Ruane, J., and J. Todd. 2009. "Protestant minorities in European states and nations." *National Identities* 11 (1): 1–8.

Ryan, S. 2012. "Bishop Leo O'Reilly expresses concern about secular schools plan." *Catholic Ireland News*, July 18.

Seanad Éireann Debate. 2009. Vol. 197, No. 5, *School Capitation Grants*, October 8.

Smyth, E., M. Darmody, F. McGinnity, and D. Byrne. 2009. *Adapting to Diversity: Irish Schools and Newcomer Students*. Research Series Number 8. Dublin: ESRI.

# Liberal equality and toleration for conservative religious minorities. Decreasing opportunities for religious schools in the Netherlands?

Marcel Maussen and Floris Vermeulen

*Department of Political Science, University of Amsterdam, Amsterdam, The Netherlands*

> Liberal democratic states face new challenges in balancing between principles of religious freedom and non-discrimination and in balancing these constitutional principles with other concerns, including social cohesion, good education, and immigrant-integration. In a context of increased prominence of secular and anti-Islamic voices in political debate, there are demands to reduce legal 'exceptions' for (conservative) religious groups in the Netherlands. This article focuses in particular on public debate and jurisprudence with regard to education and explores discussions of associational freedoms that are of importance to religious schools, including the right to select and refuse pupils (the debate on the so-called duty to enrol (*acceptatieplicht*)), the possibilities for schools to refuse hiring staff who do not support the school's philosophy (for example in relation to sexual orientation), and teaching on sexuality and sexual diversity. The article concludes by arguing that the Netherlands is undergoing a shift in the conceptualisation of religious freedom in relation to liberal equality, which in the longer run may destabilise a tradition of toleration and substantial collective freedoms for conservative religious groups.

## Introduction

Education of children and young adults is deemed important to parents, communities, and the state, all having their own motives and ideas with regard to raising and socialising new generations. In this context, there are different and sometimes conflicting views about the appropriate role of religion in public schools, and about whether there should be faith-based primary and secondary schools. All states with liberal-democratic constitutions leave room for religion in education, but the modalities and degrees in which they do vary, for example when it comes to religious instruction and teaching in schools (Pépin 2009), expressions of religion and religious identity in the school context (prayer, rituals, religious feasts, wearing symbols, and dress), and opportunities for faith-based educational institutions (including primary and secondary schools) (Bader and Maussen 2012). Space for religion in schools is based on two basic rights. First, the *freedom of religion*, which entails, amongst other things, the right to manifest one's religion 'in public and in private' and 'in worship, teaching, practice and observance' (article 9 European Convention on Human Rights [ECHR]). Second, there is the constitutional protection of the *freedom of education*. This

---

This is an Open Access article. Non-commercial re-use, distribution, and reproduction in any medium, provided the original work is properly attributed, cited, and is not altered, transformed, or built upon in any way, is permitted. The moral rights of the named authors have been asserted.

freedom involves a 'right to teach' that is granted to individuals (as citizens, parents, or professionals) and to collectives (including families, denominational communities, and 'like-minded' groups), and a 'right to learn', which is primarily a right of individuals (including children) but also entails the right of parents to ensure that the teaching of ideas, attitudes and skills that they value is being provided to their children (De Groof and Noorlander 2012, 60–61). The freedom of education thereby also protects the right of groups or individuals to 'establish and operate state-independent primary and secondary schools according to their own religious, philosophical, or pedagogical principles', *and* the freedom of parents 'to choose the school they want their children to attend' (Vermeulen 2004, 31).

In this article, we explore debates about the position of religious schools in the Dutch educational system. Our focus is on schools that are 'out of the mainstream' for different, sometimes overlapping, reasons, for example because they are (perceived as) 'conservative' or 'strict', because their religious identity is relatively unfamiliar to Dutch society (as is the case for Islamic, Hindu, and, to a lesser extent, Evangelical schools), because they mostly cater to children belonging to ethnic and cultural minorities, or because doubts are voiced concerning the wider social consequences of the relatively homogeneous composition of the school population, particular teaching styles, or internal school rules (such as gender segregation in class).[1] For some of these schools, the discussion about their religious identity intersects with concerns about their performance[2] and management. We study the extent to which the position of religious schools in the Netherlands has changed, or is changing, because of new legislation and/or new legal interpretations of the associational freedoms of religious schools.

To some it may come as a surprise to hear that there are discussions about reducing the opportunities for religious schools in the Netherlands. After all, the Dutch approach to governance of religious pluralism has often been applauded, and labels such as 'pragmatism', 'tolerance', and 'pillarization' are sometimes used to argue that the Netherlands illustrates how in a modern society deep moral and cultural differences can be recognised and institutionalised without undermining opportunities for social peace, welfare, and political stability. The domain of education certainly has been viewed as exemplary in this respect, and in their comparative discussion of religious governance and state neutrality, Monsma and Soper concluded: 'There is much to learn from the Dutch experience' (2009, 85). However, over the past two decades this superlative image of the Netherlands has changed quite dramatically. The Dutch are said to have distanced themselves from 'multiculturalism' and the 'model of pillarization', not only in political discourse but also, and more importantly for the purposes of this article, in terms of the legal-institutional opportunities and freedoms granted to religious minorities, especially those minorities that are (perceived to be) 'pervasively religious' (i.e. orthodox, conservative, strict, and fundamentalist) or 'religiously different' (notably Muslims) (Maussen and Bogers 2012). This institutional re-orientation is said to be illustrated by a series of legal-constitutional changes that ended long-standing privileges held by dominant Christian religious groups, such as direct financing of church building and clergy (which ended in 1975 and 1983, respectively) or the criminalisation of blasphemy (which only ended in 2013). Also the passing of legislation that for long was resisted by confessional parties – on abortion (in 1984), euthanasia (in 2001), and same-sex marriage (in 2001) – is taken to illustrate an institutional turn towards more strict 'state secularism'. Perhaps most striking has been the sharp turn away from multicultural policies over the past 20 years.[3] Our goal is to explore whether we witness major institutional changes that, when taken together, are changing the Dutch regime of governance of cultural and religious pluralism in fundamental ways.

Transformations of Dutch institutional arrangements result not only from broader social and institutional changes, but also from political contestations (see Maussen and Bader 2015). In this article, our aim is also to analyse changes in terms of shifts in underlying ideas and principles, which legitimise particular ways of doing as normatively appropriate. In recent literature on governance of citizenship and cultural pluralism, there has been much interest for particular understandings of 'national models' that play a role in justifying particular approaches and policy programmes, whilst discrediting others (see Bowen et al. 2014). In this light our hypothesis is that we are witnessing a reorientation of Dutch institutional arrangements (i.e. of 'the Dutch model') *away from* a model grounded in a paradigm of toleration and an understanding of religious freedoms in terms of rights of communities. In that model groups and minorities enjoyed substantial rights of non-interference and had effective opportunities to shape the conditions of their collective lives. We hypothesise that this model is shifting *towards* a model based upon a liberal-egalitarian understanding of religious freedom, in which individual rights and non-discrimination are firmly protected, but where there is less room for far-going associational and collective freedoms for minority groups, especially for those groups that are believed not to share liberal values.[4] In order to analyse whether such a shift is occurring in the field of education, we need a precise understanding of how to understand the associational freedoms of religious schools.

We use the terms 'associational autonomy' and 'associational freedoms' to refer to the effective opportunities of schools to express their religious identity. Associational freedoms include the liberty to decide on membership, to have internal rules and procedures, to decide on the policy of an association, and so on (Bader 2007, 141ff.). In the case of schools we can think of the right not only to select and recruit staff, admit certain pupils, and decide on curriculum and teaching styles and methods, but also to decide on priorities in the budget, the organisation and use of space, activities (within and outside the curriculum), and so on (Maussen and Bader 2015).

In the remainder of this article, we will focus on three core elements of the associational freedoms of Dutch religious schools and analyse whether fundamental legal changes are being prepared or have been implemented, and/or whether prevailing understandings and interpretations of guiding principles have been significantly changing. We begin by providing the necessary context information.

## Religious schools in the Netherlands: institutional context, associational freedoms, and political contestation

The majority of Dutch schools continue to be religious, at least in name. In 2011–2012, 61.5% of all primary schools were religious, and of all secondary schools this was 56.1%. However, the vast majority of these are relatively 'nominally' religious,[5] meaning for example that they are open to pupils and staff belonging to other groups and that they tend to teach in an open or ecumenical fashion (emphasizing the importance of different religious and secular worldviews), and they do not have internal rules that directly follow from their religious identity, for example with regard to dress. A small percentage of religious schools (less than 5%) still has a quite 'strong' religious identity and cater predominantly to specific Christian communities. Amongst these are Reformed and Evangelical schools. There are about 274 primary Reformed schools

(4.1% of the total number) and 12 secondary schools (1.9% of the total number).[6] These schools cater to children belonging to orthodox Calvinist communities mostly living in the so-called Bible Belt stretching from the South West Province of Zeeland to the North East part of the country (see Versteegt and Maussen 2011, 13–14). Further, since 1997 'evangelical schools' have been recognised as a separate denomination, and their number has steadily been growing to about 18 primary schools and 4 secondary schools.[7] However, in the summer of 2014, six evangelical schools were closed simultaneously, following a critical report by the Inspectorate of Education about the functioning of the platform organisation to which these schools belonged, the Foundation for Evangelical Schools (Inspectorate of Education 2014). Besides these Christian examples, there are Islamic and Hindu schools that also cater to distinctive communities. Most of these schools do not tend to be 'strongly religious'; they are set up as religious schools because this is the type of school identity that the Dutch constitution facilitates, but they basically cater to children of distinctive cultural-religious and ethnic communities, mainly of immigrant origin (Merry and Driessen 2012, 638). At present there are 43 primary Islamic schools, but the 2 secondary Islamic schools that also existed have been closed down (in 2010 and 2013 respectively) because of structural underperformance and problems with their management (Merry and Driessen, forthcoming). It is important to mention that only 10% of the total population of children with a Muslim background attend an Islamic school and that most Islamic schools have a 'native Dutch' management and staff, most of whom are non-Muslims. This stands in contrast to the situation of the more conservative Christian schools and Jewish schools, which tend to have a staff that exclusively belongs to and identifies with the religious denomination of the school. There are three Jewish schools in the Netherlands, all in Amsterdam, including a more 'liberal' primary school, and a primary and secondary school that are administrated by a more orthodox association.

Article 23 of the Dutch constitution guarantees freedom of education and 'statutory equality' of governmental or public (*openbare*) and non-governmental[8] or denominational (*bijzondere* lit. 'special') schools. Both are funded according to identical and equivalent criteria (Vermeulen 2004, 34). The freedom of education guarantees (1) the freedom to found a school (*vrijheid van stichting*) which is entitled to be financed *if* the founders of a school can demonstrate that the school represents a 'philosophy' (lit. 'direction' (*richting*)) corresponding to a particular religious or ideological worldview *that also is of relevance in other societal domains*,[9] that the school will be able to attract a sufficient number of pupils, and that there is no similar school within five kilometres of the proposed area. (2) The freedom of direction (*vrijheid van richting*) entails the freedom to express the fundamental orientation of the school, related to its particular philosophy, for example in selecting staff and pupils, in choosing how to teach on specific (sensitive) topics, and in deciding on specific behaviours or dress codes in the school. (3) Finally, the freedom of 'internal organization' (*vrijheid van inrichting*) protects pedagogical and organisational autonomy, allowing both governmental and non-governmental schools to select a specific pedagogical approach (Montessori, Dalton) and allowing schools to make decisions on teaching materials, buildings, and how to set up their own internal administration. In the case of non-governmental schools, there is often a division of authority between the school board that usually includes representatives of denominational organisations and parents, and the school management (director and teaching staff).

In a recent publication offering policy advice on the future of article 23, the National Council of Education discusses important trends that affect the understanding of freedom of education (Huisman et al. 2011; Onderwijsraad 2012a, see also the official reaction of the government, Ministry of Education, Culture and Science 2013a).[10] First, in an increasingly globalised and competitive economy and knowledge-society, parents, especially higher educated parents, are very conscious of the importance of good schools for their children. They are also increasingly sensitive to variation between schools in terms of pedagogical approach and school performance, and many parents are not, or are no longer, primarily interested in the denominational identity of the school (for example they will send their children to a Catholic school because it has a good reputation and uses Montessori as a pedagogical approach). Parents are also less inclined themselves to participate in school boards, further strengthening a trend in which schools have become larger, professionalised, and bureaucratic organisations and school boards are increasingly governed by 'professionals'. In such a context, a logic of 'offer and demand' will shape freedom of education with regard to the selection of a school, and parents will be more inclined to 'vote with their feet' (i.e. leave a school and move the children to another school) than to be founders of new schools or demand a say in school policy.

Against the background of these structural trends the Council of Education discusses two important possibilities to adjust the Dutch interpretation of the freedom of education to modern times. First, it should be more clear who the main 'carrier' (*drager*) is of the freedoms to found and operate religious schools: the actors who *de facto* run the school *or* the parents (in the interest of children)? Historically and in its phrasing, article 23 was mostly interpreted as protecting the 'interests of institutions, notably of non-governmental (*bijzondere*) schools' (Onderwijsraad 2012a, 85). In the new context, the balance may shift towards the need for schools to respond to demands of parents (and children) who are seen as carriers of a 'right to education'. As the Council of Education observes, such an interpretation of the freedom of education is also visible in the ECHR that is more 'individual oriented' and that stresses that children and parents have a right to education that corresponds to their religious and philosophical convictions (article 2) (Onderwijsraad 2012a, 80).

Second, the Council argues that there may be good reasons to re-consider the concept of 'philosophy of life' (*levensovertuiging*) or 'direction' (*richting*) in the context of education. The fact that in order to qualify as a 'direction' that can form the basis for the right to found a school, an ideology or doctrine should be 'comprehensive' and should be visible, if not institutionalised, in different societal spheres, creates a bias in favour of religious worldviews (especially those of more established religious communities) and in favour of some secular 'worldviews' that are more comprehensive in their expression (such as Humanism). In upholding this understanding of what constitutes a 'worldview', so the Council argues, the state is insufficiently neutral, given the new meanings identity and ideology have for different groups in present-day Dutch society. In our times, the state should more even-handedly accommodate all kinds of 'viable and socially articulated views' (Onderwijsraad 2012a, 45). Furthermore, the pedagogical philosophy of schools may matter more for parents than the broader (religious) 'worldview'. It seems, therefore, reasonable to make it more easy to found a school on the basis of a recognisable *educational* identity. At present the choice for a particular method and pedagogy (e.g. Jenaplan, Montessori, or Dalton) does not in itself, according to the legal-constitutional texts, constitute sufficient ground to found a new school (Huisman et al. 2011). Yet, in jurisprudence often the category 'general special' (*Algemeen Bijzonder*) has been used to grant the right to found a school also to schools that were mainly based on a specific pedagogy (such as Montessori).[11] The Council advised to allow for the creation of new schools that correspond to demands and wishes of parents, and that in a plausible way add to the diversity of schools on offer in a specific region, without making denominational 'direction' the leading criterion to grant recognition and financing.[12] Interpretations of the ways in which 'school identity' and 'associational freedoms' should be balanced with other legal or constitutional requirements (such as non-discrimination) could then be diversified. For example it should not be possible for a denominational school to discriminate against pupils on the basis of its 'pedagogical identity', whereas this should remain possible for schools founded on the basis of a religious identity (e.g. for a Jewish school to select only Jewish pupils) (Onderwijsraad 2012a, 51).

Against the backdrop of the discussion initiated by the Council of Education, we focus in the next section on three core elements of the associational freedom of religious schools in the Netherlands: the extent to which religious schools based on the school's religious identity have the right to (1) select and admit pupils, (2) recruit and select staff, and (3) decide on important parts of the curriculum. For each element we briefly describe important political discussions, as well as new legislation and/or new interpretations by courts. Further, we include the reactions of school directors of religious schools in our analysis. We conducted qualitative interviews with two principals of Reformed schools, four principals of Islamic schools, and one principal of a Jewish school.[13] The goal of these interviews was to gain a deeper understanding of the significance of associational freedoms in practice and 'on the ground', to explore the particular justifications of associational freedoms and their boundaries as they were articulated by the directors, and finally to learn about the ways school directors experience changes in public opinion with regard to their schools. We also use data from other interviews that were conducted with representatives of the main religious and secular umbrella organisations.[14]

**Institutional change? Public and political debate and (proposals for) legal amendments with regard to three core elements of associational freedom of religious schools, 2008–2014**

*Admission of pupils*

Religious schools have the right to select and admit pupils based on the school's religious identity (Onderwijsraad 2010). Schools can require that pupils and their parents support the mission of the school. In 2005 an initiative bill was issued by the Social-Democrat Party (PvdA), the Socialist Party (SP), the Green Party (GroenLinks), and the Liberal Democrats (D66) that proposed the introduction of a so-called duty to enrol (*acceptatieplicht*) for non-governmental schools.[15] Whereas at present schools may demand that parents 'endorse' (*onderschrijven*) the philosophy of the school, meaning they can justify not accepting a pupil by arguing that by their behaviour or statements parents demonstrate they do not (truly) subscribe to the philosophy or direction of the school (e.g. by being member of another church or by being divorced), in the new situation only if parents explicitly *refuse to declare they agree to respect* this philosophy, there will be the possibility to refuse a pupil. One of the motives behind this proposal was to strengthen the freedom of parents to have their child accepted in a particular school, whilst another was to reduce inequalities between governmental and non-governmental schools with regard to opportunities to select pupils. An important underlying motive, according to the MPs who submitted the initiative bill, was to prevent denominational schools from making strategic or disingenuous use of their admission rules to refuse 'weaker' pupils. Some religious schools with good educational performance were said to refuse pupils with an immigrant background in order to remain middle-class, 'white' schools. In the subsequent advisory reports it became clear that as a matter of fact this concern was ill-founded because there were few proven cases of this 'disingenuous use' of the right to select on the basis of the denominational identity of the school. Also the possibility only existed for schools that had an explicit policy in this regard, and which had consistently applied this policy over many years. Effectively these were the more conservative religious schools, such as the Reformed schools. They did not, however, appear to use the principle to refuse weaker pupils with an immigrant background (Onderwijsraad 2010, 17–18; van den Berg and van Egmond 2010).[16]

A few legal cases have set the tone for the debate on the so-called duty to enrol. Actually the cases that ended up in courts and received media attention show how difficult it is to detect explicit refusal of a pupil because parents do not subscribe to the philosophy of the school, which also make it difficult to assess how widespread this phenomenon is. Moreover, what is sometimes at stake is that a specific internal school regulation, for example with regard to dress, will constitute an obstacle for children belonging to a different religious group, and will subsequently become a tool for the school to refuse pupils 'unwilling to respect the rules'. In 2003, the Equal Treatment Commission ruled for example that a Catholic secondary school was entitled to demand that a female student did not wear the headscarf in school (Equal Treatment Commission, Judgement 112, 2003). In 2007, the Court in Arnhem decided against a Reformed secondary school, the Hoornbeeck College in Amersfoort, that had refused a student because (in the words of the court) 'his parents have a TV and open internet access, they use different translations of the Bible and their daughter wears trousers occasionally' (Reformatorisch Dagblad 2007). Another, more recent, case involved the Don Bosco College in Volendam, a Catholic secondary school. Confronted with four female Muslim pupils who indicated they wanted to begin wearing the headscarf, the school decided to change the article in its internal regulation on forms of dress that were not allowed (which included caps, hats, and so on) to now also include 'headscarves'. On the basis of this rule that was implemented the following school year, the school denied their Muslim pupils the right to wear the headscarf, saying this was also considered as 'an infraction upon the Catholic identity of the school'. Strictly speaking, and in the legal procedures that followed, this was not a case of refusing to admit a pupil, but about an internal rule with regard to religious expression that, according to the school, was related to its religious identity. As a matter of fact, the pupil remained in the school pending the legal procedures, and was first allowed to work in a separate room (with her headscarf on) and then decided not to wear it awaiting the outcome of the legal procedures (which lasted until 2011). In the media and in parliamentary debate the case was represented as paradigmatic for the need to have a 'duty to enrol' and as yet another illustration of the ways in which religious schools used their denomination 'to keep pupils [from] wanting to express another religion [than that] of the school'.[17]

As is often the case, the incidents and cases that result in legal proceedings may shed light on fundamental issues with regard to constitutional arrangements, but they do not necessarily clarify the importance of the matter: How many similar cases are there? How important is the right to select on the basis of denomination for schools and parents? We draw on our interviews with directors of a number of Reformed, Jewish, and Islamic schools to get an idea of the reasons they have to value the right to select pupils on the basis of their religious identity, to what extent it is an issue in day-to-day school management, and why they may be opposed to the initiative bill.

The platform organisations of Reformed schools have been very concerned with the political debate on the 'duty to enrol' (*acceptatieplicht*) (VGS 2013). For these schools it would mean they would have to accept children as long as parents say they respect the identity of the school, whilst they may have different religious views and may not follow the strict rules of the Reformed religion in their personal life. A principal of a Reformed school explains why the school does not have any Muslim pupils, and why he feels there should remain a right to refuse children with other religious backgrounds:

> the crucial difference between Muslims and Christians is of course the work of the Lord Jesus Christ, I will not ignore that or change that because of a number of Muslim children that I should respect ... So, that won't work. And so in reality, those Muslim parents, they simply don't enrol their children here. (Interview 1)

According to this director, then, the relatively 'pervasive' religious identity of the school has a self-selecting effect, and non-Christian parents will be disinclined to try and enrol their children in these schools. Interestingly, an important additional motive for Reformed schools to want to hold on to the constitutional right to refuse pupils was a fear of a growing influence of evangelicals. Parents and children with an evangelical interpretation of Protestantism tend to diverge from the strict rules of the Reformed, and there is a fear that they will undermine the Reformed community 'from within'.[18] The need to uphold the orthodox norms in the school may also arise when a child's family is less strict. An example given in one of the interviews was that the role of the teacher was to point out that Sunday is meant for Church attendance and to be critical if children would mention they had been on an outing during the weekend. The teacher and the school should instruct children about what kind of behaviour is intolerable for Reformed Christians. However, even these internal rules also hardly become reasons to 'expel' children from the school and schools tend to pursue a strategy of dialogue with parents.

For Islamic schools the issue of refusing certain students hardly arises. Most directors we interviewed emphasised that all pupils are welcome. When asked about whether the school would refuse students on the basis of religion, one of the Islamic directors said that pupils 'should not be refused on the basis of religion'. At this school a Catholic child would be admitted, but, so the principal added, it should 'abide with the rules of the school' (Interview 5). However, it became clear that the issue of refusing pupils because they do not respect the identity of the school remained basically hypothetical for these schools. There were interesting exceptions though. One school principal mentioned the example of Salafist parents who wanted the school to be stricter in its religious teachings and dress rules. The school would not accept that these parents would take their children out of the religious classes and suggested that they ought to look for another school (Interview 6). As a matter of fact, this type of decision by the school would still be protected under the new law.

As this article goes to press, the proposed bill for a general 'duty to enrol' has not (yet) been voted on in parliament. In a reply to the advice on the future of article 23, the

Secretary of Education has indicated that the trend was that 'equal treatment legislation would be applied more consistently to schools, both with regard to the selection of students and the hiring of staff' (see below) (Ministry of Education, Culture and Science 2013a, 14). Importantly also, the government intends to give more weight to parents when deciding whether a school might want to 'change' or 'redirect' its denominational identity. This might imply that the power balance may shift in favour of parents who want the school identity to correspond to what they want for their children, and that the school board will have less power to refuse pupils and impose rules in an attempt to protect the identity of the school the board supports. Also there is less political support for public subsidies to cover the transportation costs of children whose parents want them to attend a religious school that is outside of their region ('bussing'), even though a decision on this issue is not imminent (Ministry of Education, Culture and Science 2013a, 11). According to many members of the orthodox Reformed community, however, all these measures point in one direction, namely that the dominant groups in society and the government intend to give priority to equal treatment and non-discrimination over freedom of education and toleration for religious groups.

## *Selection of staff*

The Constitution requires the government to respect the freedom of non-government schools to appoint teachers. Teachers in non-governmental schools are employees of the foundations or associations that own or direct the school. The board of the organisation can use the purpose of the school, if it is clearly stated in the school's mission statement, as a selection criterion when selecting or assessing teachers (Zoontjens and Glenn 2012, 354). Board members of religious schools find the selection of staff to be the most important element of protecting the identity of their school, often more important than selection of pupils or issues concerning curriculum. Wim Kuiper, president of the Dutch organisation for Protestant schools, explains how the selection of staff is central to the Dutch system of religious education:

> See, the heart of the freedom of education really is one's own personnel policy and not the freedom of choice of parents (although that of course is an important aspect as well), nor is it the acceptance policy of the children. The heart [of the matter] really is the policy of selecting personnel. That this is free, that you can ask the question about someone's philosophy of life (*levensovertuiging*), while normally of course you can't do this as an organisation.

There are definite limits, however, upon the freedom of a school board to make direct distinctions on the basis of gender, sexual orientation, and marital status when selecting personnel. Article 5 of the General Law on Equal Treatment (1994) indeed makes an exception for non-governmental schools allowing them to set conditions for employment related to the religious mission of school, *but* it then states that different treatment cannot be based exclusively on race, gender, marital status, sexual orientation, or religion (Zoontjens and Glenn 2012, 355). This so-called 'the sole fact construction' (*enkele feit constructie*) makes it illegal for non-government schools to discriminate on the basis of 'the sole fact' of gender, sexual orientation, or civil status. Still, a school may refuse to hire staff if it has 'additional reasons' justifying why it expects or finds the person unfit to work under the school's mission.[19] These additional reasons are, however, not specified and remain rather vague. Very few cases concerning the 'sole fact' construction have been brought forward to either the Equal Treatment Commission or courts.[20] An example of such case is a teacher of a Reformed school, who was no longer allowed to teach at his school after he told the school principal in the year 2009 that he was in a homosexual relationship (Oomen et al. 2009). Despite the fact that the teacher did not press charges against the school and came to a personal agreement about the situation, there was an appeal at the Commission for Equal Treatment, which was initiated by the COC, an advocacy organisation defending the rights of lesbian women, gay men, bisexuals, and transgenders. Another example concerned a female teacher who was not hired at an evangelical school because she lived together with a man but was not married to him.[21] In this case, the school did provide 'additional reasons' for making this distinction, namely the fact that the person did not belong to a church and had a different religious conviction from the one mentioned in the mission statement of the school. The Commission of Equal Treatment still decided that the school had made a direct distinction on the basis of the 'sole fact' of marital status, which is not allowed. Legal scholars reacted to this verdict by stating that in practice it was impossible for schools to provide plausible 'additional reasons' that would justify not selecting gay or divorced people.[22]

Legally the chances of courts supporting schools that supposedly make use of the 'sole fact' construction thus have been quite small. Nonetheless, there has been increasing societal and political opposition to this exemption from the Equal Treatment Act. Also the Council of Europe and the European Commission have been extremely critical in this regard and have argued that the Netherlands has not adequately implemented European guidelines regarding the protection of rights of homosexual employees (Oomen et al. 2009, 26; Platform Artikel 2009; European Union Agency for Fundamental Rights 2010, 26). Already in the discussions following the critique of the European Commission, politicians of the Green Left party suggested to abolish the 'sole fact' construction. The proposal gained momentum when the new coalition government of Liberal Party (VVD) and Social Democrats (PvdA) included it in their official government agreement under the heading 'emancipation and equal treatment': 'Schools are not allowed to fire teachers who are gay, nor may they refuse pupils who are homosexual or send them away because of their sexual orientation. In schools there will be education about sexual diversity' (Government Agreement 2012, 19). In May 2014, a large majority of Parliament, including almost all members of the Christen Democratic Party (CDA), voted in favour of a motion to abolish the 'sole fact' construction. Now it will be decided by the Senate before it can be enacted formally.

Interestingly some of the school directors we interviewed stated that the new legal situation will not have great impact on choices they make in appointing teachers. During one of our interviews the director of an orthodox Jewish high school stated:

> Regarding Jewish teachers, we [ ... ] expect them to identify with the religious viewpoint of the school, in mind and in practice. We can only hire a Jewish teacher if he or she lives his or her life in line with the school's religious identity, so in line with orthodox Judaism. We demand this freedom and we get it. If the government tries to interfere in this, we will not let it happen.

Most other schools, especially the Islamic, Hindu, and Protestant schools, tend to be more careful in expressing themselves in relation to these sensitive issues. A director of a Reformed school explained that he believed that schools were justified in discriminating against homosexuals when selecting teachers, as long as they would follow the right procedure. In his view, the issue did not arise so often, but the media always created a hype and therefore schools had to choose their words in an extremely careful manner (Interview 1). When we asked the director of an Islamic school whether they would tolerate that a staff member was homosexual, he gave a more ambiguous answer. During the application procedure the rules of the schools would be mentioned and candidates should understand this meant they could not 'propagate' that they were gay (Interview 6). It remains to be seen in what ways these ideas and practices will change when the legal amendment has entered into force.

Interestingly, the interviews also brought to light in what ways directors of religious schools have concerns about their right to select (and refuse) staff on the basis of their religious identity. Teachers at Reformed schools must be members of one of the orthodox Protestant churches. However, sometimes teachers who are already working at the school may change their perspective on religion, for example because they become evangelicals. This is regarded as problematic, because, as one school principal explained, there is a fear that the teacher may communicate his changed views on religion to the pupils and then 'the school could be used as some sort of institute for evangelization'. He believed teachers should not actively talk about their alternative religious views (Interview 1). Again the fear of a growing influence of evangelicals motivated Reformed schools to make use of their associational freedoms to refuse non-Reformed staff, and a general obligation to abide by religious non-discrimination guidelines was seen as a threat to their attempts to defend the mission and identity of the school. Another issue that sometimes arises in these schools concerns discrepancies between the strict religious rules that the schools uphold (for example with regard to school attire) and the choices staff members make in their private life.

Islamic schools have problems finding enough certified teachers, which seems to influence their position in the earlier discussion on selecting staff members. The staff in Islamic schools can have another religion, or no religion, but they are asked not to (actively) try to communicate their own views to the pupils. Actually only a minority of the teachers in Islamic schools is Muslim and in this particular school, only one-third of the staff members had a Muslim background (Interview 3).

In sum, the political debate on the 'sole fact' construction has been primarily concerned with combating discrimination on the basis of gender and sexual orientation, whereas it remains to be seen whether it will be possible for the state to demand that religious schools cannot recruit and select staff on the basis of their religious identity.

## *Curriculum*

The Dutch constitution provides the State with the competence to set quality standards in schools. During the last decades, government policies aiming to enhance educational quality in governmental and non-governmental schools have gained top priority, which resulted in the formulation and implementation of several new requirements and guidelines. Most importantly, in 1993, Parliament established a series of national outcome standards, so-called 'core goals' (*kerndoelen*), to which schools are to be held accountable. The Act on Educational Supervision of 2002 gave the Inspectorate new powers to judge school education. Inspectors visit schools periodically, observe classes, make recommendations, and report to the minister in cases where there is a violation of one of the requirements. Since 2010, there is also the legal obligation for schools to reach minimum learning results in the areas of language and mathematics. The funding for non-government schools that have serious and lasting shortcomings will be ended (Zoontjens and Glenn 2012, 355–358).

There can be tensions between some of these requirements and the freedom of non-governmental schools to organise teaching as they see fit. In 2010, two members of Parliament, Mr Pechtold and Mr Van der Ham, both representatives of the Liberal Democrat party (D66), successfully filed a parliamentary motion demanding a change of the formulation of the 'core goals' (*kerndoelen*) concerning the teaching about pluralism in Dutch society, both in primary schools (article 38) and in secondary schools (article 43). These articles specify that pupils learn about the diversity of 'life convictions', about 'differences in culture and philosophies of life', and to see the importance of 'respecting one another's views and life styles'. Both articles should be changed to include the phrase: 'with attention to sexuality and sexual diversity'.

One of the reasons for the MPs to demand this change was the assumption that in some schools (read: especially in religious schools) there was hardly any attention to 'sexual diversity' and/or homosexuality was being represented as wrong and sinful. Indeed, an important study conducted by the Netherlands Institute for Social Research showed how widespread the lack of acceptance of sexual diversity was in schools (especially in vocational schools), and underlined that in specific communities (such as Reformed, Muslim, and Evangelical communities, as well as in certain ethnic communities) anti-gay prejudice was particularly widespread (SCP 2010).

In an advice on the matter, issued in 2012, the National Council for Education questioned whether this motion would be effective, given the goal pursued, namely, creating more respect and a safer environment for homosexual, bisexual, and transgender pupils and staff in schools. Violence and discrimination for reasons of sexual orientation are important facts of life in many schools in the Netherlands, and the Council argued that changing the (cognitive) core goals was not a plausible strategy to create a 'safer climate' within schools (Onderwijsraad 2012b, 4). The Council also pointed to the more principled issue that by changing 'core goals' the freedom of schools to give more precise content to these goals was at stake. The existing texts of articles 38 and 43 mention the need to teach about, and make pupils aware of, pluralism and differences of background and culture, or more generally a diversity of 'opinions, philosophies of life and ways-of-being' (Onderwijsraad 2012b, 5). In the law, this is a *general* goal and there is no mention of the need to teach about cultural or religious or linguistic diversity in specific. Therefore, demanding that all schools specifically teach about sexuality would demand a more fundamental change of the law, going against the more basic idea that this type of 'core goals' should remain relatively unspecified to allow for autonomy of schools. Despite these reservations of the Council of Education, the government has decided to implement the motion, and since 1 December 2012 teaching on sexuality and sexual diversity is amongst the core goals in primary and secondary education. In addition, the Inspectorate of Education will monitor whether and how schools take measures to implement the new goals in their teaching programme, with special focus on 'risk groups' (Ministry of Education, Culture and Science 2013b).

Teaching on sexuality is one of the main issues where (some) religious schools may experience tensions between the legal output requirements and their own school mission statement, another issue concerns teaching about evolution. Teaching about the theory of evolution actually is one of the core goals of schools, but it is possible for religious schools to critically engage with the theory. The Foundation for the

Bible and Education for example suggested that Christian schools might also seek to teach 'pupils to obtain knowledge of both theories of creation and of evolution, and learn to distinguish between facts and opinions' (B&O 2008). This suggested that reformulation or reinterpretation of the core goals has no formal legal standing, but it demonstrates what opportunities may exist in practice for schools to decide on the way they want to teach these issues, and still attain required goals set by the state. Still, a director of a Reformed school mentioned the teaching of evolution theory as a domain in which associational autonomy increasingly was threatened. According to him 'evolution is in fact a belief as well ... because of a lot of things are not clear and not proven' (Interview 2). The principal of the Jewish school was even more explicit about the refusal of his school to teach evolution theory as defined in the attainment targets by the Dutch state. He explains how his school, in discussion with the inspection, is until now still allowed to ignore one of the 58 targets:

> A [non-governmental] school has to justify to the Inspectorate why they do not teach evolution theory. I find it ridiculous that we have to do this. The state should just accept the fact that non-government schools decide to do this. [ ... ] I must admit that the Inspectorate is willing to help us [after negotiations and explanations the school is allowed to not teach evolutionary theory]. (Interview 4)

The directors of Islamic schools whom we interviewed mentioned sexual education as a 'sensitive issue'. Teachers would teach about sexuality and procreation in the biology lessons using a general textbook; 'we just follow the method, what is in there we simply must present, one way or the other' (Interview 3). During religious classes these issues would also be discussed, and more emphasis was put on Islamic norms with regard to sexuality. In practice in all religious schools decisions on issues related to curriculum and activities are negotiated between school boards, school management, and parents, within the constraints set by the Ministry of Education. It seems that at Islamic schools the school-management (director and teacher), who are often non-Muslims, believe that considerations concerning educational goals should take priority and that they often stand for a more liberal course than some of the school board members or parents would like to see. One director spoke of a shift in the school's policy upon his arrival as manager. The more conservative members of the school board had been removed and the new policy was that the focus should no longer be on everything that should, for religious reasons, potentially be seen as forbidden (*haram*) but on what should be allowed (*halal*) (Interview 6).

## Concluding observations

There are major concerns in the Dutch public debate about the ways Reformed, orthodox Jewish, and Islamic schools use their associational freedoms. In the media and political debate the tone is often set by a small number of controversial legal cases and incidents, and over the past 10 years the proposals for legal amendments concerning the 'duty to enrol', rescinding the 'sole fact' construction, and obliging all schools to 'teach on sexual diversity' have constituted a kind of agenda for thinking about a different balance between non-discrimination and associational autonomy in the domain of primary and secondary education. We have explored not only the legal framework and the possible consequences of legal amendments, but also how these associational freedoms play a role in practice in Reformed, Jewish, and Islamic schools. In our view, there is clearly a trend to give priority by the Dutch State to non-discrimination. Two proposals to reduce the scope for exemptions for religious schools from equal treatment legislation have already been accepted (with regard to hiring of staff and teaching on sexual diversity), whereas the government intends to also follow up on the motion for a 'duty to enrol' for pupils. It remains to be seen, however, what the impact will be of the legal amendments and the normative pressure surrounding the interpretation of associational freedoms of schools. The legal opportunities granted to religious schools to make distinctions on the basis of religion, sexual orientation, or marital status have become more restricted, but they may find alternative ways to defend what they see as their core identity. This may involve both their constitutional rights and opportunities that exist in practice when teachers are recruited or decisions are made about how to teach about certain topics. At the same time, we have also shown how school policies and practices change in reaction to societal pressures, and exemplified for example by attempts to be more open and self-critical with regard to gender discrimination and acceptance of sexual diversity.

In our view it is accurate to speak of a regime shift occurring in the Netherlands with respect to understandings of religious and educational freedoms, and especially with regard to the balancing of associational freedoms and non-discrimination. We witness increased unwillingness of the government to defend legal and constitutional arrangements that allow for discrimination on the basis of religion, gender, sexual orientation, and marital status. In that context, the government is responding both to domestic and European pressures. However, in the field of education this broader trend intersects with two other important developments. First, because of a series of structural changes in the education system, the understanding of 'school autonomy' has changed. To a significant extent schools have become *more* 'autonomous' because they operate under a regime of governance based on 'steering at-a-distance' and 'privatization' (admittedly subject to strict monitoring and control by the state), and have professionalised further over the past decades. Nowadays school managements are less keen on listening to institutional actors that used to have an important say in the day-to-day management of religious schools, such as religious leaders and representatives of religious organisations. In addition, most religious schools in the Netherlands no longer function as one amongst several institutions constituting the 'organizational infrastructure of a subculture', which was exactly what the tradition of 'pillarisation' was about. In some cases, there also exists a substantial cultural gap between the school board and the management of the school (director and teachers), notably in Islamic schools. Only those religious schools that cater to communities that are still in a sense 'pillarised' (such as orthodox Jewish groups and Reformed groups) can still pursue a school policy based on consensual views that are shared by the school board, the management and staff, religious elites, and the parents. Second, the reorientation of fundamental freedoms and principles in the education system is also greatly affected by a 'diversification of cultural pluralism', which in this field has destabilised the idea that 'denominational direction' should be leading in understanding freedom of education. New forms of religious diversity have become more important, in part because of immigration, but simultaneously also all kinds of other 'views', 'life convictions', and 'value differences' have become more salient for parents and children. These structural changes, in interaction with a principled political choice in favour of non-discrimination, will make it more difficult for conservative religious groups in the Netherlands to organise education for their children in ways they were used to.

## Acknowledgements

We specially acknowledge the work of Inge Versteegt who conducted the interviews with principals of Reformed and Islamic schools and co-authored the ACCEPT-Pluralism report 'The Netherlands: Challenging diversity in education and school life' (2011) on which some parts of this article draw. Special thanks to Veit Bader and Michael Merry for their extensive comments on earlier drafts of this article.

## Funding

This article draws on research conducted in the context of two projects funded by the European Commission, DG Research, seventh Framework Program, Socio-Economic Sciences and Humanities: 'Tolerance, Pluralism and Social Cohesion: Responding to the Challenges of the twenty-first Century in Europe' (ACCEPT PLURALISM) (2010–2013) (call FP7-SSH-2009-A, grant agreement no. 243837), Coordinator: Prof. Anna Triandafyllidou, Robert Schuman Centre for Advanced Studies, European University Institute. And 'Religious diversity and Secular Models in Europe. Innovative approaches to Law and Policy' (RELIGARE) (2010–2013) (Grant agreement no. 244635). Coordinator: Prof. Marie Claire Foblets, Catholic University of Leuven.

## Notes

1. See Merry (2013), chapter 5 for a thoughtful discussion of these issues.
2. Two main indicators for primary school quality are commonly used in the Dutch context: the outcome of the assessment of the inspection of education (which is published online) and the three-year school average SAT score based on student achievement scores (CITO scores). Dutch Reformed schools and Islamic schools are often perceived as performing relatively poorly in this respect. However, this relative underperformance can be explained largely by controlling for factors such as the composition of the school population in terms of immigrant background, social class, and educational background of parents. Religious schools often perform slightly better than public schools. For a brief comparative overview of schools, see Inspectorate of Education (2013). See also Dronkers and Avram (2015). See Merry and Driessen (forthcoming) on the performance of Islamic schools.
3. There is some debate on the significance of these shifts in public and in political discourse, and especially about whether or not they illustrate the end of a 'Dutch model' of immigrant integration policies. See recently Duyvendak et al. (2013).
4. For the normative discussion on the limits of tolerance and liberalism, see Maussen (2012, 2014), Dobbernack and Modood (2013), and Calder, Bessone, and Zuolo (2014).
5. We borrow the term 'nominally' religious from Monsma and Soper (2009).
6. This number includes both Reformed (*Reformatorische*) and Reformed Liberated (*Gereformeerd vrijgemaakt*) schools. See http://www.stamos.nl/index.rfx?verb=showitem&item=5.24.5&view=table (retrieved July 1 2014).
7. In 2014, the main umbrella organisation, the Platform for Evangelical Education (PEON), counted 11 primary schools and 4 secondary schools. See www.peon.nl.
8. We use the terminology governmental and non-governmental schools for reasons explained in the introduction to his special issue (Maussen and Bader 2015).
9. As the National Council for Education (Onderwijsraad 2012a, 19) explains the freedom to found schools also includes the freedom to create private schools, so the key issue is whether there is an obligation for (equal) funding of these schools. Not all (sub-)cultural identities or worldviews can be drawn upon to demand respect for this constitutional right, which is reserved to more established collective, denominational identities that are 'comprehensive' and institutionally present in different societal spheres. Hence, this understanding of what a 'direction' (*richting*) is is said to be biased in favour of more established, religious denominations (see below).
10. The advice was prepared in response to the question by the Minister in 2011 for an 'authoritative interpretation' of article 23 of the Constitution.
11. The case of the Free Schools (*Vrije Scholen*) is different, because they correspond to a 'philosophy of life' (*levensovertuiging*), namely Rudolf Steiner's philosophy.

12. In the reply to the advice, the Secretary of State indicated she intended to follow up on this advice in favour of 'planning irrespective of direction' (*richtingsvrije planning*) (Ministry of Education, Culture and Science 2013a).
13. As mentioned in the acknowledgements, these interviews were conducted in 2010–2011 as part of two European Research Projects. The interviews with directors of Reformed and Islamic schools were conducted by Inge Versteegt. The interview with the director of a Jewish school was conducted by Floris Vermeulen.
14. In this article, we only refer to the interview by the number in our own files in order to guarantee confidentiality to our interviewees. The interviews with representatives of platform organizations and scientific bureaus of political parties were conducted by Floris Vermeulen. These interviewees have consented to being cited and named. For a full list of the respondents, see Vermeulen and El Morabet Belhaj (2013, 137).
15. Initiative Bill Hamer, Vergeer, Jungbluth, and Lambrechts, TK 2005–2006, 30417. Because of the formation of a new government and election, a new Initiative Bill with similar demands was issued in 2006.
16. Still, one could argue that the general pattern shows there is clearly a disproportionally small number of children from 'disadvantaged social classes' or 'with an immigration background' in Christian schools, which shows that there is evidence of structural discrimination or that 'something is skewing the results', to use Anne Phillips phrase (2004, 8). See also Merry (2015).
17. See the response of the Minister of Education, Culture and Science, 12 April 2011. See also Merry (2015) for a further discussion on mechanisms of exclusion in the Dutch school system.
18. As we mentioned earlier in the article, Evangelical schools have been founded since 1997 and their number has been growing. Opportunities for parents to demand that a school changes its 'denominational identity' further strengthen the concerns of the boards and directors of Reformed schools. They think there is a need to have a large majority of children and parents who firmly adhere to the denominational views of the school.
19. These discussions are, therefore, about the 'right' of religious schools to 'discriminate' on the basis of their religious identity and not about the issue of how religious people are protected from discrimination, for example when working in public schools. On the latter issue (in the UK), see Vickers (2011) and Sandberg (2011).
20. Many people expected a lot of cases concerning the hiring and firing of teachers by the boards of non-governmental religious schools; however, only a few cases did come to the Commission of Equal Treatment or Courts. Most cases concerning teachers and non-governmental religious schools have been about equal payment, salary problems, and legal positions, but not related to identity issues (Zoontjens and Glenn 2012, 355).
21. CGB Oordeel 2011-102.
22. Overbeeke Annotaties bij Oordelen CGB 2011-102, 471–472.

**References**

Bader, V. 2007. *Secularism or Democracy? Associational Governance of Religious Diversity.* Amsterdam: Amsterdam University Press.

Bader, V., and M. Maussen. 2012. "Religious Schools and Tolerance." In *Tolerance and Cultural Diversity in Schools. Comparative Report*, edited by M. Maussen and V. Bader, 87–107. Accept-Pluralism, Working paper, 2012/01. http://cadmus.eui.eu/handle/1814/20955

van den Berg, W., and J. Van Egmond. 2010. "Acceptatieplicht scholen is symboolpolitiek" [Duty to Enroll is Symbolic Politics]. *De Volkrant*, April 13.

B&O (Bijbel en Onderwijs). 2008. "Kerndoelen Biologie" [Core Goals Biology], March 12. http://bijbelenonderwijs.nl/bijbel-en-onderwijs/kerndoelen-biologie/

Bowen, J. R., C. Bertossi, J. W. Duyvendak, and M. L. Krook, eds. 2014. *European States and their Muslim Citizens. The Impact of Institutions on Perceptions and Boundaries*. Cambridge: Cambridge University Press.

Calder, G., M. Bessone, and F. E. Zuolo, eds. 2014. *How Groups Matter. Challenges of Toleration in Pluralistic Societies*. New York: Routledge.

Dobbernack, J., and T. Modood, eds. 2013. *Tolerance, Intolerance and Respect. Hard to Accept?* Basingstoke: Palgrave MacMillan.

Dronkers, J., and S. Avram. 2015. "What can International Comparisons Teach us about School Choice and Non-Governmental Schools in Europe?" *Comparative Education* 51 (1): 118–132.

Duyvendak, J. W., van Reekum, R., El-Hajjari, F., and Bertossi, C. 2013. "Mysterious Multiculturalism: The Risks of Using Model-Based Indices for Making Meaningful Comparisons." *Comparative European Politics* 11 (5): 599–620.

European Union Agency for Fundamental Rights. 2010. *Homophobia, Transphobia, and Discrimination on Grounds of Sexual Orientation and Gender*. Luxembourg: Publication Office of the EU.

Government Agreement [Regeerakkoord VVD-PvdA]. 2012. "Bruggen Slaan" [Building Bridges], October 29.

de Groof, J., and C. W. Noorlander. 2012. "Nieuwe contouren van de vrijheid van onderwijs. De vrijheid van onderwijs in de dynamische 21$^e$ eeuw" [New Contours of the Freedom of Education. The Freedom of Education in the Dynamic 21st Century]. *Tijdschrift voor Constitutioneel Recht* 2012 (1): 54–85.

Huisman, P. W. A., M. T. A. B. Laemers, D. Mentink, and P. J. J. Zoontjes. 2011. *Vrijheid van stichting. Over de mogelijkheden en consequenties van een moderne interpretatie van de vrijheid van richting bij de stichting van bijzondere scholen* [Freedom to Found Schools. The Opportunities and Consequences of a Modern Interpretation of the Freedom of Direction for the Founding of Non-governmental Schools]. Den Haag: Ministerie van Onderwijs, Cultuur en Wetenschap.

Inspectorate of Education. 2013. "The State of Education in the Netherlands." http://www.onderwijsinspectie.nl/actueel/publicaties/the-state-of-education-in-the-netherlands-2011–2012.html

Inspectorate of Education. 2014. "Onderzoek bestuurlijk handelen Stichting voor Evangelische scholen (SVES)" [Research into Management Foundation for Evangelical Schools]. Accessed June 4. http://www.rijksoverheid.nl/ministeries/ocw/documenten-en-publicaties/rapporten/2014/01/30/onderzoek-bestuurlijk-handelen-stichting-voor-evangelische-scholen-sves.html

Maussen, M. 2012. "Pillarization and Islam: Church-State Traditions and Muslim Claims for Recognition in the Netherlands." *Comparative European Politics* 10 (3): 337–353.

Maussen, M. 2014. "Religious Governance in the Netherlands: Associative Freedoms and Non-Discrimination After 'Pillarization'. The Example of Faith-Based Schools." *Geopolitics, History, and International Relations* 6 (2).

Maussen, M., and V. Bader. 2015. "Non-Governmental Religious Schools in Europe: Institutional Opportunities, Associational Freedoms, and Contemporary Challenges." *Comparative Education* 51 (1): 1–21.

Maussen, M., and T. Bogers. 2012. "Discourses on Tolerance and Diversity Challenges in the Netherlands." In *Addressing Tolerance and Diversity Discourses in Europe*, edited by R. Zapata-Barrero and A. Triandafyllidou, 103–124. Barcelona: CIDOB.

Merry, M. S. 2013. *Equality, Citizenship, and Segregation. A Defense of Separation*. Houndmills: Palgrave/MacMillan.

Merry, M. S. 2015. "The Conundrum of Religious Schools in Twenty-First Century Europe." *Comparative Education* 51 (1): 133–156.

Merry, M. S., and G. Driessen. 2012. "Equality on Different Terms: The Case of Dutch Hindu Schools." *Education and Urban Society* 44 (5): 632–648.

Merry, M., and G. Driessen. Forthcoming. "On the Right Track? Islamic Schools in the Netherlands After an Era of Turmoil."
Ministry of Education, Culture and Science. 2013a. *Reactie op Onderwijsraadadvies Artikel 23 Grondwet in maatschappelijk perspectief.* September 18.
Ministry of Education, Culture and Science. 2013b. *Uitvoering motie Dijkstra (D66) and Van Ark (VVD) over monitoren voorlichting seksualiteit en seksuele diversiteit op scholen voor PO en VO en de situatie in MBO en VMBO,* December 17.
Monsma, S., and C. Soper. 2009. *The Challenge of Pluralism. Church and State in Five Democracies.* 2nd ed. Lanham: Rowman & Littlefield Publishers.
Onderwijsraad. 2010. *Het recht op toelating nogmaals bezien. Advies bij het initiatiefwetsvoorstel regeling toelatingsrecht (scholen)* [The Duty to Enrol Reconsidered]. Den Haag: Onderwijsraad.
Onderwijsraad. 2012a. *Artikel 23 grondwet in maatschappelijk perspectief* [Article 23 of the Constitution in a Societal Perspective]. Den Haag: Onderwijsraad.
Onderwijsraad. 2012b. *Advies aanpassing kerndoelen* [Advice on the Adaptations of Core Goals]. Den Haag: Onderwijsraad.
Oomen, B., J. Guijt, I. Meijvogel, M. Ploeg, and N. Rijke. 2009. *Recht op verschil? Percepties en effecten van de implementatie van gelijke behandeling wetgeving onder orthodox-protestanten in Nederland* [A Right to Difference? Perceptions and Effects of the Implementation of Equal Treatment Legislation among Orthodox Protestants in the Netherlands]. Middelburg: Roosevelt Academy.
Pépin, L. 2009. *Teaching about Religions in European School Systems.* NEF. London: Alliance Publishing Trust.
Phillips, A. 2004. "Defending Equality of Outcome." *Journal of Political Philosophy* 12 (1): 1–19.
Platform Artikel. 2009. *Factsheet enkele-feit constructie. Europese richtlijnen en de Algemene wet gelijke behandeling* [Fact-sheet Sole-fact Construction. European Guidelines and the Equal Treatment Act], September 13.
Reformatorisch Dagblad. 2007. *Hoornbeeck moet leerling toelaten* [Hoornbeeck College Must Enrole a Pupil], July 25.
Sandberg, R. 2011. "A Uniform Approach to Religious Discrimination? The Position of Teachers and Other School Staff in the UK." In *Law, Religious Freedoms and Education in Europe,* edited by M. Hunter-Henin, 327–346. Farnham: Ashgate.
SCP (Sociaal Cultureel Planbureau). 2010. *Just Different, that is all. Acceptance of Homosexuality in the Netherlands.* The Hague: SCP.
Vermeulen, B. P. 2004. "Regulating School Choice to Promote Civic Values: Constitutional and Political Issues in the Netherlands." In *Educating Citizens: International Perspectives on Civic Values and School* Choice, edited by P. Wolf and S. Macedo, 31–66. Washington, DC: Brookings Institution Press.
Vermeulen, F., and R. El Morabet Belhaj. 2013. "Accommodating Religious Claims in the Dutch Workplace: Unacknowledged Sabbaths, Objecting Marriage Registrars and Pressured Faith-Based Organizations." *International Journal of Discrimination and the Law* 13 (2–3): 113–139.
Versteegt, I., and M. Maussen. 2011. *The Netherlands: Challenging Diversity in Education and School Life.* Accept-Pluralism, Working Paper, 2011/11. http://hdl.handle.net/1814/19798.
VGS (Vereniging voor Gereformeerd Schoolonderwijs). 2013. "VGS plaatst kritische kanttekeningen bij voorstellen Dekker" [Critical Comments by VGS on Proposals Dekker]. Accessed July 16. http://www.vgs.nl/besturenorganisatie/nieuws/vgs-plaatst-kritische-kanttekeningen-bij-voorstellen-dekker
Vickers, L. 2011. "Religious Discrimination and Schools: The Employment of Teachers and the Public Sector Duty." In *Law, Religious Freedoms and Education in Europe,* edited by M. Hunter-Henin, 87–104. Farnham: Ashgate.
Zoontjens, P. J. J., and C. L. Glenn. 2012. "Netherlands." In *Balancing Freedom, Autonomy and Accountability in Education,* edited by C. L. Glenn and J. de Groof, vol. 2, 333–362. Nijmegen: Wolf Legal Publishers.

# The continued existence of state-funded Catholic schools in Scotland

Stephen J. McKinney and James C. Conroy

*School of Education, University of Glasgow, Glasgow, UK*

> Catholic schools in Scotland have been fully state-funded since the 1918 Education (Scotland) Act. Under this Act, 369 contemporary Catholic schools are able to retain their distinctive identity and religious education and the teachers have to be approved by the Catholic hierarchy. Similar to the position of other forms of state-funded and partially state-funded faith schools in Europe, the position of state-funded Catholic schools in Scotland has been contested. This paper initially locates the debate and discussion about Catholic schools in Scotland in the history and development of the wider faith schools debate in the UK, particularly England and Wales. The paper outlines the key themes in the debate on faith schooling in England and Wales identifying the similarities between the debate in Scotland and England and Wales and the distinctive features of the debate in Scotland. The paper will then focus on a critical examination and analysis of two key themes concerning state-funded Catholic schools in the Scottish context. The first theme is the debate over the continuation of government funding of Catholic schooling as it is effectively government funding of religious beliefs and practices for a particular Christian denomination. The second theme is more unique to Scotland and has some tenuous links to the debate on faith schools in Northern Ireland: the claims that Catholic schools are the root cause of sectarianism or contribute to sectarianism.

## Introduction

There are national disputes throughout Europe about the extent to which children can be educated within a context that accommodates, in some way, their religious beliefs. Some of the key and highly contested issues focus on whether religious schools should not be *tolerated* or be *tolerated* and, in some cases, even accorded *recognition* and whether there should be any form of state funding for religious schools (Maussen and Bader 2102). This paper examines the position of Catholic schools in Scotland which are fully state funded. First, the paper provides a brief outline of state-funded or partially state-funded faith schools in the context of the UK, explaining that the government has moved from a position of *tolerance* to *recognition* and support for faith schools. Nevertheless, the continuation of state funding for faith schools remains highly contested. The paper then examines the Scottish education system and the position of Catholic schools within this system, incorporating a brief account of the origins of Catholic schools and the agreed conditions for the state funding of Catholic schools. The paper also locates the continued existence of state-funded Catholic schools within the contemporary demographical patterns of the Catholic community in Scotland.

The first of two key themes is then discussed: the continuation of state funding for Catholic schooling in Scotland. The arguments against the continuation of state funding will be presented, as will the counter arguments and the importance of the political support from the leader of the government, albeit contested by his own political party. The paper will then discuss the second key theme: the debate that Catholic schools are the cause of sectarianism or contribute to sectarianism. The claims that Catholic schools are the cause of sectarianism or contribute to sectarianism are critiqued as unsubstantiated and contrary to the extant research evidence.

**Faith schools in the UK**

In all parts of the UK, privately funded religious schools predated the introduction of mass compulsory state-funded school education (e.g. Roman Catholic in all parts of the UK; Church of England and Jewish schools in England) (Miller 2000; McCulloch 2005; Gallagher 2007). Through processes of negotiation, these faith schools were accommodated within the national school systems and a variety of funding models emerged in the UK. The recent Labour government (1997–2010) promoted the expansion of existing faith schooling and incorporated new forms of faith schooling in England and Wales (Gardner 2005). The government white paper, *Schools Achieving Success* (2001), recognised the significant historical contribution of faith schools and welcomed new faith schools (Muslim, Greek Orthodox and Sikh) into the maintained sector (DfES 2001 section 5.30). The white paper also called for faith schools to be more inclusive (Section 5.31). The variety of faith schools grew as faith groups were encouraged to publish proposals for new schools (5.24). This white paper effectively provided government *recognition* for the position and value of faith schools in England and Wales and the current situation is that approximately one in three contemporary maintained schools in England is a faith school (Department for Education 2013).

Faith schools in the UK have an important role in the contemporary education systems of the member states of the UK (England, Northern Ireland, Scotland and Wales). These education systems are not uniform; they have different funding systems, curricular models and public exam structures. In England state primary and secondary schools follow the National Curriculum. Faith schools that are state funded also follow the National Curriculum though have more freedom in the content of religious education. Privately funded schools (Independent schools) and academies (publicly funded independent schools) do not have to follow the National curriculum. In Scotland, state-funded schools, including state-funded denominational schools, follow the Curriculum for Excellence (for ages 3–18). The public exams for England, Northern Ireland and Wales are the General Certificate of Secondary Education and A levels (though there is a variety of awarding body), and in Scotland the public examination structure consists of National Qualifications and Highers.

Despite the recognition of faith schools by the government, the continued existence of a significant number of state-funded or partially state-funded faith schools in England and Wales has attracted considerable philosophical debate about their position in twenty-first century education systems (Francis and Robbins 2011). This debate shares many aspects of wider international debates on the *non-tolerance, tolerance* or *recognition* of the existence of faith schools in state education systems. Arguments that support *non-tolerance* of faith schools include: desirability of state funding for faith schooling which is essentially state funding for religious nurture; the divisiveness of faith schooling; the accusation that faith schools covertly exclude children with special educational needs to maintain high positions in league tables; the potential in faith schools for indoctrination and the inhibiting of rational autonomy; parental choice of faith schooling that impedes the rights of the child and the potential for faith schooling to contribute to the deliberate self-exclusion of religious-ethnic groups (Mason 2005; Gibbons and Silva 2006; Law 2006; Marples 2006; Ameen and Hassan 2013). There are, however, also strong arguments that promote the *tolerance* of the continued existence of faith schools and even *recognition* of the value of faith schools: faith schools provide a choice of state-funded schooling that is offered to citizens and tax-payers who have religious beliefs and wish these beliefs to be transmitted to their children through schooling; religious pluralism is recognised and validated through the expansion of newer forms of faith schooling; the apparent success of some forms of faith schooling in school league tables; the values and perceived successful ethos in faith schooling; faith schools promote community cohesion and appear to enjoy enhanced social capital (McCreery et al. 2007; Pugh and Telhaj 2008; Scott and McNeish 2012).

## The historical and contemporary position of Catholic schooling in the Scottish context

Contemporary Scotland draws on a long tradition of national autonomy in curriculum, education of teachers and regulation of the teaching profession in school education. This autonomy is currently configured as devolved responsibility for education (The Scottish Government 2014). The Scottish Government has political responsibility for education and the 32 local authorities in Scotland own the schools and have responsibility for operational matters in the schools. The vast majority of state-funded primary and secondary schools are comprehensive and coeducational (Paterson 2007). State-funded faith schools in Scotland are identified as denominational schools and they are predominantly Catholic schools; there is also one Jewish primary school and three Episcopalian schools (The Scottish Government 2013a). Non faith schools are identified as non-denominational schools. There are a small number of privately funded independent denominational and non-denominational schools in Scotland.

The complex history of Catholic education and Catholic schools can ultimately be traced back to pre-Reformation Scotland, but the foundations of contemporary state-funded Catholic schools are located in the few voluntary Catholic schools that were established in the early nineteenth century (Skinnider 1967; Fitzpatrick 2000). The influx of large numbers of Irish Catholics in the mid-nineteenth century precipitated a rise in demand for Catholic schooling to preserve Catholic Christianity and culture (Lynch 1991). After protracted negotiations with the government, denominational schools were state-funded under the Education (Scotland) Act 1918 (H. M. Government 1918; O'Hagan 2006; O'Hagan and Davis 2007). Under this Act, Catholic schools were able to retain their distinctive identity, religious education and the teachers have to be approved by the Catholic hierarchy (Act, Section 18 (3) (i), (ii), (iii)). The Act also provided scope for the construction of new Catholic schools (Act (18 (8)). There are currently 369 state-funded comprehensive Catholic schools in Scotland. This figure incorporates 313 primary schools, 53 secondary schools, 3 Additional Support Needs schools. There are also three privately funded independent Catholic schools. The approximate total pupil enrolment is around 120,000 (approximately one-sixth of all pupils in Scotland) (SCES 2014). The majority of the Catholic schools are located in the west central belt of Scotland.

Catholic schools continue to exist within the context of the diminishing sociological prominence, critical mass and influence of some of the religious groups in Scotland, especially some mainstream Christian groups (Bruce et al. 2004; Bruce and Glendinning 2007). The recent census in Scotland (2011), on first sight, can be interpreted as providing evidence to confirm this seemingly inexorable process. The 'headline news' reveals an 11% decrease in the number of people who stated that their religion is Christianity (54% in 2011; 65% in 2001) and 9% increase in the number of people who state that they had no religion (37% in 2011; 28% in 2001) (Scottish Executive 2005a; Donnelly 2013; The Scottish Government 2013b). Nevertheless, the overall number of people who stated that they had some religion is 56.3%, which is still a sizeable number of the population of Scotland. Despite the overall decrease in the number of people who stated that their religion is Christianity, there has been, perhaps surprisingly, a slight increase in the number of people who have stated that their religion is Roman Catholic Christianity (15.88% in 2001; 15.9% in 2011). Whether this is an identification of religious belief or some form of cultural or historical association, it can be assumed that a significant amount of the 15.9% support state-funded Catholic schooling.

As has been stated above, the national curriculum is the curriculum used by Catholic and non-denominational state schools, offering the same choices and opportunities. Teachers in Catholic schools, similar to all teachers in state-funded schools, must be educated to graduate level and be qualified teachers. All teachers who work in Catholic schools must also be approved in terms of their religious belief and character by representatives of the Catholic Church. The Young people in Catholic schools and non-denominational schools sit the same public exams that are set and awarded by the Scottish Qualifications Authority (SQA 2014; Education Scotland 2014a). The only curricular difference is in religious education: Catholic schools follow a confessional Religious Education, while non-denominational schools follow a non-confessional Religious and Moral Education. This distinctive Catholic Religious Education has historically consisted of a curriculum and syllabus created on behalf of the Bishops of Scotland. Interestingly, Catholic Religious Education remains distinctive but has been incorporated as a curricular area into the two most recent national curricular innovations (5–14 and Curriculum for Excellence) suggesting a move from *tolerance* to greater *recognition* for Catholic Religious Education and for Catholic schools by the government and the education agency, Education Scotland (Gillies 2013; Priestley 2013).

## The continuation of Catholic schooling in Scotland
### Introduction

The range of state-funded faith schooling in Scotland is less diverse than the range in England and, as the vast majority of denominational schools are Catholic schools, the debate is focused on the position and continued existence of state-funded Catholic schools in Scotland. This means that issues shared with the UK and Europe are debated exclusively in relation to Catholic schools, and there are also some issues that are distinctive and unique to the debate in Scotland, most notably: (1) the claims that Catholic schools are the cause of sectarianism or contribute to sectarianism and (2) Catholic schools were founded to help an economically disadvantaged community progress and become more socially mobile – this aim has now been achieved and these schools have become anachronistic.

The discussion will be restricted to exploring two key themes in the debate in Scotland on the continued existence of Catholic schools. The first theme to be explored is one that is shared with the faith schools debate in England and Wales: the continuation of government funding for faith schooling – but in this case, focusing exclusively on the funding for Catholic schooling, and the desirability of this funding as it is effectively government funding of religious beliefs and practices for Catholic Christians. The second theme to be explored is more distinctive, though superficially appears to share some similarities with the faith school debate in Northern Ireland: the allegation that Catholic schools are the cause of sectarianism or have some form of association with sectarianism.

### *The debate on the continuation of state funding for Catholic schools*

Since the Act of 1918, there have been repeated calls by the Presbyterian Church of Scotland to repeal the 1918 Act. The Church of Scotland is the majority Christian denomination in Scotland but has no state-funded religious schools and has not supported the *tolerance*, never mind the *recognition* of Catholic schools. Instead the Church has advocated the *non-tolerance* of Catholic schools and has periodically lobbied the government for the removal of what they have described as a privileged status of denominational schools and proposed an alternative: the introduction of an integrated school system. These repeated calls failed to attract government support (Brown 1991; Lynch 1991; Devine 2006). Over the last 20 years, the Humanist Society Scotland and the Scottish Secular Society have engaged in well-publicised and concerted campaigns of *non-tolerance* in opposition to state-funded Catholic schools. The Humanist Society Scotland are opposed to Catholic schools because they do not believe that schools should be based on one set of religious beliefs and the government should not endorse any form of religion (Humanist Society Scotland 2014). They state that all schools in Scotland should be totally inclusive and be open to all children. They also state that there should be no separate curriculum and no separate school buildings. This refers to Catholic schools being traditionally located in separate buildings and employing their own teaching and support staff as required. The Secular Society considers the state funding of faith schooling to be an inappropriate response to the expansion of religious diversity and advocate a secular education system that retains religious education, though as the study of objective and neutral study of religious and non-religious viewpoints (National Secular Society 2014). The National Secular Society also points out that there can be further costs accrued by faith schools – the cost of free transport for children to the faith school. While this is discussed in reference to England, it applies equally to Scotland as Catholic schools, especially secondary schools, often have a wide catchment area and necessitate expenditure on transport for the pupils.

State funding or partial funding of faith schools is perceived by those who support faith schools as an acknowledgement of their democratic rights to be offered the choice of the most appropriate form of state schooling for their children. This argument is formulated in a number of ways. First, Kenneth (1972) argues that state-funded Catholic schools are a legitimate option in Scottish society because those who support faith schools are tax-payers and have a right to be supported in their choices of publicly funded school education. Second, applying the arguments of Morris (2008) to the Scottish context, state-funded Catholics schools are a public acknowledgement of the validity and application of Article 27, section (3) of Universal Declaration of Human Rights (Morris 2008):

> Parents have a prior right to choose the kind of education that shall be given to their children. (United Nations 1948)

This section of article 27 is consolidated and extended in article 2 of the first protocol of the European Convention on Human Rights (1950, protocol added 1952)

> ... the State shall respect the right of parents to ensure such education and teaching in conformity with their own religious and philosophical convictions.

However, the UK has a reservation to article 2 of the first protocol (Allen and Thompson 2011)

> ... only so far as it is compatible with the provision of efficient instruction and training, and the avoidance of unreasonable expenditure.

The reservation outlines two conditions and these can be applied to Catholic schools in Scotland. The first condition is that Catholic schools are to be compatible with the provision of efficient instruction and training. This is not a major challenge for Catholic schools as they are state-funded and subject to the national and local quality assurance systems such as Quality Improvement Officers (local authority level) and Her Majestys' Inspectors (national level) (Education Scotland 2014b). Arguably this support is supplemented by the work of SCES (Scottish Catholic Education Service), the operational arm of the SCES and the Catholic Religious Education Advisors. If a Catholic school was not demonstrating efficient instruction and training, the school would be provided with targets for improvement and the progress in achieving those targets would be closely monitored. The second condition is more problematic as there are different viewpoints on what constitutes unreasonable (and reasonable) expenditure in publicly funded school education. SCES, on its website, argues that Catholic schools thrive because they are actively supported by parents, who consider the state funding to be a reasonable expenditure. The Humanist Society Scotland, the Scottish Secular Society and the Church of Scotland who support *non-tolerance* of Catholic schools consider state funding to be unreasonable expenditure. This appears to be a profound clash between contrasting ideologies – Catholic Christian on one hand, and (perhaps ironically) Protestant Christian and secular beliefs systems on the other hand. All parties involved in this debate, the Catholic Church, the Church of Scotland and the Humanist and Secular Societies, actively pursue and lobby government support for their positions.

### *Political divide on support for Catholic schools*

On a long-term historical perspective, the political support for Catholic schools has been, at times, ambivalent, and can possibly be best described as an uneasy *tolerance*. However, the leadership of the Scottish Executives and Government has been resolute in their support (and praise) in the last 15 years. This can be illustrated in the statements and actions of Alex Salmond, the first minister (2007–). He accepted an invitation to deliver the annual Cardinal Winning lecture at the University of Glasgow on Saturday 2 February 2008 to celebrate Catholic Education Week (The Scottish Government

2008). This lecture highlighted the historical importance of Catholic schools and celebrated the contribution of Catholic schools to the school system and to Scottish society. Mr Salmond's view was clearly one of *recognition* and his public support for Catholic schools was not restricted to this lecture – he has consistently articulated his support and praise and Catholic schools in his term of office as First Minister (McKenna 2013).

This *recognition* and support for Catholic schools by Mr Salmond has not always been shared by the membership of his party, the Scottish Nationalist Party (SNP), and a recent survey of SNP members revealed that 65% adopted a view that can be described as *non-tolerance,* believing that state-funded Catholic schools should be phased out (McLaughlin and Peterkin 2012). This marked disjuncture between the *recognition* views of the leadership and the *non-tolerance* views of the SNP party members highlights the pragmatic approach of the leadership who support Catholic schools and the clash with the ideological and educational ambitions of a significant number of the membership (Mitchell et al. 2012). Mr Salmond's support for Catholic schools is consistent with the inclusive approach that he has adopted to Scottish society, including religious groups (Clark 2012). It is also consistent with the trend in UK politics since the late 1990s to 'enlist faith as a political resource' to help realise societal goals such as community cohesion (Beckford 2011).

This *recognition* and support for Catholic schools can be partly understood within a political position that is rooted in a deeper agenda of support for religious groups and the inclusion of religious groups within Scottish society and may be interpreted as political expediency with an expectation of reciprocal support and the ultimate aim of acquiring votes. It does bring the leadership and the government into conflict with the aims and ambitions of the Church of Scotland, the humanist and secular lobby and with the membership of the SNP. The debate about reasonable and unreasonable expenditure on state-funded Catholic schools, for these protagonists, is also rooted in this deeper agenda of government support for religious groups, as humanist and secular organisations recognise that state-funded Catholic schools are a long-term public manifestation of not just *tolerance* but *recognition*, support and active relationship with religious groups. It is reasonable to interpret the position of the Church of Scotland as being partly motivated by the perceived advantage accorded to the Catholic Church in the *tolerance* and *recognition* of Catholic schools. It remains open to question if the *recognition* and support for Catholic schools is dependent upon the individual views of the leadership of the government and if that *recognition* and support would return to a position of uneasy *tolerance* with a change in leadership or a greater degree of independence for Scotland. It would seem unlikely that leadership of Scottish government in the foreseeable future would move to a position of *non-tolerance* as this may conflict with the continuation of multifaceted strategies of inclusion, accommodation and expediency with religious groups.

## The debate that Catholic schools are the root cause of sectarianism or contribute to sectarianism

### Claims that Catholic schools are the root cause of sectarianism or contribute to sectarianism

A number of prominent politicians, legal experts and academics have claimed that Catholic schools are at the root of sectarianism or, in some way, contribute to sectarianism in Scotland. The real challenge in engaging with these views is that they tend to be communicated through widely disseminated media reporting, television and newspapers. The views are mediated through 'production processes' and are presented in sound bites and quotes from interviews rather than methodical argument (Hartley 2002). A number of important examples will illustrate these points. In 2007, Sam Galbraith, a former government minister, claimed that Catholic schools are the root cause of sectarianism and 'entrench a religious divide in society' (*The Scotsman* 2006). The Scotsman newspaper stated that he had the support of a number of leading figures, though the leading figures make different claims. Lord Moonie, an MP, stated that religion should have no role in educating children and the Moderator of the Church of Scotland stated that faith schools were an anachronism. Neither of them referred to sectarianism. In 2012, John Downie, a director of the Scottish Council for Voluntary Organisations (SVCO), stated on a blog on the SVCO website that denominational schools was one of the key causes of sectarianism in Scotland (Hutcheson 2012). In 2013 Sheriff Richard Davidson adjudicating on a case of alleged sectarianism, stated to the court that the best way to tackle sectarianism in Scotland is to 'do away with' denominational schools (McGlone 2013). In April 2013, A.C. Grayling, on a visit to Scotland, stated that the 'argument against faith-based schools can be summed up in two words – Northern Ireland. Or perhaps one word – Glasgow' (Dinwoodie 2013). The challenge of engaging with these views is compounded by the fact that none of protagonists is represented as providing any evidence to substantiate their views.

Despite the serious limitations of the arguments above, this is a recurring theme and arguably the media functions in the construction (and as custodian) of a collective memory of this link between Catholic schools and sectarianism (Zelizer and Tenenboim-Weinblatt 2014). Sectarianism in Scotland has been described as Scotland's 'secret shame' – the historical and continued inter-denominational hostility between Roman Catholic and protestant Christians that is manifested in rivalry between football fans, Walks and Parades (Orange, Hibernian and Irish Republican).

Sectarianism is characterised by anti-social and bigoted attitudes and beliefs and can lead to practices of sectarian discrimination and even violence. Sectarian offences in Scotland have been classified as one of the hate crimes – crimes motivated by malice or ill-will towards a social group. Hate crimes include crimes motivated by racial or religious discrimination or homophobia. The Scottish Government has been resolute in condemnation of sectarianism and proactive in tackling sectarian activity, introducing anti-sectarian legislation (Scottish Executive 2005a, 2005b, 2006a, 2006b; The Scottish Government 2012).

The media attributes these views concerning Catholic schools and sectarianism, albeit unsubstantiated, to prominent and influential individuals and it is important to provide an academic response to these views and the possible ways in which Catholic schools can be construed to be a cause of sectarianism or contribute to sectarianism in contemporary Scotland. On a superficial level, it is tempting to view this series of arguments as similar or parallel to the arguments about Catholic schools in Northern Ireland but academic caution must be exercised. The history and manifestations of sectarianism in Northern Ireland and Scotland, while related, have evolved in different ways. Some of the clear lines of demarcation are that there is no geographical segregation on grounds of religious affiliation in Scotland nor has there been sustained armed conflict between religiously based factions (Bew and Gillespie 1993; Cochrane 2013). The voting patterns in elections are very different between Scotland and Northern Ireland, as there is no sizeable distinctive Catholic or Protestant political parties in Scotland (Bruce and Glendinning 2007). It is also important to note that the school system in

Northern Ireland is quite different from that in Scotland. The Northern Ireland school system has been dominated by two models of schooling since 1923: controlled and maintained schools (Catholic schools) (Holt et al. 1999). In 1989, integrated schools were introduced (O'Callaghan and Lundy 2002). The aim of integrated schools is to create an environment that is religiously mixed and is inclusive of both Protestant and Catholic children. These integrated schools have received a disproportionate amount of national and international media attention given that they constitute 5% of primary schooling and 10% of secondary schooling (McAndrew 2013; Department of Education Northern Ireland 2014).

### *Counter arguments to the claims that Catholic schools are the root cause of sectarianism or contribute to sectarianism*

There is a persistent message that has been communicated through government reports and government-sponsored research reports on the relationship between Catholics schools and sectarianism: Catholics schools are not the cause of sectarianism and there is no evidence to support the claims that Catholic schools contribute to sectarianism (Scottish Executive 2005a, 2005b, 2006a, 2006b; The Scottish Government 2013c). This is articulated in the documentation that emerged from the Summit of 2005 and from the two major reports on extant research: *Religious Discrimination and Sectarianism in Scotland; a Brief Review of Evidence (2002–2004)* (2005) and *An Examination of the Evidence on Sectarianism in Scotland* The Scottish Government Social Research (2013). This was further reiterated in the *Report of the Advisory Group on Tackling Sectarianism in Scotland, Independent Advice to Scottish Ministers and Report on Activity 9 August 2012–2015 November 2013* (2013). In the 2013 *Examination,* there is slight evidence provided that there is some low level of public perception that Catholic schools can inadvertently contribute to sectarianism.

The claim that Catholic schools are the cause of sectarianism is one that cannot be substantiated and betrays an ignorance of the history of Christian religion in Scotland. The Reformation in Scotland in the sixteenth century was quite unique and resulted in the Presbyterian Church of Scotland that was heavily influenced by Calvinism and vehement in its condemnation of Catholicism and Catholic practices. Sectarianism in Scotland predates the introduction of post Reformation privately funded Catholic schools in the early nineteenth century and the later introduction of state-funded Catholic schools in the early twentieth century. Catholic schools cannot be a root cause of sectarianism as the causes of sectarianism predate the introduction of both privately funded and state-funded Catholic schools.

Let us discuss the equally unsubstantiated claim that contemporary Catholic schools in Scotland contribute to sectarianism. Catholic schools in Scotland publicly promote a vision of Christian schooling that is articulated in the Charter for Catholic schools, launched in 2004 by the SCES (Catholic Media Office 2004). This is a localised rationale for Catholic schools in Scotland that draws on the wider Vatican documentation on Catholic education that has been produced and disseminated since 1964 (Vatican 2014). The Charter states that all Catholic schools in Scotland will have a commitment to 'integrated education and formation of the whole person', rooted in a Christian vision of life and aims to be inclusive and honour the dignity of each person (SCES 2010). The Charter also makes a commitment to 'ecumenical action and the unity of Christians' and promotes 'respect for different beliefs and cultures and for inter-faith dialogue'. The aims of the national Charter which emphasise inclusivity, ecumenism and respect for others indicate that at the level of a national rationale, Catholic schools do not aim to contribute to sectarianism.

This rationale for Catholic schools may not necessarily be observed in every Catholic school and there may be instances of individual Catholic schools or individuals in Catholic schools that do contribute to sectarianism by demonstrating sectarian beliefs, attitudes or even actions. This possibility cannot be dismissed as everyone may not share the inclusivity and respect articulated in the Charter, despite approval processes for the appointment to Catholic schools. If this were to happen, the specific individual or school (or schools) as a state-funded institution(s) would be subject to close scrutiny from the Scottish government which has a high-profile anti-sectarian campaign and also intervention from the local authority that owns and oversees the management of the school. If individual teachers were implicated in contributing to sectarianism, they would also face investigation by the regulatory body, The General Teaching Council for Scotland (The Scottish Government 2012, 2013d; The General Teaching Council for Scotland 2014). Presumably the individual(s) and school(s) would also be under close scrutiny and intervention from SCES as any form of contribution to sectarianism contradicts the publicly articulated rationale for Catholic schools in Scotland.

**Concluding remarks**

The faith school debate in Scotland is a debate that, for historical reasons and because of the critical mass of contemporary Catholic schools, becomes necessarily focused on state-funded Catholic schools and their continued position within the Scottish state education system. This paper has explored the quite distinct nature of the debate in Scotland and examined two key themes. The first theme is a theme shared in other national contexts, the desirability of state funding for faith schools, but with a patently distinct Scottish flavour in the sole focus on Catholic schools, the opposition by the established Protestant Church of Scotland and the Humanist and Secular bodies, by the argument from human rights and the importance of the *recognition* and support by the first minister despite the political divide within the SNP. The second theme is very unique, though there is a superficial similarity to the situation in Northern Ireland. The claims that Catholic schools are the cause of, or contribute to, sectarianism are serious claims about a link between a section of the state-funded school system and hate crime. The counter arguments, however, are very strong and, unlike the initial claims, are substantiated with evidence. This is not to close down either of the key themes. The first theme could be profoundly affected by a change in the leadership of the Scottish government and a shift in position from *recognition* to *tolerance*. The second theme could be influenced by new research into Catholic schools. Sustained evidence of individuals or Catholic schools contributing to sectarianism would suggest that Catholic schools should not be accorded *recognition* or *tolerance* but possibly *non-tolerance* because they are consistently involved in anti-social religious discrimination.

**References**

Allen, M., and B. Thompson. 2011. *Cases and Materials on Constitutional and Administrative Law*. Oxford: Oxford University Press.
Ameen, R., and N. Hassan. 2013. "Are Faith Schools Educationally Defensible?" *Research in Teacher Education* 3 (1): 11–17.
Beckford, J. A. 2011. "Religious Diversity and Social Problems." In *Religion and Social Problems*, edited by T. Hjelm, 53–66. London: Routledge.
Bew, P., and G. Gillespie. 1993. *Northern Ireland A Chronology of the Troubles 1968–1993*. Dublin: Gill and Macmillan.
Brown, S. J. 1991. "'Outside the Covenant'; The Scottish Presbyterian Churches and Irish Immigration, 1922–1938." *The Innes Review* 42 (1): 19–45.
Bruce, S., and T. Glendinning. 2007. "Religious Beliefs and Practices." In *Devolution – Scottish Answers to Scottish Questions?* edited by C. Bromley, J. Curtice, K. Hinds, and A. Park, 86–115. Edinburgh: Edinburgh University Press.
Bruce, S., T. Glendinning, I. Paterson, and M. Rosie. 2004. *Sectarianism in Scotland*. Edinburgh: Edinburgh University Press.
Clark, A. 2012. *Political Parties in the UK*. Basingstoke: Palgrave Macmillan.
Cochrane, F. 2013. *Northern Ireland: The Reluctant Peace*. New Haven: Yale University Press.
Council of Europe. 1950. "European Convention on Human Rights." http://www.echr.coe.int/Documents/Convention_ENG.pdf
Department for Education. 2013. "Faith Schools." http://www.education.gov.uk/schools/leadership/typesofschools/b0066996/faith-schools
Department for Education and Skills. 2001. "Schools Achieving Success." http://dera.ioe.ac.uk/15197/1/Schools%20-%20achieving%20success%20%28white%20paper%29.pdf
Department for Education Northern Ireland. 2014. "Northern Ireland Summary Data." http://www.deni.gov.uk/index/facts-and-figures-new/education-statistics/32_statistics_and_research-numbersofschoolsandpupils_pg/32_statist
Devine, T. M. 2006. *The Scottish Nation*. London: The Penguin Press.
Dinwoodie, R. 2013. "Argument Against Faith Schools Summed up in Two Words: Northern Ireland. Or One: Glasgow." http://www.heraldscotland.com/politics/political-news/argument-against-faith-schools-summed-up-in-two-words-northern-ireland-or-one-glasgow.12345
Donnelly, B. 2013. "Census Reveals Huge Rise in Number of Non-religious Scots." *The Herald*, September 27. Friday. http://www.heraldscotland.com/news/home-news/census-reveals-huge-rise-in-number-of-non-religious-scots.22270874
Education Scotland. 2014a. "Curriculum Areas and Subjects." http://www.educationscotland.gov.uk/thecurriculum/howisthecurriculumorganised/curriculumareas/index.asp
Education Scotland. 2014b. "About Inspections and Reviews." https://www.educationscotland.gov.uk/inspectionandreview/about/index.asp
Fitzpatrick, T. 2000. "Catholic Education." In *Scottish Life and Society: A Companion to Scottish Ethnology Volume 11*, edited by H. Holmes, 435–455. East Linton: Tuckwell Press.
Francis, L., and M. Robbins. 2011. "Teaching Secondary RE at Faith Schools in England and Wales: Listening to Teachers." *Journal of Beliefs and Values* 32 (2): 219–233.
Gallagher, J. 2007. "Catholic Schools in England and Wales: New Challenges." In *International Handbook of Catholic Education*, edited by G. Grace, and J. O'Keefe, 249–268. Dordrecht: Springer.

Gardner, R. 2005. "Faith Schools Now. An Overview." In *Faith Schools Consensus or Conflict?* edited by R. Gardner, J. Cairns, and D. Lawton, 7–13. London: Routledge.

Gibbons, S., and O. Silva. 2006. "Faith Primary Schools: Better Schools or Better Pupils? Centre for Economics of Education." http://cee.lse.ac.uk/ceedps/ceedp72.pdf

Gillies, D. 2013. "The History of Scottish Education, 1980 to the Present Day." In *Scottish Education Fourth Edition: Referendum*, edited by T. G. K. Bryce, W. M. Humes, D. Gillies, and A. Kennedy, 251–261. Edinburgh: Edinburgh University Press.

Hartley, J. 2002. *Communication, Cultural and Media Studies. The Key Concepts*. London: Routledge.

H. M. Government. 1918. *Education (Scotland) Act 1918*. London: H.M. Stationery Office.

Holt, G., S. Boyd, B. Dickinson, J. Loose, and S. O'Donnell. 1999. *Education in England, Wales and Northern Ireland*. Slough: National Foundation for Educational Research.

Humanist Society Scotland. 2014. "Education." http://www.humanism-scotland.org.uk/content/e

Hutcheson, P. 2012. "Catholic Fury as Charity Boss Blames Faith Schools for Sectarianism." *The Herald*, February 5. www.heraldscotland.com/politics/political-news/catholic-church-fury-as-charity-boss-blames-faith-schools-for-sectarianism.1328411182

Kenneth, Br. 1972. *Catholic Schools in Scotland 1872–1972*. Glasgow: John S. Burns and Sons.

Law, S. 2006. *The War for Children's Minds*. London: Routledge.

Lynch, M. 1991. *Scotland a New History*. London: Pimlico.

Marples, R. 2006. "Against Faith Schools: A Philosophical Argument for Children's Rights." In *Reflecting on Faith Schools*, edited by H. Johnson, 19–33. London: Routledge.

Mason, M. 2005. "Religion and Schools – A Fresh Way Forward? A Rights-based Approach to Diversity in Schools." In *Faith Schools: Consensus or Conflict?* edited by R. Gardner, J. Cairns, and D. Lawton, 74–82. Abingdon: Routledge Falmer.

Maussen, M., and V. Bader. 2102. *Tolerance and Cultural Diversity in Schools*. Comparative Report. ACCEPT PLURALISM. 2012/01; 3. http://accept-pluralism.eu/Research/Project Reports/CaseStudiesSchool.aspx

McAndrew, M. 2013. *Fragile Majorities and Education*. Montreal: McGill-Queen's University Press.

McAspurren, L. 2005. *Religious Discrimination and Sectarianism in Scotland; a Brief Review of Evidence (2002–2004)*. Edinburgh: Scottish Executive Social Research.

McCreery, Elaine, Jones Liz, and Holmes Rachel. 2007. "Why do Muslim Parents want Muslim schools?" *Early Years* 27 (3): 203–219.

McCulloch, G. 2005. "Introduction: History of Education." In *The RoutledgeFalmer Reader in History of Education*, edited by G. McCulloch, 1–12. London: Routledge.

McGlone, P. 2013. "Sheriff Clears Celtic Fan of Sectarian Singing and Says Solution is to End Denominational Schools." *The Herald*. April 9. http://www.heraldscotland.com/news/crime-courts/catholic-anger-at-school-claim-by-sheriff.20738798

McKenna, K. 2013. "Are We Protecting Catholic Education? Scottish Catholic Observer." January 18. http://www.sconews.co.uk/opinion/24718/are-we-protecting-catholic-education/

McLaughlin, M., and T. Peterkin. 2012. "Battle Lines Being Drawn by SNP Members Over Key Alex Salmond Policies." *The Scotsman*, February 12. www.scotsman.com/news/politics/top-stories/battle-lines-being-drawn-by-snp-members-over-key-alex-salmond-policies-1–2112801

Miller, P. 2000. *Historiography of Compulsory Schooling*. In history of education Volume II, edited by Roy Lowe. London: Routledge.

Mitchell, J., L. Bennie, and R. Johns. 2012. *The Scottish National Part: Transition to Power*. Oxford: Oxford University Press.

Morris, A. 2008. *Fifty Years on: The Case for Catholic Schools*. Chelmsford: Matthew James.

National Secular Society. 2014. "Faith Schools." http://www.secularism.org.uk/faith-schools.html

O'Callaghan, M., and L. Lundy. 2002. *Education in the United Kingdom*. edited by Liam Gearon. London: David Fulton.

O'Hagan, F. J. 2006. *The Contribution of the Religious Orders to Education in Glasgow during the Period 1847–1918*. Lewiston: The Edwin Mellon Press.

O'Hagan, F., and R. A. Davis. 2007. "Forging the Compact of Church and State in the Development of Catholic Education in Late Nineteenth-century Scotland." *Innes Review* 58 (1): 72–94.

Paterson, L. 2007. "The Renewal of Social Democratic Educational Thought in Scotland." In *Scottish Social Democracy*, edited by M. Keating, 59–84. Brussels: Peter Lang.

Priestley, M. 2013. "The 3–18 Curriculum in Scotland." In *Scottish Education Fourth Edition: Referendum*, edited by T. G. K. Bryce, W. M. Humes, D. Gillies, and A. Kennedy, 28–38. Edinburgh: Edinburgh University Press.

Pugh, G., and S. Telhaj. 2008. "Faith Schools, Social Capital and Academic Attainment: Evidence from TIMSS-R Mathematics Scores in Flemish Secondary Schools." *British Educational Research Journal* 34 (2): 235–267.

Scott, S., and D. McNeish. 2012. "Leadership and Faith Schools: Issues and Challenges." National College for School leadership. http://www.bristol.ac.uk/cubec/researchreports/leadershipandfaithschools.pdf

SCES (Scottish Catholic Education Service). 2010. "Charter for Catholic Schools." http://www.sces.uk.com/catholic-schools-charter.html

SCES (Scottish Catholic Education Service). 2014. "Schools Past and Present." http://www.sces.uk.com/schools-past-and-present.html

Scottish Catholic Media Office. 2004. "Launch of Charter for Catholic Schools." http://www.scmo.org/articles/launch-of-charter-for-catholic-schools.html

Scottish Executive. 2005a. *Analysis of Religion in the 20001 Census*. Summary Report. http://www.scotland.gov.uk/Resource/Doc/36496/0029047.pdf

Scottish Executive. 2005b. *Record of the Discussion on Sectarianism Held on 14 February 2005*. Edinburgh: Scottish Executive. http://www.scotland.gov.uk/Publications/2005/04/2193329/33313

Scottish Executive. 2006a. *Action Plan on Tackling Sectarianism in Scotland*. Edinburgh: Scottish Executive. Located at: http://www.scotland.gov.uk/Publications/2006/01/26134908/0

Scottish Executive. 2006b. *Building Friendships and Strengthening communities*. Edinburgh: Scottish Executive. http://www.scotland.gov.uk/Resource/Doc/159545/0043404.pdf

Skinnider, M. 1967. "Catholic Elementary Education in Glasgow 1818–1918." In *Studies in the History of Scottish Education 1872–1939,* edited by T. R. Bone, 13–70. London: University of London Press.

SQA (The Scottish Qualifications Authority) 2014. http://www.sqa.org.uk/sqa/5656.html

The General Teaching Council for Scotland. 2014. "Fitness to Teach." http://www.gtcs.org.uk/fitness-to-teach/fitness-to-teach.aspx

The Scottish Government. 2008. Celebrating Catholic Education in Scotland: Reflections on Partnership from 1918 to Date, and Beyond. Cardinal Winning Education Lecture Delivered by Rt.Hon Alex Salmond, First Minister on Saturday 2 February 2008.

The Scottish Government. 2012. "Offensive Behaviour at Football and Threatening Communication (Scotland) Act 2102." http://www.scotland.gov.uk/Topics/Justice/law/sectarianism-action-1/football-violence/bill

The Scottish Government. 2013a. "Schools – Frequently Asked Questions." http://www.scotland.gov.uk/Topics/Education/Schools/FAQs

The Scottish Government. 2013b. "Summary Religious Group Demographics." http://www.scotland.gov.uk/Topics/People/Equality/Equalities/DataGrid/Religion/RelPopMig

The Scottish Government. 2013c. *Advisory Group on Tackling Sectarianism in Scotland*. Independent Advice to Scottish Ministers and Report on Activity August 9, 2012–November 15, 2013.

The Scottish Government. 2013d. "Religiously Aggravated Offending in Scotland 2012–2013." http://www.scotland.gov.uk/Publications/2013/06/1944/0

The Scottish Government. 2014. "Scottish Responsibilities." http://www.scotland.gov.uk/About/Factfile/18060/11552

The Scottish Government Social Research. 2013. "An Examination of the Evidence on Sectarianism in Scotland." http://www.scotland.gov.uk/Resource/0042/00424891.pdf

The Scotsman. 2006. "Galbraith Under Fire for Claiming Catholic Schools Cause Sectarianism." December 26. http://www.scotsman.com/news/scotland/top-stories/galbraith-under-fire-for-claiming-catholic-schools-cause-sectarianism-1-735750

United Nations. 1948. "Universal Declaration of Human Rights." http://www.un.org/en/documents/udhr/

Vatican. 2014. "Vatican Internet Sites." http://www.vatican.va/siti_va/index_va_en.htm

Zelizer, B., and K. Tenenboim-Weinblatt. 2014. "Journalism's Memory Work." In *Journalism and Memory*, edited by B. Zelizer and K. Tenenboim-Weinblatt, 1–14. Basingstoke: Palgrave Macmillan.

# What can international comparisons teach us about school choice and non-governmental schools in Europe?

Jaap Dronkers[a,b] and Silvia Avram[a,b]

[a]ROA, Maastricht University, Maastricht, the Netherlands; [b]ISER, University of Essex, Essex, UK

> All European states have a primary obligation to establish and maintain governmental schools everywhere, but as the result of political struggle and constitutional guarantees, they have also allowed and often financed non-state schools based on special pedagogical, religious or philosophical ideas. Depending on the level of state grants for non-state schools, states have more or less the right to supervise these non-governmental schools and seek to guarantee that the quality of organisation and teachers are not lower than those in governmental schools. Using comparable cross-national data for all member states of the European Union, we first describe four existing basic arrangements of non-governmental and governmental schools: integrated educational systems of public and non-state schools, denomination supportive educational systems, limited-support non-governmental schools and educational systems with segregated public and non-state schools. Using the same cross-national data for all member states of the European Union, we then explore three other topics: parental background and the choice of non-governmental schools, non-governmental schools and their cognitive outcomes, and non-governmental schools and their non-cognitive outcomes. There are important differences between non-governmental-*in*dependent (without state grants) and non-governmental-*de*pendent schools (with state grants); that school choice of non-governmental-*de*pendent schools is more related to socially mobile parents, whereas schools choice of non-governmental-*in*dependent schools is more related the reproduction of social classes; that in a majority of European countries, non-governmental-*de*pendent schools are more effective cognitively than governmental schools, but that non-governmental-*in*dependent schools are more effective cognitively only in a few countries and more ineffective in a larger number of countries. Also non-governmental-*de*pendent schools are *not* more effective non-cognitively than governmental schools.

**Introduction**

This article aims to summarise some of the empirical outcomes of a Europe-wide comparison, and we focus on the functioning of religious non-governmental schools in relation with their institutional context (notably funding and social selection) and school choice in a more or less secular Europe (Smyth, Lyons, and Darmody 2013). Maussen and Bader (2015) provide an overview of the situation of non-governmental religious schools in Europe (see also Glenn and De Groof 2002; Wolf and Macedo 2004). Most of the debates and research on non-governmental religious schools follow strictly the lines of the national states and thus tend to overemphasise the uniqueness of the national religious schools, and underscore the more general trends in the functioning of religious non-governmental schools and school choice in secular Europe. However, the empirical evidence on cross-national similarities and differences in the functioning of non-governmental schools in comparison with governmental schools is scarcer, even within Europe.

The first reason for this scarcity is the omission of information about the religious background of schools in the mayor cross-national data-sets, collected by the OECD (Organization for Economic Cooperation and Development) (the so-called Programme for International Student Assessment (PISA) data of 15-year-old pupils, which we will use in this article as well) or the IEA (International Association for the Evaluation of Educational Achievement, with data-sets like PRILS (Progress in International Reading Literacy Study), TIMSS (Trends in International Mathematics and Science Study) and ICCS (International Civic and Citizenship Education Study)). Religion has become a private and irrelevant matter in Europe, at least in the eyes of the data-collecting authorities.[1]

The second reason is the political sensitivity of the religious background of schools and the possible differences in outcomes between governmental and non-governmental schools. The struggle between non-governmental schools and the state about the degree of their funding and supervision makes any comparison of educational outcomes between governmental and non-governmental schools highly sensitive. Especially in countries that have witnessed intense school struggles, and/or in which state–church relations tend to be subject to deep ideological and political contestation, and/or in which 'colour blindness' of the state vis-à-vis religious and ethnic differences is the norm, even reporting the situation of religious schools from a comparative perspective is a sensitive issue. For instance, France has deleted all school information for the public PISA data-files since the first wave, and Canada has deleted the variables, which would allow the identification of schools as governmental or non-governmental from public PISA data-files.

Alongside these non-governmental-dependent schools, there exist in a number of European countries' non-governmental schools that do not get funding from the (local, regional and national) government. Financially, they are fully dependent on student fees, donations, sponsorships and parental fundraising. The best-known example is the English public school. However, even their school autonomy can still be restricted in two ways. Authorities might set conditions (some teacher qualification, minimum quality of school buildings, rules related to home teaching, etc.) even for independent non-governmental schools in order to ensure some minimum quality of socialisation of the next generation. Although there is no recognised exam of these schools, these school had to function within their societal context and could not fully ignore the constraints of that society. For example, entrance criteria for universities will restrict the autonomy of a non-governmental school's curriculum, or pupils need an additional state exam and some preparation for that exam, either by the non-governmental-independent school or by another school. However, non-governmental school autonomy will be the largest in their student admission policies, especially given the importance of student fees for the financing of these schools.

In this article, we summarise the most important outcomes of a European project on religious schools (Smyth, Lyons, and Darmody 2013).[2] The aim of this European project was the comparison of a number of systematic case studies of religious schools in a few EU countries. As an addition to these separate national case studies, we have analysed all available cross-national data on non-governmental schools in all EU countries, among which PISA data are the most prominent (Avram and Dronkers 2011, 2013; Dronkers and Avram 2010a, 2010b). These cross-national data can show the more general trends in the functioning of religious non-governmental schools and school choice in secular Europe, and not only in the case study countries. That is also the aim of this chapter: a general overview of the functioning of religious non-governmental schools in relation with their institutional context (notably funding and social selection) and school choice in a more or less secular Europe, based on cross-national comparable data.

## Institutional opportunities and school autonomy

This chapter based on cross-national data aims to sketch a picture of non-governmental schools in all EU countries, not just in a few selected countries. That is important because non-governmental schools (which are in majority religious schools) do not only exist in Denmark, France, Germany, Ireland, the Netherlands and Scotland. They exist in many more European countries, sometimes already for a long time (for instance Belgium), sometimes interrupted by regime changes (Hungary) and sometimes recently emerged (Sweden). By comparing all European countries, we can see that the religious schools of the selected countries are not unique cases, and we make the more general trends in the functioning of religious non-governmental schools and school choice in secular Europe visible.

### *Variations among non-governmental schools within the European Union*[3]

EU countries vary greatly in terms of their educational systems and practices, including the approach taken to the provision of religious education (see Glenn and de Groof 2002, volume 2). Historical legacies relating to the relative power of church and state in influencing key aspects of education are of particular relevance in the context of this research. Avram and Dronkers (2013) analysed the cross-country variation in the role of various religious bodies in education. They used three aspects of the relationship between school and religion, namely the role of religion in state-provided education, the existence and organisation of faith schools and school autonomy. Based on 11 indicators of these dimensions, they found that substantial country divergence exists in these characteristics. Most countries have a constitutional separation of church and state, especially Roman Catholic countries (like France, Italy and Austria), where both institutions have fought for primacy for many years, and where religious and anti-clerical political parties and movements exist. By contrast, there tends to be a less clear-cut separation in predominantly Orthodox and Protestant countries, where the state has had a long tradition of incorporating the Christian church as a branch of the state apparatus. The UK is a good protestant example with the king as head of the Anglican Church and Anglican bishops as members of the Upper House.

Religious education is normally available in all of the state-provided school systems, except for France where there is a well-established principle of secularism within state-provided education. However, countries differ in the emphasis they place on and the importance they attach to religious education, with practices ranging from having compulsory religious education (in Austria, Cyprus and Greece), quasi-compulsory religious education (with a special procedure to opt out needed in England and Ireland) to offering it on an optional but regular basis (students have to opt out of religious education in Malta, Belgium, the Netherlands, Bulgaria,

Poland, Portugal and Scotland) or offering it on request (students have to opt for religious education in Estonia, the Czech Republic, Hungary, Latvia and Lithuania). Countries also differ in the extent to which they impose the obligation on schools to make religious education available in the pupils' faith, when the subject is optional.

Great variation in the size of the non-governmental sector exists as well, from under 1% of the primary school pupil population in Bulgaria and Lithuania to 100% in Ireland, where technically all primary schools are non-governmental. Not surprisingly, the non-governmental sector tends to be more developed in countries where at least some public funding is made available to non-governmental schools. The exceptions are Central and East European countries where the only recent re-emergence of the non-governmental sector is still visible in its small size relative to state-provided education.

A national curriculum, quality control as well as national examinations are all ways in which the content of teaching and the instructional process in non-governmental schools may be controlled from the central level. The strictest form of control is the setting of a national curriculum. In prescribing the content and outcomes of a sizable portion of (sometimes the entire) teaching time, it allows for less flexibility at the school level for the establishment of a certain ethos of the teachers or a more stimulating school climate. The introduction of national examinations constitutes the opposite approach. It does provide for some, albeit indirect, control of the content of the educational process (for example, by drawing examination questions from a given syllabus), but it highlights the output side, that is, the actual achievement of students. Direct quality control, most often through external inspection, represents the middle ground between curriculum setting and national testing. Depending on how the inspection is structured, and the exact characteristics of the inspectors, it can vary in emphasis on the actual content of teaching or the educational output. All countries have some form of control, either through a national curriculum, national examinations or an inspection system. In fact, the majority of countries have at least two such control mechanisms in place. A more detailed account of country variation along these lines will follow further on, in the context of a discussion on school autonomy.

Schools may also be circumscribed in their ability to set their own staff policies. Almost all countries set special teaching certification/qualifications as a necessary precondition for employment in the non-governmental educational system (clear exceptions are England and Wales). Hiring and dismissal usually fall under the remit of general employment legislation, although special additional conditions may apply either because of educational legislation (for example, Hungary and Lithuania), collective branch agreements (for example, Finland) or because the government directly pays the teacher salaries and is thus their employer (for example, France and Spain). Restrictions regarding the flexibility of pay setting may also apply, especially when schools receive funding for all or a considerable size of their personnel expenses from the state budget (for example, in Belgium, Ireland and the Netherlands).

Finally, countries differ in whether administrative responsibilities regarding schools are allocated to the central or local level. A number of countries have centralised systems in which a central body, usually the Ministry of Education, is responsible for administering schools. A slightly smaller number of countries have decentralised responsibility for running and often also for financing state-provided schools at the local level. In these countries (for instance, the UK or Germany), it is the provincial, district or municipal authorities that are in charge of taking administrative decisions (for example, establishing or closing schools, appointing staff and so on) regarding state schools. Finally, there are some countries (like Italy) that split the various responsibilities between central and local levels. Usually, the Ministry of Education retains decision-making power over more sensitive areas, while local governments are charged with settling routine issues.

The cost of attending a non-governmental school may differ considerably by country and, in some countries, by school. Very often, countries that offer public funding for non-governmental schools on an equal footing to public ones, or which shoulder the majority of non-governmental school expenses, impose limitations on the fees that non-governmental subsidised schools may ask of their pupils. The most common situation is that in which non-governmental subsidised schools are required to provide education free of charge to their students (for example, Finland, Belgium, Spain, Hungary and Slovakia for the higher subsidy amount). In a few cases, governments allow some fees to be charged but these have to be either nominal or proportional to family income (for example, Slovenia or Germany).

## *Four basic arrangements for non-governmental schools within the European Union*

No clear blueprints emerge when looking at all of the 10 indicators in conjunction. The 10 dimensions cut across each other, thus making any parsimonious grouping of countries in homogeneous clusters elusive. Nonetheless, some broad patterns may be discerned. When looking at the position of the non-governmental sector and at that of faith schools within the non-governmental sector, four basic arrangements exist from the funding point of view:

(1) countries in which non-governmental education is more or less on the same footing as state-provided education, termed 'integrated educational systems': Denmark, Finland, Ireland, the Netherlands, Poland, Slovakia, Spain and Sweden;

(2) countries where faith schools (of some or all of the denominations) receive a more favourable treatment than other schools in the non-governmental sector, termed 'denomination-supportive educational systems'; the religious bias can be more prominent, such as is the case in Austria, Malta, Portugal and the UK where almost no funding is made available for non-governmental non-faith schools, or relatively mild as in the Central European countries of Hungary and the Czech Republic where faith schools are entitled to have a larger share of their expenses borne by the state;

(3) countries that offer varying degrees of subsidisation to the non-governmental sector, but (always) less than the corresponding amount they spend on state-provided schools: Belgium, Estonia, France, Germany, Italy, Latvia, Lithuania, Luxembourg and Slovenia. This category is rather eclectic; it not only contains countries that make public funding available on generous terms such as Belgium and Slovenia, but also contains countries where no public funding is guaranteed although it is offered in some cases such as Italy;

(4) countries that fail to make any public funding directly available to the non-governmental sector, termed 'segregated educational systems': Bulgaria, Cyprus, Greece and Romania.

A brief review of the four categories of countries reveals some interesting findings. First, all the countries that have segregated educational systems are Eastern Orthodox countries. Unlike the Roman Catholic Church, Orthodox Churches have tended to be national churches and, as such, developed a special relationship with the state. Rather than running a parallel educational network, the Orthodox Church has made its influence felt in state-provided education through the state (a sign of the influence of the church can be found in the importance given to religious education in the state-provided sector). As a result, no tradition of separate faith schools developed in these countries. The non-governmental sector developed and was perceived as an (almost) exclusively commercial enterprise, and the state sees no reason to support it.

A sizable non-governmental but state-supported sector developed in particular in countries with a large Roman Catholic population (for example, the Netherlands, Belgium, France, Spain and Germany). Often, the existing arrangements came about after prolonged accommodation and protracted conflict between the state and the Catholic Church or the Calvinist Churches over the control of the educational system. As a result, faith schools have gained equal status as state-provided schools while maintaining their specific ethos. But because the state often refused to acknowledge a special position to any particular church, it extended the favourable status enjoyed by Catholic and Calvinist schools to the entire non-governmental sector.

A peculiar situation arose in Britain. Here, the church initially established its own schools but subsequently agreed to the state overtaking the financial and educational responsibilities for these schools. Consequently, faith schools have been integrated into state-provided schools; that is, they are financed almost in the same way as state-provided or municipal schools, but the church has retained considerable influence on the way these schools are run and continues to be represented on their boards. The overall result has been to accord a special position to faith schools within the educational system.

Decentralisation also encourages the emergence of favourable conditions for the funding of non-governmental schools, a situation that is typical of the Nordic countries. However, the decentralisation of the educational system does not mean that the central state can take a more unitary approach towards the various types of schools, thus making school ownership less irrelevant in an indirect way when it comes to the allocation of central funds.

The subsidisation of non-governmental schools by the state is, of course, only one side of the coin. In return for its financial support, the state has imposed and continues to impose various types of controls on schools and in the process has reduced school autonomy (for example, by setting a ceiling on the fees that may be charged). However, the most important way that the state may seek to control schools is through the educational process itself. As already mentioned, there are at least three ways by which the state can try to obtain some leverage, namely outlining a compulsory national curriculum, establishing national examinations (possibly as a precondition for certification) and by directly inspecting schools. Pooling all three aspects together yields a classification of countries based on school autonomy. Because prescribing educational content through a national curriculum is potentially the most intrusive way of exercising control, this dimension has been treated differently than the other two. Four categories have been constructed, which represent points along a continuum stretching from extensive school autonomy to strict school control:

(1) countries with significantly considerable school autonomy (only one of national testing or school inspection is used as a method of control): Belgium, Hungary, Germany and Sweden;

(2) countries with substantial school autonomy (both national examinations and school inspection are employed as methods of control): Denmark, Latvia, the Netherlands, Poland, Portugal, Slovakia, England and Wales and Scotland;
(3) countries with some school autonomy (a national curriculum exists along with either national testing or school inspection): Austria, Czech Republic, Estonia, Finland, Lithuania and Spain;
(4) countries with restricted school autonomy (all of the three control methods are present): France, Ireland, Luxembourg and Malta.

One thing that becomes immediately apparent is the interconnection between school autonomy (as defined above) and system centralisation. All countries in the group with the largest degree of school autonomy have decentralised educational systems, while all the countries in the group with the lowest level of school autonomy have centralised administration. The strong coupling of decentralisation with school autonomy points to a consistent pattern of central state involvement in the educational system. Countries that see education foremost as a state responsibility and domain for intervention tend to both directly administer the state-provided sector and limit the freedom of the non-governmental sector. The state tries to take direct charge of the system. On the contrary, countries that give more importance to non-governmental and local initiative allow both non-governmental entities and the local government more room to take decisions. In these countries, the state mainly plays the role of a facilitator and regulator.

Apart from decentralisation, school autonomy is also related to outcome of the state–church struggle. Countries in which the state succeeded in subduing the church (such as France) developed a setting that restricts further school autonomy within the national educational framework. In contrast, in countries where neither of the two parties achieved supremacy, a more flexible national framework was adopted allowing for more school autonomy within that framework (for example, Belgium and the Netherlands).

The school autonomy classification depicted above includes only countries, which make some kind of provision for public support of non-governmental schools. The four states that comprise the last category of the non-governmental sector subsidisation classification (that is, countries with no public funding available for non-governmental schools) have been intentionally omitted from the analysis. Since they do not shoulder any of the expenses incurred in the non-governmental sector, in principle, these four countries should have less of an incentive to restrict non-governmental schools' autonomy. Quite surprisingly, this expectation is not borne out. Two of them, Cyprus and Romania, have all three control measures in place, while the other two retain a national curriculum, and in the case of Bulgaria, quality inspection as well as tools to intervene within the non-governmental sector. However, a more careful reconsideration of the history of these four Orthodox nations underlines the prominent place that state agency has always held. Indeed, the strong centralisation of school administration in all four countries confirms the exceptional role of the state.

To conclude, current educational systems in Europe are very much a product of national historical developments. Past contingencies have created specific equilibria that retain a lingering influence on the way the educational system is organised and educational instruction structured. Both public support for the non-governmental sector and the various degrees of embedded school autonomy can be traced back to state formation processes, such as the emergence of a conflict for supremacy between the state and the (Catholic) church, the outcome of this conflict and, more generally, the role that the state assumed in shaping society.

**School choice and the market orientation on schools**

Since the '70s of the last century neo-liberalism and libertarianism started the current debate about school choice and the market orientation on schools. The position of the non-governmental schools in England and its former colonies has always been quite different from that of those in continental Europe. Archer (1984) has explained this Anglo-Saxon deviation by its stronger confidence on the market to organise and finance schools, which resulted in a relatively large non-governmental-independent school sector. Therefore, parental choice and non-governmental schools are often advocated in Anglo-Saxon countries as a means of introducing competition for pupils among schools and decreasing the level of bureaucracy, thereby improving the quality of teaching and reducing the cost of education (Chubb and Moe 1990). The introduction of charter schools in the USA (non-governmental, non-religious schools, but funded under certain conditions by the states) can be interpreted as a consequence of the growth of neo-liberalism and a market orientation on schools.

Another argument used in libertarianism, which is much stronger in the USA as a political stream, states that schools should offer young people an education that is in accordance with the way of life of their parents. This latter line of reasoning comes closer to the European tradition of government-dependent religious schools (Godwin and Kemerer 2002).

The growth of neo-liberalism and a market orientation on schools in the USA since the '90s influenced the discourse and policies on the relation between governmental and non-governmental schools in Europe. This influence was strongest in the UK and Scandinavia, where fully subsidised non-governmental schools were rare. But also in countries like Belgium, Germany, France and the Netherlands, these neo-liberal and market arguments became stronger and partly replaced the older religious arguments for the existence and subsidising of non-governmental religious schools. The latter was also necessary because the high level of secularisation and non-membership of churches in Europe (Bruce 2002; Davie 2002) made the religious arguments for non-governmental religious schools partly outdated. Yet, it is also possible that, as a consequence of this secularisation, religious schools are no longer keen on or successful in forcefully moulding the attitudes and beliefs of the students attending it. If religious schools are not able or willing to alter (in comparison with governmental schools) these attitudes and values of their pupils, the confessional character of a school becomes irrelevant for irreligious parents. These irreligious parents would be able to select a religious school based on their superior effectiveness in delivering academic performance and not be concerned by a potential religious, moral or values conversion of their children. This might explain the continuous existence of religious schools in a secularised and irreligious Europe (see Merry 2014).

However, migration towards the European Union since the '60s resulted also in the growth of non-Christian religions in Europe, notably Islam and Hinduism. Adherents of these non-Christian religions started to claim the same right to subsidies of non-governmental Islamic or Hindu schools, and they have been successful in a few European countries (for instance the Netherlands) in establishing these Islamic or Hindu schools within the framework of the national educational laws. One of the related debates is whether the existence of Islamic or Hindu schools is a hindrance to the integration or assimilation of these children of migrants and whether these Islamic or Hindu schools have a higher added value than governmental schools for educational performance (Driessen 2007; Driessen and Merry 2006).

This combination of religious and neo-liberal arguments for subsidised non-governmental religious schools and the additional migration controversy makes these European cross-national comparisons also relevant for the USA, not only for debates around the charter schools as a form of non-governmental subsidised non-religious schools, but also for the legal battles around funding non-governmental religious schools, and the societal consequences of the introduction of non-governmental school in immigrant societies like the USA.

## Patterns of non-governmental or governmental school choice processes[4]

State legislation can facilitate or, on the contrary, impede the development of the non-governmental sector in general and of faith schools in particular. But the ability of faith schools to secure a firm foothold hinges on whether parents choose to send their children to non-governmental schools instead of state ones. So the question arises as to how this choice regarding the decision between state and non-governmental schools is made.[5] More specifically, who are the parents who are more likely to send their offspring to non-governmental schools and what are the characteristics of the schools that are most successful in attracting students? Unfortunately, no comprehensive cross-national data exist on attendance of state-provided versus faith schools at the primary level. Nonetheless, a valuable insight into school choice processes can be gained from the PISA, developed by the OECD. It not only collects cross-nationally comparable information on student achievement and skills among 15-year-olds, but also contains rich data on student and school background.

The PISA survey does not distinguish between faith and non-faith schools. However, it does provide information on both school boards and funding. While the exact details vary, most countries allow faith schools to be run autonomously from the public system and make available substantial public funds for them, often on a par with public establishments. Consequently, we have opted to use the government-dependent category as an indicator for faith schools. Although a reasonable assumption, it has to be kept in mind that the overlap between the two categories is not perfect. In particular, some non-governmental-dependent schools are not affiliated with religious organisations, as freedom of establishment is a right enshrined in the constitution in countries such as the Netherlands, permitting a wider range of organisations to establish their own school networks. For instance, there exist in Dutch non-governmental primary education six non-religious school sectors (for instance anthroposophy), eight Christian religion school sectors (for instance Catholic and various protestant orthodoxies) and three non-Christian school sectors (for instance Hindu and Islamic). Thus non-governmental schools are not equal to religious schools in the Netherlands. Although the Netherlands is an extreme case, and the degree of overlap between religious schools and non-government-dependent schools is likely to be much higher in other European countries, it might be different across countries.

Based on existing literature comparing non-governmental and governmental schools, as well as on the availability of comparable data in the three waves of PISA, a variety of family and school characteristics that are likely to influence school choice by parents are been included. Gender, immigrant status, cultural possessions (like books, painting, own desk), wealth, both maternal and paternal education and occupational status have been incorporated to account for family background variation in the population of non-governmental and state schools. The school's social composition (the percentage of students having at least one parent with a university degree), size, admission policies (whether it considers parental endorsement of the school's educational philosophy and attendance of its special programmes as criteria when admitting students) as well as variables related to the school's resources, namely student–teacher ratios, computer–student ratios and a composite index of educational resources, have been considered as potential factors influencing school choice on the school side. Finally, to gauge the potential deterrent effect that financial costs of attending a school might have, a variable on whether the school charges tuition fees has been included.

We found that two roughly equal groups of choice patterns in the choice of a non-governmental-dependent school over a state-provided one can be discerned. The first group contains Belgium, Hungary, Italy, the Netherlands, Portugal, Slovakia and Spain. The second group is made up of Austria, the Czech Republic, Denmark, Finland, Ireland, Germany, Luxembourg and Sweden. In the first group, non-governmental-dependent schools appear to be chosen more for their *specific school philosophy* and less for their favourable student composition. The parental background of their student body is mixed, including both working-/lower middle-class parents and immigrants alongside middle-class families. In the second group, non-governmental-dependent schools tend to educate students from *families with the most financial resources*. They also tend to be smaller and have lower student–teacher ratios. Girls are more likely to be sent to non-governmental-dependent schools in these countries. Maternal and/or paternal high occupational statuses along with cultural capital also increase the chances of attending a non-governmental-dependent school instead of a state-provided one. Higher social class together with enhanced resources seem to constitute the prevailing reason for choice of non-governmental-dependent schools in the second group of countries, with these schools tending to cater especially to children of upper-class professionals.

We also found that two roughly equal groups of choice patterns in the choice of a non-governmental-independent school over a state-provided one can be discerned. The first group consists of Austria, Switzerland, Italy, Greece and the UK. Non-governmental-independent schools in these countries are chosen by native-language-speaking pupils from more wealthy families who choose non-governmental-independent schools for their high socioeconomic school composition and the special programmes of these schools. One might characterise the non-governmental-independent school choice in these countries as a *social class reproduction choice*. The second group contains Belgium, Portugal and Spain. Non-governmental-independent schools in these countries are chosen by foreign-language-speaking pupils from less wealthy families who choose schools with many material resources. One might characterise the non-governmental-independent school choice in these countries as *an outsider's choice for a well-equipped school*.

As we have seen above, the school philosophy or a well-equipped school, next to social composition and social reproduction, is important for the choice of public and non-governmental schools (dependent or independent). Therefore, it is important to investigate whether the cognitive and non-cognitive performance of pupils at non-governmental schools differs, and to what extent these differences in cognitive and non-cognitive performance are related to the social composition of these schools.

## Performance of non-governmental schools: cognitive outcomes

The results we present in this section are based on a precise and restricted comparison, using propensity score matching analysis. We only compare pupils who have a comparable chance to attend a non-governmental-dependent or a governmental school. We omit those pupils in non-governmental-dependent schools who have no comparable match among pupils in governmental schools. This leads to the loss of quite a large number of pupils in the sample, particularly in countries where the non-governmental-dependent sector is small or obviously skewed towards better-off families. The big advantage of this precise and restricted comparison is that it provides a fairly better proof of eventual different outcomes between dependent, independent and governmental schools.

If we do not take into account the comparability of dependent and governmental schools, we would find that the pupils of non-governmental-dependent schools in Austria, Belgium, Germany, Hungary, Ireland, Norway, Slovakia, Spain, Sweden and Switzerland have higher reading scores on average, and that pupils of non-governmental-dependent schools in Italy and Luxembourg score significantly lower compared to those in governmental schools. However, if we would only select those pupils who have a comparable chance to attend a non-governmental-dependent or a governmental school, and match each pupil attending a non-governmental-dependent school to another pupil with a similar chance but attending a governmental school, the only significant positive differences in the reading score between pupils of non-governmental-dependent schools and governmental schools are still found in Belgium, the Czech Republic, Germany, Hungary, Ireland, the Netherlands and Portugal. Pupils of non-governmental-dependent schools in Austria score significantly lower than their counterparts in governmental schools.

We apply the same procedure of a precise and restricted comparison to independent schools. Given the school choice selectivity discussed earlier, it is no surprise that pupils of non-governmental-independent schools in nearly all countries have higher readings scores on average (except Switzerland). But if we apply the same comparison, we find only significant positive differences in the average reading score of pupils attending non-governmental-independent and governmental schools in Belgium and Greece, and pupils of non-governmental-independent schools in Switzerland score significantly lower than their counterparts in governmental schools. In the remaining countries, the differences in the reading score between pupils of non-governmental-independent schools and those of governmental schools are no longer statistically significant.

## Performance of non-governmental schools: values and attitudes as non-cognitive outcomes[6]

Hitherto, especially in the European context, an important aspect of legitimacy of religious schools is not related to any academic superiority but to producing positive outcomes, like certain (religious) values and desirable attitudes towards life and the world. Religious schooling, with its deep historical roots, makes up an important part of European educational systems (especially in the Western and Central parts of the continent). Given its specificity, religious schooling can be expected to place a greater weight on values teaching and moral education. Churches themselves played an overwhelmingly important role in norms and tradition preservation and transmission in the ancient regime (before the French Revolution); although diminished, it still retains this function nowadays. As such, it may be more effective in bringing about certain attitudes and opinions. It also may be more successful in creating a warm and caring atmosphere, thus helping students to better emotionally connect to the school community.

However, differences in non-cognitive achievements are not found in most national studies. This contradicts the raison d'être of state-funded religious schools, because the right of parents to determine the moral and religious education of their children always has been more or less explicitly the basis of state recognition and funding of religious schools. But the higher cognitive effectiveness of state-funded religious schools also contradicts this raison d'être of religious schools, which maintain throughout that they do not want to compete with state schools for better academic outcomes. As a consequence, most state-funded religious schools and their organisations in various European societies tend to deny any higher cognitive effectiveness and try to avoid any research in that direction. Also state schools and their organisations tend to avoid research on their lower cognitive effectiveness in order to avoid embarrassment and political defeat by religious organisations, with which they have struggled so long for hegemony. This avoidance of political difficulties and embarrassment around a politically sensitive topic can explain why the research on effectiveness of public and state-funded non-governmental schools in Europe is not as extensive as one might expect given the disproportionate size of and the current increase in the state-funded school sector in various European countries. To show the problems around non-cognitive outcomes, we analyse non-cognitive outcomes by making use of three waves of data collected in the framework of the PISA study.

More specifically, public and publicly supported non-governmental (as our proxy for religious) schools have been compared on two dimensions, the emotional integration with the rest of the school community, as reported by students,[7] and the concern and feelings of responsibility towards the environment.[8] In the first case, except for Austria, Belgium and Spain, no evidence could be found that the type of the school has any impact on the reported psychological adaptation to the school. In these three countries, publicly supported non-governmental schools tend to be more successful in integrating their students. In the latter case, students in public and non-governmental-dependent schools were equally environment oriented, taking into account several student and school characteristics. Thus, whereas differences in emotional integration between non-governmental and governmental schools are only found in three countries, differences between non-governmental and governmental schools in environmental responsibility are not found.

The lack of schooling-sector differences in attaining non-cognitive aims (psychological well-being/integration, environment preservation) may have at least three causes. First, ecological issues could be salient enough not to necessitate any special religious or moral reinforcement in order to gain traction. They are, in fact, among the few examples where a strong public consensus exists on the desirable course of action. Second, governmental schools may use religious education or ethics just as fruitfully and consequently they are just as successful in values and norms transmission. In fact, a variant of moral, civic or ethics education is always present in the official curricula for public secondary education in all countries. Further research is needed to probe into these hypotheses.

It should be kept in mind that we only analyse one normative dimension, namely concern and willingness to protect the environment. This debate is a fairly recent one in which the Christian churches have only just begun to take part. Religious and governmental schools may foster much more contrasting attitudes in more traditional areas such as gender roles, abortion, euthanasia, tolerance and respect for diversity and one's fellows and so forth. Yet, it is also possible that confessional education is no longer keen on or successful in forcefully moulding the attitudes and beliefs of the students attending it. If such were the case, the lack of school sector differences on non-cognitive dimensions could shed light on the mechanisms behind the success of religious schools in secularised societies. If religious schools are not able to alter the attitudes and values of their pupils, their confessional character could be irrelevant for irreligious parents. If parents are interested in cognitive skill development, they would be able to select a religious school based on their superior effectiveness in delivering academic performance and not be concerned by a potential religious, moral or values conversion of their children. For the moment, such a mechanism remains a hypothesis. Further research is needed to probe into the ways non-governmental school characteristics are intertwined with parental school preferences.

## Conclusions

Using comparable cross-national data for all member states of the European Union, we first described four existing basic arrangements of non-governmental and governmental schools. Then we explore three other topics: parental background and the choice of non-governmental schools, non-governmental schools and their cognitive outcomes, and non-governmental schools and their non-cognitive outcomes. Most of the debates and research on non-governmental religious schools follow strictly the lines of the national states and thus tend to overemphasise the uniqueness of the national religious schools, and underscore the more general trends in the functioning of religious non-governmental schools and school choice in secular Europe. By comparing all European countries, we can see that the religious schools of the selected countries are not unique cases, and we make the more general trends in the functioning of religious non-governmental schools and school choice in secular Europe visible.

We summarise first the most important points of this cross-national comparison of school choice and performance of governmental and non-governmental schools.

The first point is the importance of the distinction between non-governmental-independent and non-governmental-dependent schools, next to governmental schools. Lumping non-governmental-independent and non-governmental-dependent schools together into one category as 'market-driven' schools is misleading (Vandenberghe and Robin 2004). That would underestimate the seriousness of the restrictions, which go with the state grants in most countries and ignore the still powerful history of the struggle between the state and the church. This distinction between non-governmental-independent and non-governmental-dependent schools might have different names in different countries, but that does not mean that they function differently. On the other hand, the same name in different countries does not necessarily mean that their function is equal.

The second point is that school choice and subsidised (faith) non-governmental schools are widespread phenomena in European countries, although not always visible like in France where the image of a dominant governmental school sector is wearing thin. However, there is a large variation in the relations between countries' religiosity and the existence of subsidised faith schools, caused by the historical path dependency in the different countries. As a consequence, there are different arrangements and patters of these relations in the different European states.

The choice of non-governmental schools seems driven not only by parental class and inequality. The choice of non-governmental-dependent schools seems more related with parents who are or wish to be socially mobile. On the other hand, the choice of non-governmental-independent schools seems to be more related to the intergenerational reproduction of existing inequalities.

Non-governmental-dependent schools are more effective cognitively than governmental schools, but not in all countries. In a few countries, non-governmental-dependent schools are less effective than governmental schools, and in the remaining countries, they are as effective cognitively as governmental schools. Non-governmental-independent schools are more effective cognitively than governmental schools in only a few countries and more ineffective in a comparable small number of countries. In the remaining countries, they are as effective cognitively as governmental schools.

The main argument for religious schools in the nineteenth and the first part of the twentieth centuries has been the assumption that faith schools would socialise the pupils in the religious values and attitudes better than governmental schools could. Therefore, parents had the right to send their children to subsided faith schools in order to ensure the socialisation of their children by the school in the values and attitudes of their religion (non-cognitive performance of schools). However, non-governmental-dependent schools (of which the majority are faith schools) are not more effective non-cognitively than governmental schools. This contradicts the raison d'être of state-funded religious schools, because the right of parents to determine the moral and religious socialisation of their children always has been more or less explicitly the basis of state funding of religious schools. This ineffectiveness of non-governmental-dependent schools in the non-cognitive domain is compensated by the larger effectiveness of non-governmental-dependent schools in the cognitive domain. The latter might be a good explanation for the survival and even growth of faith schools in a secular European Union.

**Notes**
1. This omission of the religious background is not unique for education. In a cross-national data-set on fertility from the late '90s (Family & Fertility Survey, collected by the United Nations Economic Commission for Europe), there was no question about the religious background of the surveyed women, although it is generally acknowledged that religion relates with fertility.
2. Financed by the European Commision within the seventh Frame Work (FP7-SSH-2007-1-REMC).
3. In this and the next section, we used extensively Avram and Dronkers (2013).
4. In this and the next section, we used extensively Avram and Dronkers (2012) and Dronkers and Avram (2010a, 2010b).
5. It goes without saying that governmental and non-governmental schools are not the only or the most important school characteristic that parents will consider when they have to choose a school.
6. In this section, we use extensively Avram and Dronkers (2011).
7. The index of the items – my school is a place where: I feel like an outsider, I make friends easily, I feel like I belong, I feel awkward and out of place, other students seem to like me, I feel lonely.
8. The index of items like: do you see the environmental issues below as a serious concern for yourself and/or others? Air pollution, energy shortages, extinction of plants and animals, clearing of forests for other land use, water shortages and nuclear waste.

## References

Archer, M. S. 1984. *Social Origins of Educational Systems*. London: Sage.
Avram, S., and J. Dronkers. 2011. "School Sector Variation on Non-cognitive Dimensions: Are Non-public but Publicly Supported More Effective?" *Educational Research and Evaluation* 17 (2): 115–139.
Avram, S., and J. Dronkers. 2012. "Social Class Dimensions in the Selection of Non-governmental schools: A Cross-National Analysis using PISA." In *Non-governmental Schulen in Deutschland. Entwicklungen, Profile, Kontroversen*, edited by H. Ullrich and S. Strunck, 201–223. Wiesbaden: Springer VS.
Avram, S., and J. Dronkers. 2013. "Religion and Schooling: the European Context." In *Religious Education in a Multicultural Europe: Children, Parents and Schools*, edited by E. Smith, M. Lyons and M. Darmody, 15–36. Houndmills: Palgrave Macmillan.
Bruce, S. 2002. *God is Dead: Secularization in the West*. Oxford: Blackwell.
Chubb, J. E., and T. M. Moe. 1990. *Politics, Markets and America's Schools*. Washington, DC: Brookings Institution Press.
Davie, G. 2002. *Europe: The Exceptional Case*. London: Darton, Longmann and Todd.
Driessen, G. 2007. *Opbrengsten van islamitische basisscholen. Prestaties, attitudes en gedrag van leerlingen op islamitische scholen vergeleken*. Nijmegen: ITS.
Driessen, G., and M. Merry. 2006. "Islamic Schools in the Netherlands: Expansion or Marginalization?" *Interchange* 37 (3): 201–223.
Dronkers, J., and S. Avram. 2010a. "A Cross-national Analysis of the Relations of School Choice and Effectiveness Differences between Non-governmental-dependent and Governmental Schools." *Educational Research and Evaluation* 16 (2): 151–175.
Dronkers, J., and S. Avram. 2010b. "A Cross-national Analysis of the Relations of School Choice and Effectiveness Differences between Non-governmental-independent and Governmental Schools." *Sociological Theory and Methods* 25 (2): 183–206.
Glenn, C. L., and J. de Groof. 2002. *Finding the Right Balance. Freedom, Autonomy and Accountability in Education*. Utrecht: Lemma Publishers.
Godwin, R. K., and F. R. Kemerer. 2002. *School Choice Tradeoffs. Liberty, Equity, and Diversity*. Austin: University of Texas Press.
Maussen, M., and V. Bader. 2015. "Non-Governmental Religious Schools in Europe: Institutional Opportunities, Associational Freedoms, and Contemporary Challenges." *Comparative Education* 51 (1): 1–21.
Smyth, E., M. Lyons, and M. Darmody, eds. 2013. *Religious Education in a Multicultural Europe. Children, Parents and Schools*. Houndsmills: Palgrave Macmillan.
Vandenberghe, V., and S. Robin. 2004. "Evaluating the Effectiveness of Private Education across Countries: A Comparison of Methods." *Labour Economics* 11 (4): 487–506.
Wolf, P. J., and S. Macedo. 2004. *Educating Citizens. International Perspectives on Civic Values and School Choice*. Washington, DC: Brookings Institution Press.

# The conundrum of religious schools in twenty-first-century Europe

Michael S. Merry

*Department of Educational Sciences and Department of Philosophy, University of Amsterdam, Amsterdam, Netherlands*

> In this paper Merry examines in detail the continued – and curious – popularity of religious schools in an otherwise 'secular' twenty-first century Europe. To do this he considers a number of motivations underwriting the decision to place one's child in a religious school and delineates what are likely the best empirically supported explanations for the continued dominant position of Protestant and Catholic schools. He then argues that institutional racism is an explanatory variable that empirical researchers typically avoid, though it informs both parental assessments of school quality as well as selective mechanisms many mainstream religious schools use to function as domains of exclusion. He then distinguishes between religious schools in a dominant position from those serving disadvantaged minorities and argues that the latter are able to play a crucially important function other schools only rarely provide and hence that vulnerable minorities may have reason to value.

Many contributions in this issue have discussed the historical development, state support and perceived legitimacy of religious schools in Europe, each of them focussing in detail on variations of education policy in different national contexts. Implicitly or explicitly, different authors also have tried to answer this question: *why do religious schools continue to garner the support that they do in twenty-first-century Europe?* Why indeed. With few exceptions such as France (Pons, van Zanten, and Da Costa 2015), the market share of religious schools in Europe has remained largely unchanged over the last 45 years, and in at least one country – Germany (Scheunpflug 2015) – the demand for religious schools appears to have *increased*. Given what many consider to be an inexorable 'secularisation' trend across Europe (Berger 1967; Bruce 2002),[1] what are we to make of these seemingly inexplicable trends?

To try and answer this question, empirical studies on religious schools in Europe typically focus on fairly uncontroversial institutional features, such as core objectives. Or, concerning parental motives for selecting religious schools, studies usually report explicitly observed and reported – and hence measurable – characteristics and responses. However, I would argue that the existing empirical research does not tell us all that we need to know. But that fact should not stop us from reasoned speculation. Thus given the unfortunate lacunae in the empirical literature, some of what I will argue will be couched in terms of warranted conjecture, both as this concerns the reasons why religious schools remain as popular as they do as well as what I think are reasonable grounds to support and defend religious schools serving marginalised groups likely to suffer a far worse fate in another school environment. My aim in this paper, then, will not be to recapitulate or synthesise what others have said, but rather to argue that there are other – often well hidden and non-quantifiable – variables relevant to our question than what we presently may 'know'.

The structure of the paper is as follows. In order to sketch the background for what is to come, in Section 1, I dispute the notion of a 'secularised' Europe, and then summarise a number of recent policy-related developments related to religious schools, as well as several criticisms directed against them. Then, to see why religious schools continue to enjoy such a dominant market share, in Section 2, I examine a number of motivations underwriting the decision to place one's child in a religious school and delineate what I think are likely the best empirically supported explanations for the continued dominant position of Protestant and Catholic schools in twenty-first-century Europe. In Section 3, I hypothesise that institutional racism informs both parental assessments of school quality as well as selective mechanisms many mainstream religious schools use in order to function as domains of exclusion. Finally in Section 4, I distinguish between religious schools in a dominant position from those serving disadvantaged minorities. I argue that the latter are able to play a crucially important function other schools only rarely provide and hence that vulnerable minorities may have reason to value. I then sketch the outlines of a circumscribed case for what I will call 'voluntary separation'.

## *Religion in Europe*

A traveller moving through Europe is likely to be confronted with evidence on all sides of religion in decline: empty cathedrals and just as nearly empty parish churches, many of which now serve as museums, or which have long been annexed by universities or local authorities to house art exhibits or to facilitate a variety of other municipal functions. Even when churches are still used to exhibit religious art, much of the time they serve merely to enchant a secular public intrigued with exotic relics from the past. Indeed religion in Europe seems marked chiefly by its absence. It would therefore be understandable if this same traveller was to find the persistence of *religious schooling* in Europe to be something of a conundrum. It is a conundrum, she might say, because so few Europeans count themselves as religious, and so many Protestant and Catholic schools no longer explicitly serve to propagate religious teaching (Casanova 2006; Pickel 2009). Having lost their divinely inspired raison d'être, they exist merely as artefacts, something that in due time will pass away.

Many people doubtless hold this view, and there is much evidence – as many of the authors in this issue have demonstrated – to suggest that the importance of religion in Europe has indeed dramatically decreased. Yet while it certainly is true that far fewer indigenous Europeans profess to be religious, or that mainstream Protestant and Catholic institutions do not wield the power they once did, or even that explicit references to religion in politics are rare, it would be a non-sequitur to claim that religion has ceased to matter to individuals, let alone that it has ceased to play a significant cultural and political role. Indeed, as Maussen and Bader (2015) articulate in their opening essay, that view would betray too casual an understanding of religion as an important social and political rallying force in Europe. At least three reasons are apposite.

First, Christianity continues to enjoy unrivalled status as the dominant religion and numerous institutions remain assiduously Christian: Christian universities, hospitals, schools and even churches often receive generous support from the state; virtually every European country has a Christian political party – often in the majority – and in some countries, there are more than one (in the Netherlands, for instance, there are three prominent Christian parties that punch above their weight); multiple countries bear Christian crosses on their national flags; Christian holidays of all sorts (e.g. Good Friday, Pentecost, Ascension Day and Easter) are public holidays in many countries, even when most of the public is unlikely to know or understand the religious significance of these occasions to the devout. These and other phenomena are so ubiquitous as to go virtually unnoticed by the larger 'secular' public.

Second, we are unable to deduce anything reliably true about religiosity from available figures on institutional membership. Indeed, it would be mistaken to infer much at all about the religiosity of persons from how frequently they attend the local temple, mosque, church or synagogue. While it is true that large numbers of Europeans now report having no religion at all, or no longer belong to a church, alternative spiritualities among Europeans are well known.[2] Indeed, sociologist Peter Baldwin has observed, 'In the most secular nations [of Europe] there seems to be a belief in some higher power that is not captured by a simple question on a survey about faith in God' (Baldwin 2009, 169; cf. Pickel 2009).

Third, there continues to be a cultural narrative that implicitly (and sometimes explicitly) draws upon the notion of a 'Christian Europe'. Perhaps nowhere is this more in evidence than in the populist – and unabashedly racist – rhetoric that has swept the European continent in the past quarter century. Indeed, many clearly believe Europe's 'norms and values' to be currently *under threat.* Invoking a 'Judeo-Christian' culture as the foundation of Europe, this quasi-religious account separating the indigenous from the non-indigenous resonates with, and easily galvanises, a large public unable to come to terms with the sizable presence of non-Western, and not incidentally, non-Christian, others.[3] And the cultural nexus with state-supported education is a seamless one, for until relatively late in the twentieth century even public schools continued to operate as de facto denominational schools owing to the dominance of Christianity as a cultural force.[4] The upshot is that institutionalised Christianity remains deeply embedded both in the European identity and also in its cultural and educational traditions.

## *Recent developments in education*

Several significant changes in Europe have occurred – to greater or lesser degrees depending on the location in question – since the early 1970s and many of these changes have impacted education. First, with the massive influx of ethnic and religious minorities after the second World War and in particular from the mid-1960s onwards, states have struggled to come to terms with what it means to 'accommodate' this new diversity. Official recognition of the 'new religions' began in the early 1970s and by the 1980s, there were halting attempts in many countries to include – somewhat tokenistic – changes to the curriculum in a feeble effort to 'recognise' the large presence of minority children in schools. In some places, there even was some (modest) attempt to offer religious instruction for non-Christian faiths, notably Islam.[5]

Second, by the late 1980s, there was a gradual realisation that migrant (and principally Muslim) populations had more or less permanently settled in their host countries. By the end of the decade, some European countries had witnessed the establishment of the first state-supported Islamic and Hindu schools. Concurrent with these developments came the rapid rise of far-right populist political parties with an openly anti-immigrant – and, more often than not, anti-Muslim – message. Often couched in terms of a 'culture clash' or a concern about 'social cohesion', these political parties stoked latent anti-immigrant and racist sentiment and galvanised support from a public unnerved by dramatic demographic changes coinciding with a sluggish economy. Though immigrant policies had already begun to change in the 1990s, it was particularly following the New York City attacks of 9/11 that demands of 'integration' became increasingly strident. Anti-immigrant populism across the continent and in the UK gained an ever-expanding support base for their racist rhetoric, even in countries such as Sweden and the Netherlands where this previously had been (publicly) taboo. From mainstream politicians, too, there was a new urgency to the 'politics of integration', and outspoken concerns about segregated minority groups became common place. Notably, as several papers in this issue have already shown, religious schools serving minority groups – especially Islamic schools – were singled out for condemnation as evidence for a 'failure to integrate' (Maussen and Bader 2015; Merry 2007a; Olsen 2015).

Finally, a series of neo-liberal reforms began to take hold in the early 1990s that would alter how school systems in most European countries worked. Many of these reforms were framed as increasing parental choice and school autonomy. Indeed, attempts were made to 'devolve' the chain of authority to the local level as much as possible. At the same time, however, stricter top-down directives began to gather steam. Parallel with these reforms was a new kind of school competition taking root in which, partly because of the emergence of published school quality ranking lists, but also better educated and media savvy parents (capable of navigating a confusing array of school options as well as ensuring that their children would have the transportation necessary to reach those schools), began more actively to seek out 'better' schools for their children. For their part, schools have responded to these developments by increasingly marketing themselves to parents, sometimes carving out a distinctive niche in order to set themselves apart from the fray (Ackerman 1997; James and Phillips 1995; Smedley 1995).

## *Criticisms of religious schools*

Each of foregoing developments has coalesced to create a very different kind of atmosphere in which religious schools in Europe operate. However, none of them has led to a decline in the religious school market share, even, as we have seen, when fewer persons profess to be religious. Yet as several contributions in this issue illustrate, religious schools have increasingly come under fire (Maussen and Vermeulen 2015; McKinney and Conroy 2015; Olsen 2015).

Criticisms of religious schools have circulated for decades, but as inter alia Maussen & Bader demonstrate, because religious schools across Europe enjoy basic constitutional protections, these typically have focussed on issues of public financing, degrees of organisational and pedagogical autonomy, and educational practices and management. But there are other criticisms. By far the criticism most frequently registered by sceptics and secular philosophers is that religious schools serve to indoctrinate young children. Here the worry is that faith-based instruction functions as a substitute for critical thinking and as such undermines a child's capacity for autonomous decision-making (Dwyer 1998; Hand 2002; Merry 2005a). A second criticism, one that is more likely to focus exclusively on the recent expansion of Islamic schools in Europe, is that they serve to promote extremism. Here the worry is that Islamic schools harbour young Muslim children away from mainstream thinking, instil anti-Western dispositions generally, and sexist and homophobic attitudes more specifically. A third criticism is that funding religious schools violates state neutrality. Here the concern is that in doing so the state exhibits favouritism towards the dominant religion on the one hand, and unwisely endorses sectarian doctrines on the other. A fourth criticism is that minority religious schools instantiate segregation; as such they co-conspire with parents in keeping minority children separate from their mainstream counterparts and the norms and values of the dominant society. Hence, the argument runs, these children are denied opportunities to cultivate attitudes and skills necessary for participation in a democratic society.

I postpone my treatment of the last criticism until later in the paper because it deserves more attention. Conversely, in the following paragraphs I will dispense with the first three criticisms rather quickly, not because they are trivial concerns but because, in the first two cases, the empirical evidence for these claims is extremely weak, and with respect to the third claim, the criticism rests upon a needlessly restrictive reading of state neutrality.

With respect to indoctrination, several things tell against this. First, outside of the British context, which has a large independent sector, most full-time religious schools are *state funded and supervised,* notwithstanding different funding and supervisory schemes in each country. Hence Western European states have made good on their constitutional guarantees vis-à-vis educational liberty by incorporating religious schools into their institutional structures. Even where religious schools are given some latitude in determining *how* they meet their learning targets (e.g. the Netherlands), governmental ministries of education still largely determine what they are, which subjects schools must teach, teacher certification requirements, the language of instruction and also how much instruction time can be spent on religion. These quality standards, combined with an absence of a strong religious ethos in a large percentage of mainstream Protestant and Catholic schools, mean that worries about indoctrination in most European state-funded schools are almost certainly exaggerated.

With respect to the claim that extremism is being taught in Islamic schools on the European continent, this allegation has repeatedly yielded no solid evidence (Merry & Driessen, forthcoming). In contrast to what may be said of certain mosques, there is in fact no evidence of 'home-grown' terrorism in Europe being linked to state-funded Islamic schools. Analogous to worries about indoctrination, state-supported religious schools across Europe have their mandates issued by the respective governments and precious little time is actually allocated for explicit religious instruction. In any case, feelings of isolation and alienation conducive to extremist attitudes arguably are more likely to occur in environments – educational or otherwise – where persons feel stigmatised and socially excluded, something, as we shall see, less likely to be the case for Muslim children in an Islamic school. Indeed, extremist religious perspectives are far more likely to be fostered in non-regulated environments, such as weekend Qur'anic instruction or in salafist chatrooms (Becker 2009; Boyle 2004).

What can be said about the claim that funding religious schools violates state neutrality? First, as many of the papers in this issue also have shown, in all liberal-democratic societies, and certainly in all European countries, there are constitutional guarantees to choose a school for one's child in conformity with one's conscience, and a majority of European states have ensured that religious schools are among the available choices. Of course, funding religious schools does not logically follow from this; it could be argued (and often is, for example, in the USA) that the state should remain 'neutral' by *not* directly supporting religious causes.[6]

But it is far from obvious whether the best way to demonstrate 'neutrality' is to pull back from supporting religious schools. One can be faithful to the principle of neutrality, for instance, by *expanding* recognition, not by restricting it (Bader 2007; Laborde 2002, 2008; Merry 2007b). First, doing so demonstrates equal concern for the quality of education all children receive irrespective of the type of school they attend. Second, doing so demonstrates equality of recognition, both in facilitating parental choice and, more controversially, in assisting with (marginalised) group self-determination. Third, doing so is more likely to strengthen the case for legitimacy, for if we proceed with a robust notion of democratic equality, then an *inclusionist* model arguably will be more legitimate than a model that excludes. In short, educational choices that include religious options are more likely to reflect the ideals of a liberal-democratic society, certainly when both pluralism and voluntary association play a central normative role.

Of course even in school systems offering a variety of educational options, constitutional freedoms alone could not explain the persistent selection of *religious* schools, particularly, as we have seen, when a great number of religious schools no longer offer a distinctly religious ethos[7] and also when we have evidence to support the suspicion that these schools remain popular among decidedly non-religious parents. Therefore in the next section, I want to explore a number of voluntary and involuntary factors that may help us better understand the strong market share of religious schools. I frame this discussion against the background of neighbourhood and school segregation.

## Religious schools and segregation

Even when liberal-democratic societies endorse normative ideals like pluralism and voluntary association, the reasons for selecting *religious* schools in such high numbers do not appear to make sense. What we need is an account of the reasons for selecting religious schools at rates more or less equivalent to 40 or 50 years ago, when church attendance levels were still quite high. In the following paragraphs I delineate a variety of plausible explanations. Several of these are well supported in the empirical literature, while others are less explicitly identified. However, this is where I think we are justified in looking to a large empirical literature on segregation for clues to other explanations. And it is appropriate that we look at this literature, for segregation is one of the predictable consequences of 'school choice', and religious schools importantly count among the favourite choices. As the literature in Europe grows (Bakker et al. 2011; Harris 2012; Karsten et al. 2006; Rougier and Honohan 2015), the findings mirror those elsewhere, namely that segregation indices (irrespective of the instruments sociologists use to measure this) are very high, and environments are often 'spatially concentrated' rather than 'spatially mixed' (For Dutch figures, see Ladd and Fiske 2009; Musterd and Oostendorf 2009; Vedder 2006). The reasons for this are of course complex. Both voluntary and involuntary mechanisms play a role.

## Voluntary factors

Voluntary mechanisms seem beguilingly simple. These include choices to live near, and socialise with, others like oneself. These choices can facilitate modes of identification and interaction on the basis of shared backgrounds, habits, interests and preferences. Here we recognise the elements of *voluntary association* and this has an effect both on where persons live and with whom they interact. Voluntary association also will have a strong effect on parents' motives for choosing a particular school for their child. Yet because neighbourhood patterns already reflect some form of voluntary association, parental motives may not require much intentionality at all but may simply indicate an 'obvious' choice owing to facts about where and how one is situated. Let us look at three motivations for selecting religious schools that are well supported in the empirical literature.

## *Location*

Though perhaps rather banal, locality plays a central role in school selection and hence the preference for religious schools for many parents largely comes down to a matter of convenience. In most European countries, the virtual omnipresence of denominational schools means that they effectively function as the school preference by default. Particularly when parents are largely responsible for transportation, and hectic schedules can prove a serious impediment to making different choices, the distance between home and school matters a great deal. In many communities, it is the local denominational school that meets this requirement. Because much of Europe shares a religiously segregated past, many neighbourhoods and their schools remain either Protestant or Catholic, even if in name only. However, so long as the school is perceived to be a part of the local community and the quality of the school is acceptable, for some parents choosing a religious school for this reason alone will suffice (Burgess et al. 2009; Denessen, Driessen, and Sleegers 2005).

## *Piety*

The second explanation also might go without saying, but we would be remiss to ignore explicitly religious motives. Devout parents wishing to reinforce their own religious worldview often consciously choose a religious school. In many European countries, a distinct minority of conservative Jewish, Christian and Islamic schools succeed in marketing themselves as an *alternative* to nominally religious schools. Devout Jews, Muslims, Catholics and Protestants (particularly of the Reformed and Evangelical variety) rank a school's authentic religious ethos high on the list of priorities. Religious schools catering to this market niche can make themselves more appealing to these parents by not only emphasising the centrality of faith (e.g. scripture reading, a weekly sermon, liturgical celebrations), but also in maintaining traditional practices (e.g. ritual cleansing, dress codes) that many religious parents have reason to value. Conservative religious schools will aim to incorporate religious doctrine in all subjects, including curricular items (e.g. how Darwinian evolution theory is handled in a biology class) that many believe are at loggerheads with their faith. Being able to select an *authentically* religious school[8] therefore becomes a marker of distinction.

## *Academic reputation*

Our third explanation for selecting religious schools concerns the academic reputation of the school. In their analysis of OECD data earlier in this issue, Dronkers and Avram maintain that there are different 'choice patterns' in Europe. They argue that higher social class, together with enhanced resources, seems to constitute the prevailing reason for choice of what they call 'non-governmental dependent schools' in a select group of countries, with these schools tending to cater especially to children of upper-class professionals (Dronkers and Avram 2015). Stating this more candidly, we might say that parents with greater social capital are likely to act similarly when selecting schools, and choosing schools that are able to offer one's own child something *distinguishable* from what 'other people's children' receive is a behaviour consistently documented in the sociology of education literature (Ball 2002; Brantlinger 2003, Holme 2002; Reay et al. 2007).

To ascertain a school's academic reputation, some parents may consult published test scores and school rankings or government inspection reports available on the Internet, but for most parents it is rather difficult to determine the quality of a particular school beyond a few obvious features (e.g., location and pupil composition). Hence parents are very likely either to fall back on word-of-mouth – and this means the opinions of others like oneself – or else by selecting the 'brand' of the school.[9] But whether a particular religious school actually succeeds in maintaining a good academic reputation may in fact depend less on what the school itself can provide and more on the fact that persons of similar social class background congregate together, as Dronkers and Avram suggest. The upshot is that a school's 'better' quality may in fact simply be a more homogenous school comprised of mostly middle-class children.

Now it is of course not always true that denominational schools offer a better quality education than the alternatives. School quality will in any case depend upon a variety of background variables. However, there is data to suggest that many religious schools are able to offer a better quality education and hence often outperform their non-confessional counterparts (Avram and Dronkers 2010; Driessen and Merry 2006; Merry and Driessen 2012). These studies point to the fact that many confessional schools facilitate favourable informal relations between school administration and teachers conducive to a better overall school climate (Hofman 1997). Consequently, they do a better job of maintaining strong leadership, smaller class size, stricter discipline and higher academic achievement. There are also criticisms of these studies, pointing for instance to the fact that religious schools often reserve the right to exercise some degree of selectivity with respect to both its hiring of teachers and its pupil intake. Although state-supported religious schools may not openly discriminate against pupils, they generally *are* able to refuse children with disabilities on the grounds that they do not have the appropriate facilities or staff, and they generally *are* able to expel pupils with behaviours that staff find difficult to manage.[10]

Readers conversant with the empirical literature on religious schools and religious education in Europe (and elsewhere) will be familiar with each of the foregoing explanations. However, in my view these and other empirically supported explanations do not tell the whole story. Indeed, as I aim to show, there arguably are other camouflaged factors; as a result they remain understudied and inadequately understood. In what follows I will argue that there are reasons for weighing other relevant factors rarely made explicit (and hence difficult to measure) but which nevertheless are germane to the continued popularity of particularly Protestant and Catholic schools in Europe.

**Involuntary factors**

The explanations discussed in the previous section all serve to illustrate an assortment of 'voluntary' parental motivations. But *involuntary* mechanisms also shape – often in profound ways – the choices that we all make. As we have seen, parents may choose a school on the basis of its location, but one's original location is rarely *chosen*. Neither are one's first language, social class, skin colour and religion, to take only a few examples. When combined with a limited selection of resources and opportunities, choices may become constrained. Even for the relatively privileged, acting on one's *first preferences* may not be an option. But for those who are significantly disadvantaged – and stigmatised[11] – the options often are far more severely restricted.

Certainly in the educational domain disadvantaged and stigmatised minorities rarely have the same options available to them as more advantaged members of the dominant group. I say more about this below. For now it will suffice to point out that in the European context, and particularly in mixed urban environments, demographic changes in Europe, particularly during the past forty years, have made previously existing patterns of segregation (e.g. along the lines of social class, race, ethnicity and religion) more *visible*.[12]

How does any of this bear upon our subject of religious schools? First, as we have seen, many religious schools, owing to their core values and expectations, have much less difficulty constructing and maintaining a cohesive school mission that will be attractive both to teachers and to parents who share them. Further, schools with a strong core mission and strong leadership often are able to produce virtues conducive to higher levels of teacher job satisfaction and pupil well-being. Core values such as respect, cooperation and self-discipline translate into better behaved pupils and higher morale within the school, and these generally will be less difficult to attain than in other schools where these are absent. We also can expect to see a strong correlation between these non-cognitive features and the cognitive outcomes of the pupils (Agirdag et al. 2012; Dijkstra, Dronkers, and Karsten 2004; Merry and Driessen, forthcoming). Second, in Europe's larger cities, a high percentage of non-confessional state schools are now majority–minority schools. That is, a majority of pupils attending 'urban' public schools[13] are now of non-Western background (read: non-white) and the achievement levels of these schools are often subpar relative to schools that have a more exclusive pupil intake. And here it is important to consider how Protestant and Catholic schools, even in majority–minority urban environments, often succeed in remaining overwhelmingly white.[14]

I examine this further below. Some of what I will argue remains speculative owing both to the paucity of empirical research and to the presence of social desirability bias. Yet I think the *absence* of explicit empirical support constitutes an even stronger reason to investigate this. Indeed, if my earlier conjecture is true, namely that parents may select religious schools for reasons other than piety, convenience and educational quality, then it certainly is not far-fetched to hypothesise that confessional schools in many European countries facilitate exclusion under the guise of religion.

## Religious schools and institutional racism

How might the involuntary and the voluntary converge in ways that produce more privilege for some and less for others? In addition to the reasons I canvassed earlier, there is evidence to suggest that Protestant and Catholic schools in Europe continue to operate in arguably 'discrete' ways that attract white parents in sufficiently high numbers so that the net effect is a homogeneous environment, i.e. a de facto white middle-class school (Ball 1994; Vedder 2006).[15] My conjectures here do not pertain to Protestant and Catholic schools per se, but rather to one of the functions they wittingly or unwittingly serve in mixed urban environments. But if and when schools also actively seek to attract and retain these parents through selective means, then religious schools effectively come to function as *domains of exclusion*.

Now even when religious schools no longer have a strong religious profile,[16] they nevertheless are able to serve an important comparable function. Indeed, there is a sense in which religion serves to bind persons together who share similar backgrounds. It has long been recognised that religion signifies a *mode of belonging* to a group and its way (s) of life, and religious schools can do this without imparting any theological content. Indeed, there is evidence to suggest that religious schools may partly serve this purpose for ethnic minorities as well (Merry and Driessen 2012). Less attention, however, has been paid to how religious schools may serve this same function for *majority* groups.

The point here is simply that religious schools need not be about dogma or belief but rather about *being with others whose backgrounds are similar and whose interests and preferences happily converge*. Religious schools may therefore facilitate social interactions and networks that supply meaning, membership, solidarity and purpose to their members. Hence parents may select a religious school not in order to inculcate religious teachings – indeed they may prefer that the school not be *too* religious – but rather to congregate with others with whom they share educational (and other) priorities in common, and doing so certainly satisfies what most of us understand voluntary association to entail. This all sounds harmless enough.

Yet by and large empirical researchers in Europe have neglected to study – or even speculate about – another side of the so-called 'religious school effect', namely the intersection between religious school selection, segregation and racism.[17] And so when we come to studies that examine whether there is a 'religious school effect' in Europe, these studies typically report only the motivations that parents *explicitly* express, and hence owing to social desirability bias[18] *and* implicit bias,[19] we unsurprisingly learn almost nothing about other – less admirable – motivations that *coincide* with voluntary association and contribute to religious school segregation. This is an odd omission given how endemic to Europe both segregation and racism are (Huggan and Law 2009; Lentin 2004; MacMaster 2001; Wieviorka 2010).

Racism need not take crude or obnoxious forms, such as is common in racist behaviour exhibited at European football matches towards black players. It also need not take the form of openly xenophobic remarks, such as those of Dutch parliamentarian Geert Wilders, who recently celebrated an electoral victory by inciting his supporters to demand that fewer Moroccans be allowed to live in the Netherlands.[20] Racism typically is more insidious than that. Given the stigma associated with being a 'racist' – indeed, few persons willingly espouse the label – I think 'institutional racism' best captures the sense in which I am using the term.

*Institutional racism* corresponds to the sociological notion of stratification in that it broadly describes differential access to goods, services and opportunities among society's members owing to the ways in which its institutions are designed and structured to benefit dominant groups.[21] Importantly, the mechanisms of institutional racism typically privilege members of dominant groups *quite irrespective of* how 'well-intended' our attitudes or choices may be, for our perceptions and understandings more often than not are shaped through *habituation*, and hence the injustices to which we contribute may not rise to the level of conscious reflection (Bourdieu 1984). Hence one need not consciously be a *racist* for one's thoughts and actions to be complicit with *racism*[22] (Bonilla-Silva 2003; Bonilla-Silva and Baiocchi 2001; Lawrence 1987). Second, the features of racism are imprecise; they frequently intersect – or may be conflated with – ethnicity, gender or social class. In the European context, racism may also incorporate *religion*, given the ways in which anti-Semitism perpetuates harm towards Jews and 'Islamophobia' operates to stigmatise Muslims (Cesari 2004; Modood 2005).

And we also can recognise racism's cosy relationship to stigma, for stigma entails strong disapproval by the majority of some unspecified person(s) or the group(s) with which they identify, and again these often take subtle forms of expression – euphemisms and codes – including how minorities (e.g. 'allochthonous,' 'Muslims') and the schools they attend are labelled (e.g. 'black schools' in the Netherlands or 'concentration schools' in Belgium). Finally, racism is expressed in the disapproval of *spatial concentrations* of stigmatised minority groups, buttressed with the concomitant – and patronising – belief that minorities are incapable of 'integration' or self-determination without the 'help' of an already beneficent and 'integrated' majority. The racist import of these 'liberal' beliefs is not lost on stigmatised minorities simply because they are expressed with 'good intentions'.

None of these everyday features of institutional racism should surprise scholars. Indeed, it has long been established in the sociology of education literature that (stigmatised) non-white minorities are far more likely to be labelled with behavioural problems, to be tracked low, to be singled out for discipline and special education assignment, and to receive advice from teachers that pushes them into lower forms of vocational training (Agirdag et al. 2011; Harry and Klingner 2006; Hilberth and Slate 2014; Kelly and Price 2011; Merry 2013). Moreover, the way that most schools – as state institutions – are designed and organised combines with the often lowered expectations of school staff to thwart the aspirations of stigmatised minorities before they even have had a chance to germinate. And lest we forget the parents: institutional racism certainly influences the behaviours of white and middle-class parents,[23] who often assess the quality of a neighbourhood or school solely on the basis of its (poor) minority pupil population. All of these things fuse to reinforce and maintain patterns of segregation and social stratification, but also stigma and disadvantage.

So why is this factor so typically absent from empirical work? I would argue, first, because 'racism' continues to be construed by members of dominant groups in its most simple – and hence easily identifiable – form of expression. As such, racism attaches only to *unequivocal, malevolent* and *personalised* speech and actions with the *intent* to harm or exclude. Accordingly, the silent and subtle workings of power that structure relations between society's members too often remain hidden from view. Second, as members of the dominant – and also privileged – classes in Europe's universities, all too often researchers working on 'minority issues' are themselves blind both to their own privilege and to their reflexive habit of labelling minority groups, labels that all too frequently serve to impute deficits and stigma. Paradoxically, institutional racism is perhaps most disturbingly manifest in the *systematic denial* of racism by those who benefit from it and, in my experience, this certainly includes many empirical researchers. Consequently, those who routinely suffer the dastardly effects of racism are assumed either to be exaggerating the problem, or worse, imagining what is happening to them. Disguised in these ways, the explanatory power of institutional racism seldom rises to the surface in empirical studies.

But it seems to me that we need to take *this* dimension of religious school segregation and performance more seriously. Doing so, I would argue, would help illuminate ways in which *institutional racism* is linked to the *institutionally privileged status* of Protestant and Catholic schools in many urban European environments. For example, it might help us better understand how many of these schools are able to produce strong 'magnet effects', such as concentrations of white and middle-class parents attracting *other* white and middle-class parents.[24] Schools that do this also typically manage to attract and retain teachers with higher qualifications and more experience. And here we recognise the familiar Matthew Effect, for if the *perception* of excellence leads more parents with higher social capital to select these schools for their own children, this only enriches the privileged status many of these schools already enjoy. Remember, too, that religious schools are able to exercise some latitude in creating the kind of school they want through selective mechanisms in recruiting both staff and pupils. A certain measure of school board autonomy may be a positive thing, but in practice it often translates into policing who gets in and who does not.

With regularity we read that the answer to these problems is more school 'mixing' (Blum 2002; Trappenburg 2003). Yet despite what some claim, most attempts to mitigate these trends through policies aimed at mixed pupil intakes seem doomed from the start. Indeed, even in so-called mixed educational environments, constitutional protections governing school choice, sorting and selecting mechanisms of schools, the differentiated expectations of teachers and a garden variety of middle-class parental behaviours ensure that these efforts very rarely attain what they purportedly set out to (New and Merry 2014). Even in schools that remain fairly 'mixed', well-educated and better informed parents – and in Europe, again, this typically means indigenous white and middle-class parents – often know how to navigate the school system more quickly and efficiently, and it is not uncommon that parents will jump the waiting list queue to ensure that one's own child attends a school with a low minority pupil composition.[25] Again, nothing that I say here should surprise researchers, for these middle-class parental behaviours are well documented in the empirical literature. They include parents challenging personnel decisions (e.g. having one's child moved to another class), pressing for ability grouping that facilitates in-school segregation and simply switching schools when things do not go their way (Ball 2002; Brantlinger 2003; Holme 2002; Reay et al. 2007).

Parents need not *consciously* have racist or class-based motives steering their school preferences; *nearly all parents want what is best for their child*. All concerned parents look for a good atmosphere (supportive staff and peer group and favourable school climate), a school that is not too large, one that is academically challenging, etc. Moreover, in wanting what is best for their child, parents need not be consciously elitist for them to decide that what is 'best' for one's own child often means selecting schools that effectively are 'better than' other schools. But these choices, I would argue, are imperceptibly influenced by institutional racism, just as they are imperceptibly influenced by the competitive sphere that has entered the educational domain, something we have already seen. When there are a limited number of resources available and the supply does not match the demand, many parents may indeed think it necessary to 'jump the queue' just to give one's child a fighting chance (Swift 2003).

But I think this argument is a clever ruse; well-situated parents nearly always are able to transfer privileges to their own child, and mostly this occurs *outside of the school*. And this is where *implicit bias* influences school choice, for as we have seen *pupil composition* is one of the proxies that particularly middle-class and white parents use to judge the quality of a particular school. This means that parents can publicly express a desire for a 'challenging curriculum' or a 'good match' between home and school without ever having to openly discuss the coded ways in which they skilfully navigate the educational landscape and avoid schools they find 'unsuitable' (read: too many minorities).[26] Gauging school quality in this way is perhaps especially convenient in 'urban' and spatially mixed areas populated by significant numbers of (non-Christian) ethnic minorities. And importantly, *social desirability bias* means that ordinary citizens can express public outrage about segregation while engaging in precisely the routine choices and behaviours that assist in maintaining it.

Perhaps counter-intuitively, these conjectures sit comfortably alongside other seemingly positive parental motivations. For instance, nowadays it is common for many middle-class parents to report wanting more 'diversity' for their child's learning environment (McDonough Kimelberg and Billingham 2012). Encounters with diversity are believed to work in the following way: they ostensibly are important for disadvantaged children who often lack relevant knowledge and skills as well as norms and values necessary to thrive in mainstream society. But for middle-class and well-educated parents such encounters also serve a cosmopolitan purpose, for they also are believed to be important for broadening the empathies of more privileged children, whose lack of contact with marginalised and minority others erodes their capacity for recognising them as equals.

The 'diversity hypothesis' expresses a noble ideal, and, under favourable conditions such interactions can produce generally positive outcomes. The problem with the diversity hypothesis is that middle-class parents interested in 'diversity' typically have in mind a learning environment in which the balance of diversity strongly tips in their favour (New and Merry 2014). The desire for 'diversity' therefore translates as follows: the school my child attends ought to be majority white with just the 'right amount' of minority children to offer one's own child some 'exposure' to difference without interrupting the peer group effects that matter to middle-class parents, and without compromising the level of challenge the parents expect from the school. And, as we have seen, schools are rarely designed in ways conducive to the ideal encounters 'diversity' is meant to facilitate, only partly because of how they sort and select pupils. The upshot is that the outcomes 'diversity' ostensibly inspires actually require a great deal more parity of power and participation among the participants, and that seems rather difficult to achieve so long as voluntary and involuntary forces – including institutional racism and stigma – continue to have the impact that they do.

## Minority religious schools and voluntary separation

As we have seen, the expression of voluntary association tends to produce spatial concentrations – segregation – in a variety of domains, including the school. It would not be surprising, then, if religious schools *for all of the right reasons* were to replicate patterns of segregation in other domains. Yet it is *minority concentrations* that continue to alarm broad sectors of the European public.[27] Even among those known for espousing minority rights and protections for stigmatised and disadvantaged persons, we find scepticism towards the idea of schools for minority groups. For example, Canadian political philosopher Will Kymlicka (2013, 6) opines that possibly 'what immigrants need most is not separate schools, but rather a more multicultural approach to education within the common public schools.' Indeed, it is particularly the existence of religious schools[28] serving stigmatised minority groups that critics often rail against, singling out Islamic schools for special attention. In its place there has been a renewed emphasis on 'integration' across Europe (Joppke 2004, 2007).

Though its meanings and uses are manifold – they may include economic, psychological, cultural or civic expressions – *integration* typically is taken to mean that a society's minority groups – whether they be immigrants, asylum seekers or even natives – must accept the dominant political and cultural norms and values of the host society (Penninx 2004; Vasta 2007). Naturally some groups are singled out more than others.[29] Yet whether expressed as populist rhetoric or political mandate, 'integration' continues to be an ideologically ambiguous concept with many implicit features whose meanings are not entirely evident to either the immigrant or the native population. Consequently, there is much debate concerning its features and requirements (Bader 2012; Berry et al. 2006; Merry 2013).

Only on one thing does there appear to be broad consensus, and that, apparently, is that segregated schools are bad for a society that values citizenship and opportunity on equal terms. Rather, it is far better for children of different backgrounds to come together and focus on what they share in common and be educated for equal recognition and citizenship. We can discern here the elements of a 'common school' thesis. And again, it may be true that *under special conditions* the 'integrated' common school may be able to foster favourable outcomes for all children. Yet even if everyone could agree that 'integration' and the common school are worthy ideals, under *highly non-ideal conditions* the relevant attributes and requirements invariably will entail far less sacrifice for members of majority groups whose backgrounds more closely correspond to the institutionalised habits, norms and values of the mainstream. Indeed, the conditions that common school – and 'diversity' – advocates imagine typically are hard to come by, especially given (a) persistently high segregation indices – facilitated both by the normative good of voluntary association and the legal support of constitutional protection for school choice – that show little sign of reversing course; and (b) the institutionalised ways in which wealth and poverty, race/ethnicity and religion interact, for example how schools routinely engage in grouping practices, disciplinary procedures and special education labels that disproportionately affect poor and minority pupils, and arguably more so in 'mixed' schools (Agirdag et al. 2011; Ireson and Hallam 2005; Thrupp et al. 2002). Indeed these two points illustrate how voluntary and involuntary forces more often than not work in tandem.

Given the unrealistic scenarios painted by advocates of the 'integrated' common school, members of disadvantaged and stigmatised minority groups are rightly sceptical of the 'solutions' drawn up by well-intentioned (but often disingenuous) liberals. Indeed, it is pragmatic alternatives that many are likely to find both more feasible and more attractive. Therefore in what follows I briefly explore the possibility that some types of religious schools serving disadvantaged and stigmatised minority pupils may be a more realistic course to follow in pursuing outcomes favourable to stigmatised groups.

**Voluntary separation**

The reader will recall that there are both voluntary and involuntary factors to help us understand why spatial concentrations of particular groups occur in neighbourhoods and schools. As we saw earlier, environments can become homogenous – segregated – because of the ways in which voluntary association facilitates modes of shared identification and interaction. Of course not every expression of voluntary association is benign; nor can we understand the impulse to voluntarily remain separate if we fail to keep the relevant non-ideal conditions of European societies in mind. We already have seen what some of these conditions are in the previous section, and they include high levels of existing segregation, significant inequalities, racism, stigma and discrimination, and pressures to assimilate to dominant norms. However, even in the absence of intentions to exclude, we still should expect that segregation will occur. And the clustering of certain groups need not cause alarm. Indeed, as Bernard Boxill (1992, 184) observes,

> Fighting and protesting against compulsory segregation does not mean fighting and protesting against every kind of segregation. It means precisely what it says. Fight compulsory segregation. This is quite compatible with permitting, and even urging, [stigmatised minorities] to voluntarily self-segregate, and I see no reason why voluntary self-segregation cannot be a sufficient means of enabling [stigmatised minorities] to make its cultural contribution to the world.

This point needs underscoring, for even when one is not able to choose one's original predicament – those brought about by institutional racism, for instance – this does not render one powerless. Indeed, strength can be found in solidarity and resistance, and these can be facilitated by spatial concentration. Within segregated communities members of stigmatised groups often experience greater equality of recognition, treatment and self-respect than they do in mixed environments, and persons can still act wilfully and in solidarity with others, *turning segregation to their advantage*. And when spatial concentrations coincide with efforts to redirect the purposes of segregation, we may say that they typify a form of 'voluntary separation'.

Allow me to elucidate. Because the voluntary and the involuntary will almost certainly intertwine, there will be involuntary elements to any voluntary gesture. But it is proper to refer to various forms of segregation as 'voluntary' to the extent that there is *intentionality* behind decisions and actions to circumstances not necessarily of one's choosing. It is also proper to see various forms of segregation as voluntary inasmuch as inhabitants strongly identify with their dwelling space and wish to remain with others like themselves. But voluntary separation basically involves strategies that creatively *resist, rearrange* and *reclaim* the terms of one's segregation. And hence by 'separation' I am not defending the prerogatives of privileged groups but rather those of the disadvantaged. Indeed, those most likely to adopt voluntary separation as an appealing strategy will be members of groups subjected to various harms and stigma. And it turns out that stigmatised minority groups in particular often have reason to stay together for the benefits such proximity affords.

And thus where education is concerned, contrary to conventional wisdom separation as such need not compromise educational quality and may in fact enhance it. Indeed, as a pragmatic strategy separate religious schools may afford persons the right to be with others like themselves if they want to. Voluntary association is in any case a normative good. More than this, separate religious schools that consciously facilitate enabling conditions may enhance educational quality to the extent that schools facilitate the fostering of self-respect, and demonstrate equality of recognition and treatment of pupils, who, not incidentally, are less likely to receive this treatment in another school environment (Agirdag et al. 2012; Terry et al. 2014). Separation may also enhance a child's education to the extent that virtues can – arguably more efficiently – be cultivated within a homogenous environment, and these virtues potentially have civic import inasmuch as they can contribute to the good of one's community and beyond. In short, it is reasonable to assume that a variety of religious schools potentially serve an emancipatory function inasmuch as in aiding disadvantaged and stigmatised populations they are able to offer pragmatic responses to stigma, discriminatory treatment and exclusion.

Consider the case of state-supported Islamic schools.[30] Other authors in this issue have argued that they are controversial, and we have already seen how they are singled out for criticism among other minority religious schools. Yet it is undeniable that Islamic schools in Europe serve a stigmatised and marginalised group, even in cities where Muslims may constitute a majority. It is also the case that nearly all of them serve more poor pupils than other kinds of religious schools. According to one study from the UK that I referred to earlier, of the 11 state-funded Islamic schools (or, Muslim schools as they are called in the UK), all are collectively more reflective of their community, with 67% of primaries and 60% of the secondaries having more than the local authority average of free school meal pupils.[31] Islamic schools host staff and pupils who share a common history and experience – and in Europe this will include routine encounters with racism and stigma – and they aim to create a school climate capable of mitigating those harms. One of the ways they aim to do this is by strengthening the relationship between teachers and pupils as well as overall internal school cohesion. Those aims also can be reflected in the didactics, namely the fact that more individual attention can be given to the cultural needs of the pupils.

To be sure, *aims* are not enough. Resources, or what I prefer to call *enabling conditions*, must also be present in order for there to be educational successes. Enabling conditions will take different forms according to circumstance and need, but in addition to institutional supports outside of the school they certainly will include things like qualified and inspirational teachers, a caring school ethos, a challenging curriculum and high expectations. Provided that these conditions are secured and coincide with the right aims, Islamic schools can help to raise the academic achievement of their disadvantaged pupils.[32] Considering the formidable challenges most Islamic schools face, this is no trivial achievement. Perhaps more significantly, as an instantiation of voluntary separation, Islamic schools may be a justifiable response to social inequality when parity of recognition, treatment and participation for Muslim pupils in other school environments are in short supply (Merry 2007a; Shah 2012; Zine 2007). I have not the space here to offer a full account of Islamic schools. I only submit that if we consider (1) what we know about de facto segregation, and (2) the variety of problems – high pupil mobility, high teacher turnover, low expectations, a punitive school climate, etc. – associated with Muslim pupils in other schools, then voluntary separation in the form of an Islamic school may indeed be one of several compellingly pragmatic strategies to confront these challenges.

Voluntary separation is not defeatist; nor is it an argument against 'integration'. Rather it involves supporting *constructive alternatives* to institutional racism and the entrenched patterns of involuntary segregation while at the same time affirming all that is good about voluntary association. Accordingly, it accepts that many worthwhile and positive features attend segregation and that to deny their importance or seek to disrupt them is potentially to engage in harmful and unwelcome forms of social engineering – ones that wittingly or unwittingly undervalue the resources that spatial concentrations often provide. The motives and need for voluntary separation will vary from one context and group to another, and its duration may fluctuate depending on external conditions. But voluntary separation certainly will have appeal for those for whom equal treatment is lacking in mixed environments, that is, where stigma and discrimination are the normal state of affairs.

Of course, simply being a member of a stigmatised group in itself will not suffice as an argument for separation. Further, even with the benefits that 'voluntarily separate' environments may provide, separation will not be an attractive option for everyone. Many will favour 'integrated' environments for their children, and for different reasons. Nothing in my argument speaks against this. Not only are stigmatised groups just as heterogeneous as non-stigmatised groups; members of stigmatised minority groups also will inevitably interact with mainstream society, at least some of the time, if for no other reason than that minority status makes this unavoidable. Whatever the case, separation will continue to be an appealing alternative for those whose equal status is not recognised, whose opportunities are impeded or denied, and whose opportunities for parity of participation all too often are diminished in 'integrated' environments. Finally, voluntary separation offers an alternative to those for whom the possibility of seamlessly blending in with the mainstream remains a fantasy. Indeed, voluntary separation can really only make sense in environments in which segregation is already the norm.

## Conclusions

In this paper, I have examined the question why there continues to be such a high market share of religious schools in Europe. In addition to the answers available to us from extant research, I argued that institutional racism is a contributing factor that warrants closer consideration by empirical researchers. To understand this better, I believe that methods should be devised to control for social desirability bias and implicit bias. Further, I have offered a defence of voluntary separation for religious minorities for whom stigma and disadvantage continue to be hurdles to overcome. I offered by way of example the case of state supported Islamic schools.

Though I have been careful to circumscribe my defence of religious schools as an example of voluntary separation, it is important to keep the following items in mind. First, as we have seen, merely a desire to remain separate will not suffice as an adequate defence; enabling conditions must be present, and religious schools that fail in this regard either must work to improve their performance or be shut down. Second, religious schools able to satisfy the requirements of voluntary separation will have among their primary aims to serve stigmatised and disadvantaged groups. The type of religious school, then, will vary according to the group in question, the context and the need. Given the appalling history of anti-Semitism in Europe, for instance, it will likely include Jewish schools; moreover, in addition to Islamic schools, it also may include Hindu, Sikh and even some Catholic schools. It also may entail religious schools for Roma, a large percentage of whom are Pentecostal Christians. Finally, the religious schools for which I am offering a defence will be funded and supervised by the state. Here we can see again how 'neutrality' can be interpreted not only to include these schools, but also issue quality controls and assist with facilitating the self-determination of marginalised groups.

Yet even though I have defended state support of religious schools that serve vulnerable and marginalised groups, I believe the matter of state support will remain a thorny problem for religious schools, for while it arguably is a preferable expression of neutrality, it has its drawbacks. As Dronkers and Avram (2015) observe, 'in return for its financial support, the State has imposed and continues to impose various types of controls on schools and in the process has reduced school autonomy'. There are ways of improving this balance, for instance by allowing for more autonomy at the level of the school board, or by giving schools more room to cultivate a distinctive atmosphere at the school, rather than merely permitting cosmetic differences to remain. And to be sure, there also will be trade-offs, the most significant of which may very well occur between educational quality and religious identity – something that Islamic schools in Europe know too well, given how they continue to struggle to attract talented and motivated young people to teach at a time when the teaching profession continues to be held in low regard, and when more lucrative professions are drawing educated young Muslims into other fields.

**Notes**
1. It should be noted that different interpretations of 'secularisation' are in circulation, and over the years this has touched off heated debate between scholars about its meaning and application. For more on this debate, see Dobbelaere (1999) and Pickel (2009).
2. Esoteric bookshops across Western Europe remain very popular, as are a variety of New Age spiritualities and quasi-religious worldviews (Rudolf Steiner's anthroposophy) and in many European countries any of the following beliefs/practices are widely reported: belief in a 'higher power', the credibility of astrology, use of crystals, contact with the dead, belief in angels and spirits, reincarnation, life after death, etc. Each of these is consistent with the 'individualisation thesis' discussed by scholars. See inter alia Baldwin (2009), Norris and Inglehart (2011), Eagleton (2014) and Pickel (2009).
3. This is not limited to Muslim immigrants; indeed anti-Semitism against Europe's Jews is again being documented in several countries, including Hungary and France, precipitating ongoing emigration to Israel. See Bunzl (2005) and Kaplan and Small (2006).
4. Indeed in many parts of Europe 'public' schools – particularly in Catholic and Orthodox countries – continue to operate as de facto religious schools endorsing the dominant religion. See Dronkers and Avram (2015).
5. Belgium is an outlier, where Islamic instruction has been widely available in state schools for decades (Merry 2005b).
6. The fact that it is routinely argued in the USA does not mean that this is in fact what happens. Faith-based non-profits engaged in drug counselling, job training or sheltering and feeding the homeless receive government subsidies, and religious schools also receive indirect subsidies through tax exemption, not to mention other kinds of services. See Green, Baker, and Oluwole (2013).
7. Quantifying the precise number of schools matching this description is not possible. But let me clarify here that not all state-supported Christian schools are devoid of a religious ethos. Particularly for some Catholic schools, the presence of a religious ethos is even preferred by many devout Muslim parents, who can rest assured that basic religious values will not be spurned. Moreover, a number of evangelical schools have been established precisely because so many mainstream Protestant and Catholic schools remain only nominally Christian. Notwithstanding these exceptions, it is undeniable that perhaps the majority of mainstream Protestant and Catholic religious schools are indeed not playing the confessional role that they once played.
8. Or what Maussen and Vermeulen (2015) in their paper have called 'pervasively religious' schools.
9. A school's 'brand' need not involve religion. A variety of 'alternative' schools (e.g. Montessori, Steiner, Dalton and Free) are on offer in many European countries, many of which are also state supported and operate as de facto all-white schools. On Danish 'free schools', see Olsen (2015).
10. For more on the disingenuous reasons religious schools may use in refusing 'weaker' pupils, see Maussen & Vermeulen 2015.
11. Stigma can cover a variety of characteristics, including social class, ethnicity, ability, sexuality, immigrant status, weight, etc. The *locus classicus* on stigma is still (Goffman 1963).
12. Irrespective of whether continental Europeans feel comfortable talking about 'race', *racism* is a concept widely in use across Europe.
13. I indicate urban with inverted commas because 'urban' environments may not be geographically located in city centres but rather in suburban environments, placed as many are outside of the predominately white and wealthy city centres. *Les banlieus* outside of Paris come to mind, but also poorer minority neighbourhoods in Amsterdam and elsewhere.

14. There are some exceptions. Indeed, in some cities (e.g. Antwerp), it has only been possible for some Catholic schools to remain open by admitting (mostly) pupils of Muslim background. See Agirdag, Merry, and van Houtte (2014).
15. It is not a coincidence that these racially charged labels are precisely how schools are labelled in the Netherlands. Schools hosting a 'larger than usual' share of minority pupils are simply known as 'black schools'.
16. For Dutch figures demonstrating that this occurred already some decades ago, see Karsten, Meijer, and Peetsma (1996) and Vreeburg (1993).
17. I am aware that the concept of 'race' is rather imprecise and problematic, and only partly because 'races' (perhaps even more than other identity markers like gender, sexuality, ethnicity or ability) entail somewhat artificial and arbitrary constructions. Yet even with these qualifications, race constructions do not make the effects of racism less real.
18. Social desirability bias refers to the habit of responding to questions about sensitive topics (e.g. homosexuality, racial prejudice and immigration) in such a way that one believes her answers will be viewed favourably by others.
19. Implicit bias describes the phenomenon of holding consciously egalitarian assumptions or beliefs about other people (e.g. "I wouldn't base my decision about a school my child will attend on the ethnic/racial composition of the school") while simultaneously holding contradictory beliefs at a subconscious level (e.g. "a high concentration of ethnic minorities in a school is a proxy for poor educational quality").
20. But in fact several mainstream Dutch politicians – like politicians in other European countries – simply find more subtle ways of expressing their racism. See Özdil (2014) and Vandyck (2014).
21. For an excellent analysis of racism as a set of structural, ideological and cultural processes, see Bonilla-Silva (1997).
22. For example, my teenage daughter's ability to study (without permission) off campus from her high school during her lunch break without ever being stopped or even suspected of being truant – unlike her male and Latino schoolmates, who *are* routinely stopped – illustrates how her racial identity and also her gender (and class assignment) confer mobility privileges without scrutiny from school officials, irrespective of whether she has any negative thoughts towards her minority schoolmates.
23. And, as other groups join the middle classes, these same behaviours occur. Here again, institutional racism will incorporate other variables, notably social class.
24. On the European continent, there are no empirical studies that have examined this closely (notwithstanding COOL data in the Netherlands showing a strong correlation between mainstream denominational schools and indigenous majority attendance; Belgium shows similar patterns). However, in the UK, recent empirical data have slowly begun to emerge. See for example, 'Richer pupils at church schools,' *BBC News* (February 13, 2006) available at: http://news.bbc.co.uk/2/hi/uk_news/education/4707452.stm; 'Church schools shun poorest pupils,' *The Guardian* (March 5, 2012) available at: http://www.theguardian.com/education/2012/mar/05/church-schools-shun-poorest-pupils and for more figures from the UK suggesting that faith schools are becoming islands of privilege within poorer urban areas, see http://www.theguardian.com/news/datablog/2012/mar/05/faith-schools-admissions. From this report, we learn that some 73% of Catholic primaries and 72% of Catholic secondaries have a lower proportion of pupils eligible for free school meals than the average of all children schooled across its local authority. The same is the case for Church of England primary and secondary schools. Some 74% of the Church's primaries and 65.5% of its secondaries have a smaller proportion of pupils eligible for free school meals than is average for the local authority. In contrast, half – 51% – of non-religious primaries and 45% of non-religious secondaries have a lower proportion of pupils eligible for free school meals than is representative for their local authority.
25. Again, these schools need not be coded by religion; other 'alternative' schools may serve the same purpose.
26. Compare an exhaustive study in the Netherlands on school choice:

> Het doelbewust mijden van scholen vanwege de hoge aantallen allochtone leerlingen is in onderzoek lastig boven tafel te krijgen. Ouders zullen niet graag toegeven dat ze een school vanwege het hoge aantal allochtone leerlingen ongeschikt vinden. Ze zullen

eerder andere, inhoudelijke argumenten aanvoeren om niet voor een school met veel allochtone leerlingen te kiezen. (Herweijer and Vogels 2004, 107)

27. There are many claims of this sort. See for example 'Faith Schools Fragment Communities'. http://www.theguardian.com/commentisfree/belief/2011/jun/13/faith-schools-fragment-communities and 'Faith-based schools may fuel racism', http://www.irishexaminer.com/ireland/faith-based-schools-may-fuel-racism-224489.html.
28. There are of course other minority religious schools that serve members of the indigenous majority. These usually will be a variety Christian denominations (e.g. Seventh-Day Adventist but they also may be Catholic schools in predominately Protestant areas or vice-versa.).
29. For instance, there is the claim that Muslims harbour loyalties at odds with liberal democratic citizenship. Suggesting that there might be something to this, polls do indeed show that Muslims *as a whole* do not feel as attached to their host countries in Europe as much as members of the majority. Importantly, there also is no shortage of data showing that Muslims – again, as a whole – do not feel *welcome*. But it is true that a small minority of young, socially isolated men are becoming radicalised.
30. I set aside Islamic schools that operate, in England, within the Independent sector for reasons mainly having to do with the fact that most are not well-financed and also academically underperform relative to state-supported (voluntary-aid) Islamic schools.
31. Free school meals are a common (though problematic) proxy used by researchers for determining poverty. See http://www.theguardian.com/news/datablog/2012/mar/05/faith-schools-admissions.
32. A majority of Islamic schools in Europe continue to struggle to raise their academic achievement, but for growing evidence that Islamic schools in the UK – like their North American counterparts – are beginning to turn a corner, see http://www.tes.co.uk/article.aspx?storycode=6006501; for the Netherlands, see http://www.trouw.nl/tr/nl/4492/Nederland/article/detail/3268671/2012/06/11/Islamitisch-basisonderwijs-voldoet-nu-ook-aan-Nederlandse-basisnormen.dhtml and for France, see http://www.leparisien.fr/societe/decouvrez-le-palmares-2013-des-lycees-26-03-2013-2672843.php.

## References

Ackerman, D. 1997. "Marketing Jewish Education." *Journal of Jewish Education* 63 (1–2): 70–76.
Agirdag, O., J. Demanet, M. Van Houtte, and P. Van Avermaet. 2011. "Ethnic School Composition and Peer Victimization: A Focus on the Interethnic School Climate." *International Journal of Intercultural Relations* 35 (4): 465–473.
Agirdag, O., M. S. Merry, and M. van Houtte. 2014. "Teacher's Understanding of Multicultural Education and the Correlates of Multicultural Content Integration in Flanders." *Urban Society and Education*. Online Early.
Agirdag, O., M. Van Houtte, and P. Van Avermaet. 2012. "Ethnic School Segregation and Self-esteem: The Role of Teacher-pupil Relationships." *Urban Education* 47 (6): 1133–1157.
Avram, S., and J. Dronkers. 2010. "School Sector Variation on Non-cognitive Dimensions: Are Denominational Schools Different?" Unpublished Paper.
Bader, V. 2007. *Secularism or Democracy? Associational Governance of Religious Diversity*. Amsterdam: Amsterdam University Press.
Bader, V. 2012. "Associational Governance of Ethno-Religious Diversity in Europe: The Dutch Case." In *Citizenship, Borders, and Human Needs*, edited by R. Smith, 273–297. Philadelphia: University of Pennsylvania Press.
Bakker, E., D. Denessen, D. Peters, and G. Walraven, eds. 2011. *International Perspectives on Countering School Segregation*. Antwerp: Garant.
Baldwin, P. 2009. *The Narcissism of Minor Difference: How Europe and America are Alike*. Oxford: Oxford University Press.

Ball, S. 1994. *Education Reform: A Critical and Post-structural Approach*. Buckingham: Open University Press.
Ball, S. 2002. *Class Strategies and the Education Market: The Middle Classes and Social Advantage*. London: Routledge.
Becker, C. 2009. "Muslims on the Path of the Salaf Al-Salih: Ritual Dynamics in Chat Rooms and Discussion Forums." *Information, Communication & Society* 14 (8): 1181–1203.
Berger, P. 1967. *The Sacred Canopy: Elements of a Sociological Theory of Religion*. Garden City: Anchor Books.
Berry, J. W., J. S. Phinney, D. L. Sam, and P. Vedder. 2006. "Immigrant Youth: Acculturation, Identity, and Adaptation." *Applied Psychology* 55 (3): 303–332.
Blum, L. 2002. "The Promise of Racial Integration in a Multicultural Age." In *Nomos XLIII: Moral and Political Education*, edited by S. Macedo and Y. Tamir, 383–424. New York: New York University Press.
Bonilla-Silva, E. 1997. "Rethinking Racism: Toward a Structural Interpretation." *American Sociological Review* 62 (3): 465–480.
Bonilla-Silva, E. 2003. *Racism without Racists: Color-blind Racism and the Persistence of Racial Inequality in the United States*. Lanham, MD: Rowman & Littlefield.
Bonilla-Silva, E., and G. Baiocchi. 2001. "Anything but Racism: How Sociologists Limit the Significance of Racism." *Race and Society* 4 (2): 117–131.
Bourdieu, P. 1984. *Distinction: A Social Critique of the Judgement of Taste*. Abingdon: Routledge.
Boxill, B. 1992. *Blacks and Social Justice*. Lanham, MD: Rowman & Littlefield.
Boyle, H. 2004. *Quranic Schooling*. London: Routledge.
Brantlinger, S. 2003. *Dividing Classes: How the Middle Class Negotiates and Rationalizes School Advantage*. New York: Routledge.
Bruce, S. 2002. *God is Dead: Secularization in the West*. Oxford: Blackwell.
Bunzl, M. 2005. "Between Anti-Semitism and Islamophobia: Some Thoughts on the New Europe." *American Ethnologist* 32 (4): 499–508.
Burgess, S., E. Greaves, A. Vignoles, and D. Wilson. 2009. *What Parents Want: School Preferences and School Choice*. Bristol: CMPO.
Casanova, J. 2006. "Religion, European Secular Identities, and European Integration." In *Religion in an Expanding Europe*, edited by T. Byrnes and P. Katzenstein, 65–92. Cambridge: Cambridge University Press.
Cesari, J. 2004. *When Islam and Democracy Meet: Muslims in Europe and the United States*. New York: Palgrave Macmillan.
Denessen, E., G. Driessen, and P. Sleegers. 2005. "Segregation by Choice? A Study of Group-Specific Reasons for School Choice." *Journal of Education Policy* 20 (3): 347–368.
Dijkstra, A., J. Dronkers, and S. Karsten. 2004. "Private Schools as Public Provision for Education School Choice and Marketization in the Netherlands and Elsewhere in Europe." Teachers College, National Center for the Study of Privatization in Education Occasional Paper 20.
Dobbelaere, K. 1999. "Towards an Integrated Perspective of the Processes Related to the Descriptive Concept of Secularization." *Sociology of Religion* 60 (3): 229–247.
Driessen, G., and M. S. Merry. 2006. "Islamic Schools in the Netherlands: Expansion or Marginalization?" *Interchange* 37 (3): 201–223.
Dronkers, J., and S. Avram. 2015. "What can International Comparisons Teach us about School Choice and Non-governmental Schools in Europe?" *Comparative Education*, 51 (1): 118–132.
Dwyer, J. 1998. *Religious Schools vs. Children's Rights*. Ithaca: Cornell.
Eagleton, T. 2014. *Culture and the Death of God*. New Haven: Yale University Press.
Goffman, E. 1963. *Stigma: Notes on the Management of Spoiled Identity*. New York: Simon and Schuster.
Green III, P., B. Baker, and J. Oluwole. 2013. "Having it Both Ways: How Charter Schools try to Obtain Funding of Public Schools and the Autonomy of Private Schools." *Emory Law Journal* 63 (2): 303–337.
Hand, M. 2002. "Religious Upbringing Reconsidered." *Journal of Philosophy of Education* 36 (4): 545–557.
Harris, R. 2012. "Local Indices of Segregation with Application to Social Segregation between London's Secondary Schools, 2003– 2008/9." *Environment and Planning A* 44 (3): 669–687. http://www.bristol.ac.uk/geography/people/richard-j-harris/pub/2866734

Harry, B., and J. K. Klingner. 2006. *Why Are So Many Minority Students in Special Education? Understanding Race and Disability in Schools*. New York: Teachers College Press.

Herweijer, L., and R. Vogels. 2004. *Ouders over opvoeding en onderwijs*. Den Haag: Sociaal en Cultuurplan Bureau.

Hilberth, M., and J. R. Slate. 2014. "Middle School Black and White Student Assignment to Disciplinary Consequences: A Clear Lack of Equity." *Education and Urban Society* 46 (3): 312–328.

Hofman, R. 1997. "Effectieve besturen? Verzuiling en bestuursvorm." In *Verzuiling in het onderwijs*, edited by A. B. Dijkstra, J. Dronkers, and R. Hofman, 271–289. Groningen: Wolters-Noordhoff.

Holme, J. J. 2002. "Buying Homes, Buying Schools: Schools Choice and the Social Construction of Equality." *Harvard Educational Review* 72 (2): 181–205.

Huggan, G., and I. Law, eds. 2009. *Racism Postcolonialism Europe*. Vol. 6. Liverpool: Liverpool University Press.

Ireson, J., and S. Hallam. 2005. "Pupils' Liking for School: Ability Grouping, Self-Concept and Perceptions of Teaching." *British Journal of Educational Psychology* 75 (2): 297–311.

James, C., and P. Phillips. 1995. "The Practice of Educational Marketing in Schools." *Education Management and Administration* 23 (2): 75–88.

Joppke, C. 2004. "The Retreat of Multiculturalism in the Liberal State: Theory and Policy." *The British Journal of Sociology* 55 (2): 237–257.

Joppke, C. 2007. "Beyond National Models: Civic Integration Policies for Immigrants in Western Europe." *West European Politics* 30 (1): 1–22.

Kaplan, E., and C. Small. 2006. "Anti-Israel Sentiment Predicts Anti-Semitism in Europe." *Journal of Conflict Resolution* 50 (4): 548–561.

Karsten, S., C. Felix, G. Ledoux, W. Meijnen, J. Roeleveld, and E. Schooten. 2006. "Choosing Segregation or Integration? The Extent and Effects of Ethnic Segregation in Dutch Cities." *Education and Urban Society* 38 (2): 228–247.

Karsten, S., J. Meijer, and T. Peetsma. 1996. "Vrijheid van inrichting onderzocht." *Nederlands tijdschrift voor onderwijsrecht en onderwijsbeleid* 8 (2): 101–110.

Kelly, S., and H. Price. 2011. "The Correlates of Tracking Policy Opportunity Hoarding, Status Competition, or a Technical-Functional Explanation?" *American Educational Research Journal* 48 (3): 560–585.

Kymlicka, W. 2013. "The Governance of Religious Diversity: The Old and the New." In *International Migration and the Governance of Religious Diversity*, edited by P. Bramadat and M. Koenig, 323–333. Montreal: McGill-Queen's University Press.

Laborde, C. 2002. "On Republican Toleration." *Constellations* 9 (2): 167–183.

Laborde, C. 2008. *Critical Republicanism: The Hijab Controversy and Political Philosophy*. Oxford: Oxford University Press.

Ladd, H., and E. Fiske. 2009. "The Dutch Experience with Weighted Student Funding: Some Lessons for the U.S." Working Papers, Sanford School of Public Policy.

Lawrence, C. 1987. "The Id, the Ego, and Equal Protection: Reckoning with Unconscious Racism." *Stanford Law Review* 39 (2): 317–388.

Lentin, A. 2004. *Racism and Anti-racism in Europe*. London: Pluto Press.

MacMaster, N. 2001. *Racism in Europe, 1870–2000*. London: Palgrave Macmillan.

Maussen, M., and V. Bader. 2015. "Non-governmental Religious Schools in Europe: Institutional Opportunities, Associative Freedoms and Contemporary Challenges." *Comparative Education*, 51 (1): 1–21.

Maussen, M., and F. Vermeulen. 2015. "Liberal Equality and Toleration for Conservative Religious Minorities. Decreasing Opportunities for Religious Schools in the Netherlands?" *Comparative Education*, 51 (1): 87–104.

McKinney, S. J., and J. Conroy. 2015. "The Continued Existence of state-funded Catholic Schools in Scotland." *Comparative Education*, 51 (1): 105–117.

McDonough Kimelberg, S., and C. Billingham. 2012. "Attitudes Toward Diversity and the School Choice Process: Middle-Class Parents in a Segregated Urban School District." *Urban Education* 48 (2): 198–231.

Merry, M. S. 2005a. "Indoctrination, Moral Instruction and Non-Rational Beliefs." *Educational Theory* 55 (4): 399–420.

Merry, M. S. 2005b. "Social Exclusion of Muslim Youth in Flemish- and French-Speaking Belgian Schools." *Comparative Education Review* 49 (1): 1–23.

Merry, M. S. 2007a. *Culture, Identity and Islamic Schooling: A Philosophical Approach*. New York: Palgrave Macmillan.

Merry, M. S. 2007b. "Should the State Fund Religious Schools?" *Journal of Applied Philosophy* 24 (3): 255–270.

Merry, M. S. 2013. *Equality, Citizenship and Segregation: A Defense of Separation*. New York: Palgrave Macmillan.

Merry, M. S., and G. Driessen. 2012. "Equality on Different Terms: The Case of Dutch Hindu Schools." *Education and Urban Society* 44 (5): 632–648.

Merry, M. S., and G. Driessen. Forthcoming. "On the Right Track? Islamic Schools in the Netherlands after an era of turmoil." *Race, Ethnicity and Education*.

Modood, T. 2005. *Multicultural Politics: Racism, Ethnicity and Muslims in Britain*. Minneapolis: University of Minneapolis Press.

Musterd, S., and Wim Oostendorf. 2009. "Residential Segregation and Integration in the Netherlands." *Journal of Ethnic and Migration Studies* 35 (9): 1515–1532.

New, W., and M. Merry. 2014. "Is Diversity Necessary for Educational Justice?" *Educational Theory* 64 (3): 205–225.

Norris, P., and R. Inglehart. 2011. *Sacred and Secular: Religion and Politics Worldwide*. Cambridge: Cambridge University Press.

Olsen, T. V. 2015. "The Danish Free School Tradition Under Pressure." *Comparative Education*, 51 (1): 22–37.

Özdil, Z. 2014. "Spreek dat racisme maar gewoon uit." *NRC Next* (March 17). http://www.nrc.nl/next/van/2014/maart/17/spreek-dat-racisme-maar-gewoon-uit-1356715

Penninx, F., ed. 2004. *Citizenship in European Cities: Immigrants, Local Politics, and Integration Policies*. London: Ashgate Publishing.

Pickel, G. 2009. "Secularization as a European fate? Results from the Church and Religion in an Enlarged Europe Project 2006." In *Church and Religion in Contemporary Europe*, edited by G. Pickel and O. Müller, 89–122. Wiesbaden: VS Verlag für Sozialwissenschaften.

Pons, X., A. van Zanten, and S. Da Costa. 2015. "The National Management of Public and Catholic Schools in France: Moving From a Loosely Coupled Towards an Integrated System?" *Comparative Education*, 51 (1): 57–70.

Reay, D., S. Hollingworth, K. Williams, G. Crozier, F. Jamieson, D. James, and P. Beedell. 2007. "A Darker Shade of Pale?' Whiteness, the Middle Classes and Multi-ethnic Inner City Schooling." *Sociology* 41 (6): 1041–1060.

Rougier, N., and I. Honohan. 2015. "Religion and Education in Ireland: Growing Diversity – or Losing Faith in the System?" *Comparative Education*, 51 (1): 71–86.

Scheunpflug, A. 2015. "Non-governmental Religious Schools in Germany: Increasing Demand by Decreasing Religiosity?" *Comparative Education*, 51 (1): 38–56.

Shah, S. 2012. "Muslim Schools in Secular Societies: Persistence or Resistance!" *British Journal of Religious Education* 34 (1): 51–65.

Smedley, D. 1995. "Marketing Secondary Schools to Parents: some Lessons from the Research on Parental Choice." *Educational Management and Administration* 25 (2): 96–103.

Swift, A. 2003. *How Not To Be a Hypocrite: School Choice for the Morally Perplexed Parent*. London: Routledge.

Terry, C., T. Flennaugh, S. Blackmon, and T. Howard. 2014. "Does the 'Negro' Still Need Separate Schools? Single-sex Educational Settings as Critical Race Counterspaces." *Urban Education* 49 (6): 666–697.

Thrupp, M., H. Lauder, and T. Robinson. 2002. "School Composition and Peer Effects." *International Journal of Educational Research* 37 (5): 483–504.

Trappenburg, M. 2003. "Against Segregation: Ethnic Mixing in Liberal States." *Journal of Political Philosophy* 11 (3): 295–319.

Vandyck, T. 2014. De speculaas van Obama: we weten gewoon niet meer wat racistisch is. http://www.knack.be/nieuws/belgie/de-speculaas-van-obama-we-weten-gewoon-niet-meer-wat-racistisch-is/article-opinion-135531.html

Van Wyck, and P. Sleegers. 2010. *Ethnic Minorities and School Achievement*. Presented at AERA (April 30–May 4), Denver, CO.

Vasta, E. 2007. "From Ethnic Minorities to Ethnic Majority Policy: Multiculturalism and the Shift to Assimilationism in the Netherlands." *Ethnic and Racial Studies* 30 (5): 713–740.

Vedder, P. 2006. "Black and White Schools in the Netherlands." *European Education* 38 (2): 36–49.

Vreeburg, B. 1993. *Identiteit en het verschil. Levensbeschouwelijke vorming en het Nederlands voortgezet onderwijs*. Zoetermeer: De Horstink.

Wieviorka, Michel. 2010. "Racism in Europe: Unity and Diversity." In *Selected Studies in International Migration and Immigrant Incorporation*, edited by M. Martiniello and J. Rath, 259–274. Amsterdam: Amsterdam University Press.

Zine, J. 2007. "Safe Havens or Religious 'Ghettos'? Narratives of Islamic Schooling in Canada." *Race Ethnicity and Education,* 10 (1): 71–92.

# Index

accreditation 11–12
assessments, school 5
association autonomy 3, 34, 89, 99
Association of Free Christian Schools 32, 33
Atheism: growth of 51
autonomy, religious schools: financing issues, relationship between 10; pedagogy 10–11; standards 12; tensions 10

Baldwin, Peter 135
bijzonder 3, 7
*Bildung* 28

Calvinism 123
Catholic schools: history of 2; ideology 11; *see also* France religious schools; Ireland, religious schools in; Scotland, religious schools in
charter schools 9
Christian Democratic Party (the Netherlands) 96
civic education 71
Committee of the Elimination of Racial Discrimination (CERD) (Ireland) 79
Coolahan, John 81
creationism teaching 99
curriculum: national 121; *see also specific countries*

Daly, Eoin 80
Decentralization 123
Debré Act 59–61, 66
democracy 28, 32, 33
Denmark, religious schools in 6–7: autonomy of 12–13, 15, 22–3, 29; Common Goals 24, 32; costs 32; democracy clause 29, 32, 33; funding 9; *gymnasium* 29; ideological freedom 29, 31; inspection 30; integration policy package 28; legislation pertaining to 29–30, 33, 34; measurements and assessments 29; Minister of Education 26, 28, 30; Muslim schools, fears regarding 24, 31, 33; political agenda 0f 23–4; subsidies 23; *see also* People's Church (Danish)
Discrimination: EU directives regarding 6; *see also* racism
diversity: increasing cultural and religious 1; institutional 1–2; goals of 76; outcomes of 145; patronage, of 77; *see also* homosexuality; sexual diversity

Eastern Orthodoxy 123
education: history of 2
Employment Equality Act (Ireland) 82
ethics instruction 40
Europeanisation 6
European Convention on Human Rights (ECHR) 1, 6, 28, 29
European Court of Human Rights (ECtHR) 1, 6
evolution teachings 99

faith-based education: diversity, relationship between 1–2; *see also* diversity
France, religious schools in: autonomy 13; Catholic schools 58, 62, 63, 64. 65; Debré Act 59–61, 66; Education Act 59; Education Decree 59; governmental schools, versus 13; new public management (NPM) 57, 58, 62, 63, 64, 65; outcomes-based management 62, 63, 64, 65; state contracts for Catholic schools 58; state–religion balance/tension 57–8
Ferry, Jules 2
freedom, religious 72, 76, 87

# INDEX

Free School Association (FSA) 32
Free School Teachers' Union (FSTU) 32, 33
free school tradition 7, 11, 13, 25, 26, 27, 31–2
French Association of English Educators 61
funding, religious education 2: block grants 75; governmental schools 3; non-governmental schools 8–9; public funding 8–9; *see also specific countries*

gender diversity 5
Germany, religious schools in 7: attractiveness to parents 50; autonomy 11; charity education 45; constitutional framework 39–40, 41–2; decline in 46–7; denominations 43; elite education 45; ethics instruction 40; funding 45; governmental schools 42, 43; gymnasium 49, 50; heterogeneous religious landscape 44; homogeneity, religious 47–8; homosexuality, teachings on 44; legal status of 39; Muslim schools, issues regarding 45; non-governmental Christian religious schools 38, 43–4, 45, 46; non-governmental schools, non-Christian 43–4. 45, 46; performance standards 49–50; secularization 44; socioeconomic status of families 48, 51; state–religion balance 52–3; tracking school system 42
Grundtvig, N.F.S. 25

headscarves, banning of 44, 93
Hickey, Tom 80
Hindu schools: founding of 12; increase in 135–6; subsidization of 125–6, 135–6
Homosexuality 42, 44, 96
humanism 110

indoctrination 137
International Civic and Citizenship Education Study 119
International Covenant on Civil and Political Rights (ICCPR) 79
Ireland, religious schools in: block grants 75; Catholic schools 74, 75; Constitution, basis of education within 73–74; curriculum 79; diversity issues 76, 79; Education about Religion and Beliefs (ERB) 82; Education Act 73; fees/funding 75; hybrid nature of typical schools 73; Minister of Education 78; parental choices 79–80; patronage 77, 78, 80, 83; Protestant schools 74–5, 75–6; Rules for National Schools 81; secularization of schools 80–1; segmentation of education 72, 83; state support for 72–3; structure of education system in Republic of Ireland 73
Irish National Teachers' Organisation (INTO) 81
Islamic schools: cultural gaps regarding 100; radicalization fears 12, 24, 33; resistance to 2–3; rise in 135–6; subsidization of 125–6; 135–6; *see also specific countries*

Jewish schools: Dutch 99; France 58; homosexuality and sexuality issues 99

Kold, Christen 25–6
Kuyper, Abraham 11

Lalouette, Jacqueline 61
Lang-Couplet Agreement 61
Lander religious schools 9, 13
libertarianism 80
loi Carle 9
Lüster Resolution 9

Marxism 26
migrant populations, Europe 135–6
Montesorri schools 11

Neo-Calvinism 11
neo-liberalism 125, 136
Netherlands, the, religious schools in 3, 7, 8: admissions 92–5; associational autonomy 89; Catholic schools in 11; curriculum 97–9; dominant religious groups 88, 89–90; educational freedoms 13–14; evolution teaching 99; funding 9–10; homosexuality issues 96; Muslims, discomfort with 88, 93, 94, 95; National Council of Education 91, 92; overview 87–8, 89–90; pluralism, religious 88; religious identity 88; Salafist parents 94; sexuality issues 96, 99; staff 95–7; tolerance 88
new public management (NPM) 5: French schools, in 57, 58, 62, 63, 64. 65
neutrality 138
non-governmental schools: arrangements for 122–3; autonomy 124; governmental schools, versus 127–8; performance

158

# INDEX

128–30; subsidization 123–4; *see also specific countries*

O'Reilly, Leo 80–1
Organisation for Economic Co-operation and Development (OECD) 23, 28, 57, 81, 119, 126, 139

parents' rights 27
pedagogy: climate of schools 12; financing, relationship between 10–11
People's Church (Danish) 24, 26
philosophies, school 127
plurality cultural 5, 83
plurality, religious 5, 51, 72, 88
privatization of school systems: issues regarding 57; tensions 57–8; worldwide 57
Programme for International Student Assessment (PISA) 23, 24, 28, 49, 81, 119, 120, 126, 129

Quinn, Ruairi 78

racism: insidious 142–3; institutional 17, 143–4; overt 142; relationship to 143–4; religious segregation, stigma 143
religion in Europe: Christianity 134–5; overview 134–5; *see also specific countries*
religious schools: choosing, factors in 139–40, 140–41; criticisms of 136–8; legal status 3, 6; legitimacy issues 2–3; power issues 3–4; structural pressures on 4–5; *see also* autonomy, religious schools; *specific countries*

Scotland, religious schools in 7–8: Catholic schools 105–6; Charter for Catholic Schools 113–4; curriculum; 107, 108; funding, state 109–10; history of faith schools in 106–7, 108; political divide regarding 110–1; pupil enrollment numbers 107; sectarianism 111–2, 113–4; tolerance, recognition to 114
Scottish Council for Voluntary Organizations (SVCO) 112
Scottish Qualifications Authority (SQA) 108
secularization of society 4–5; 44, 80–1; 111–2; 113–4, 125
segregation: racism, relationship between 144–5; voluntary separation 145–6, 146–9
sexual diversity 5, 99, 100; *see also* homosexuality
sexuality, teachings on 42, 44, 96, 100
Sikh schools: founding 12
Small Schools Association 32, 33
state–religion balance: France 58–9; Germany, in 52–3; pluralist approach 72
Steiner, Rudolf 11

Tvind school 28

van Prinsterer, Groen 11
vocational schools 50
Voluntary Aided and Voluntary Controlled schools 3

Waldorf schools 11
William I (Dutch King) 2

Zelman ruling 10